The European Union Decoded

The European Union (EU) and the Eurozone became the economic integration example to follow for years. However, the worldwide economic crisis that unfolded in 2007 put the whole economic integration process in question, the European project in jeopardy, and the euro under pressure, with serious doubts that it can survive its first crisis.

The core argument of this book is twofold. First, it seeks to explain the difficult political, economic, and fiscal idiosyncrasies of all member states in order to put the reasons for the economic crisis into a new and clear perspective. Second, it argues that the institutional response put forward to explain this tremendous crisis is flawed and dangerous because it does not solve the main underlying problem: the deep differences between member states on their understanding of economic and financial behavior. This study counters the leading institutional explanation for the economic crisis that has impacted the entire EU.

It presents a unique and provocative explanation of why the EU and the Eurozone are still immersed in an economic crisis and will be of key interest to students and scholars of European Politics and Economics.

Maria Lorca-Susino is Lecturer in Economics at the School of Business Administration, University of Miami, USA.

The International Political Economy of New Regionalisms Series
Series editor Timothy M. Shaw

The International Political Economy of New Regionalisms Series presents innovative analyses of a range of novel regional relations and institutions. Going beyond established, formal, interstate economic organizations, this essential series provides informed interdisciplinary and international research and debate about myriad heterogeneous intermediate-level interactions. Reflective of its cosmopolitan and creative orientation, this series is developed by an international editorial team of established and emerging scholars in both the South and North. It reinforces ongoing networks of analysts in both academia and think-tanks as well as international agencies concerned with micro-, meso- and macro-level regionalisms.

1 **Crisis and Promise in the Caribbean**
   Politics and convergence
   Winston Dookeran

2 **Contemporary Regional Development in Africa**
   Edited by Kobena T. Hanson

3 **Eurasian Regionalisms and Russian Foreign Policy**
   Mikhail A. Molchanov

4 **Africa in the Age of Globalisation**
   Perceptions, misperceptions and realities
   Edited by Edward Shizha and Lamine Diallo

The European Union Decoded

Challenges beneath the surface

Maria Lorca-Susino

LONDON AND NEW YORK

First published 2017
by Routledge

2 Park Square, Milton Park, Abingdon, Oxfordshire OX14 4RN
52 Vanderbilt Avenue, New York, NY 10017

Routledge is an imprint of the Taylor & Francis Group, an informa business

First issued in paperback 2019

Copyright © 2017 Maria Lorca-Susino

The right of Maria Lorca-Susino to be identified as author of this work has been asserted by her in accordance with sections 77 and 78 of the Copyright, Designs and Patents Act 1988.

All rights reserved. No part of this book may be reprinted or reproduced or utilised in any form or by any electronic, mechanical, or other means, now known or hereafter invented, including photocopying and recording, or in any information storage or retrieval system, without permission in writing from the publishers.

Notice:
Product or corporate names may be trademarks or registered trademarks, and are used only for identification and explanation without intent to infringe.

British Library Cataloguing in Publication Data
A catalogue record for this book is available from the British Library

Library of Congress Cataloging in Publication Data
Names: Lorca-Susino, Maria, author.
Title: The European Union decoded / Maria Lorca-Susino.
Description: New York, NY : Routledge, 2016. | Includes bibliographical
    references and index.
Identifiers: LCCN 2016002127| ISBN 9781472474933 (hardback)
Subjects: LCSH: European Union countries—Economic integration. |
    European Union countries—Economic integration—Political aspects.
    | European Union countries—Economic policy. | European Union
    countries—Economic conditions—21st century. | Global Financial
    Crisis, 2008-2009.
Classification: LCC HC241 .L675 2016 | DDC 337.1/42—dc23
LC record available at http://lccn.loc.gov/2016002127

ISBN: 978-1-4724-7493-3 (hbk)
ISBN: 978-0-367-28156-4 (pbk)

Typeset in Times New Roman
by Swales & Willis Ltd, Exeter, Devon, UK.

Every effort has been made to contact copyright holders for their permission to reprint material in this book. The publishers would be grateful to hear from any copyright holder who is not here acknowledged and will undertake to rectify any errors or omissions in future editions of this book.

To Victoria

Contents

List of illustrations	ix
Foreword	xi
Acknowledgments	xv

PART I
Historical and theoretical introduction to the EU — 1

1 The European Union and the Eurozone: united we stand, divided we fall — 3

2 The birth of the European Union and the Eurozone: history, myths, truths, and lies — 13

PART II
The European Union and the economic crisis: the challenge — 27

3 The economic crisis: political and economic problems — 29

4 Fiscal austerity or government spending — 39

5 The Transatlantic Trade and Investment Partnership in times of crisis: the euro and the price of crude oil — 50

PART III
EU countries: different political, social, and cultural idiosyncrasies — 67

6 Germany: the big brother of the European Union — 69

7 Spain: before and after the euro — 78

8 Greece and the battle of ideas — 95

9	The United Kingdom and Turkey: it's complicated	108
10	Trends in immigration into the EU: history and challenges	119

PART IV
The European Union and the challenges beneath the surface — 135

11	The future of the European Union: the Union must go	137

Bibliography — 147
Index — 156

Illustrations

Figures

1.1	GDP in the USA and Europe, 1997–2011	10
1.2	Public opinion on the euro, 2006–2012	11
2.1	Levels of public trust in EU institutions, 2004–2012	20
2.2	Levels of public discontent with the handling of the crisis and the economy, 2012	21
2.3	Levels of public dissatisfaction with the U.S. economy by state, 2012	22
2.4	Public opinion on the EMU and the euro, 2006–2012	23
2.5	Public opinion on Europe at two speeds, 2004 and 2011	24
2.6	Public opinion on the consequences of the introduction of the euro, 2008–2012	24
2.7	Public opinion on the best time to introduce the euro, 2004–2012	25
4.1	Estonian public debt and budget, 1995–2011	47
5.1	U.S. GDP, chained (2009) dollars, 1947–2014	51
5.2	Price of Light Crude, 1983–2011 (US$ per barrel)	53
5.3	Brent–WTI spread, 2006–2013	56
5.4	Spot prices for selected benchmark crude oils, 2011–2014	57
5.5	Real GDP and WTI crude spot price, 1990–2016	58
5.6	Dow Jones Industrial Average, 2008–2011	59
5.7	Economic indicators for the U.S. economy, 1967–2015	61
5.8	The relationship between the U.S. dollar and the European Brent Spot Price	63
7.1	The peseta and the U.S. dollar, 1972–1999	83
7.2	Public finances in Spain, 1995–2012	84
7.3	Spain: real estate price index, 2007–2011	86
7.4	Spanish labor market, 1976–2010	87
7.5	Misery Index under U.S. presidents, 1974–2011	88
7.6	Misery Index for Spain, 1990–2010	89
7.7	Misery Index for European countries, 1990–2010	90
7.8	Misery Index for the Eurozone, 1996–2011	91
7.9	Census of Spaniards resident abroad by place of origin, 2008 and 2012	92
7.10	Census of Spaniards resident abroad by destination, 2008 and 2012	92

9.1	The 35 Chapters of the *acquis communautaire*	113
11.1	Proportion of residents expressing European identity, Summer 2009	139
11.2	Voter turnout in European elections, 1994–2014	141
11.3	Voter turnout by state, 2014	142

Tables

2.1	To be a euro-millionaire	18
2.2	Europe of Freedom and Democracy	19
3.1	The Greek Loan Facility or First Economic Adjustment Programme	35
3.2	The Second Economic Adjustment Programme for Greece financed by the European Financial Stability Facility	36
3.3	EFSF aid to Ireland, Portugal and Greece	36
3.4	Capital subscriptions by member states to the European Stability Mechanism	37
5.1	Crude oil consumption by year, 1980 and 2011	52
7.1	Spain, macroeconomic data, 1967–1995	83
11.1	European Parliamentary election results: 2009 and 2014 compared	143

Foreword

Professor Lorca-Susino has written a book with the suggestive and intriguing title of *The European Union Decoded*. It is aimed at the U.S. public, although I hope that many Europeans and others around the world will read it. It would be useful to them. Given Lorca's background as an economist, one might think that her reflections would focus and be limited to the crisis of the euro. But her work is not limited to an economic analysis. It places her ideas in the historic and political context of the European Union and some of its member nations. It is a work of political economy that perfectly matches Clemenceau's famous phrase that "War is too important to be left to the generals." The creation and implementation of the euro as a currency is not an issue limited to economists, bankers, and speculators. Understanding this required digging into political as well as economic questions.

One very interesting aspect of the book is that it looks at the euro from the point of view of the United States. This is not only an exercise in comparative economics, because the DNA of the European currency includes some U.S. genes, as shown by the passions displayed by prominent American economists who study the creation and survival of the euro.

The start of Chapter 1 sums up the aim of the book as being "to explain that the current crisis is not the result of a number of unconnected financial and economic imbalances, because they are all rooted in the political, social, religious, and even ethnic structures of the member states." The quote from Milton Friedman that it uses next belongs to that type of prediction, somewhere between meteorological and magical, that various Nobel prize-winning economists like Paul Krugman and Milton Feldstein have issued for the euro. They have gone from viewing the creation of the single currency as an unattainable dream to defending it as a lesser evil. More interesting is the analysis in Chapter 2 of Canadian Nobel prize winner Robert Mundell, father of the theory of optimum monetary areas, as a precursor of the euro and defender of its viability.

In his keynote address to the Jean Monet conference in 2011, Mundell proposed a series of profound reforms, based on the lessons drawn from historic comparisons with the United States. His proposals focused on the creation of a single Finance Ministry with budgeting powers over member states. In his opinion, Europe's fundamental choice is either to move backwards to recover the independence of member states in the areas of fiscal controls and debt, or to move forward toward a strong central power. Both options are difficult, although not impossible, because this system requires a large transfer of sovereign powers. Member states that do this would earn a positive financial image and a financial system similar to the one in the United States. It would also benefit greatly from the creation of eurobonds for the Eurozone, although it would be dangerous to create them before controls on budgets and policies are put in place.[1]

In fact, the euro was created and survived the crisis because of support from citizens. In the words of Joseph Schumpeter, the Austrian-American economist who served as Austria's Finance Minister after World War I and before he migrated to the United States, "a nation's monetary system reflects everything that its people are, want and lack." The history of the euro shows that the Europeans who share it not only adopted it as a currency but have clearly declared their support for keeping it, as shown by the cases of Greece, Portugal, Ireland, Spain, Italy, and even Germany when faced with the populism reflected in the case of the Herren Professoren Doktoren. The proof is that the Eurozone, created by 12 member states, has grown to 19 members and has a waiting list. And not because of blind faith, but because people understand the power of galloping globalization and the need to confront it in a united manner.

Another original and interesting part of the book is its analysis of some of the member states, specially Germany, the big brother as well as the largest brother. In fact, the creation of the Federal Republic of Germany is intriguing because it included some of the founding principles of the European undertaking. The three victorious Western powers—United States, Great Britain, and France—knew to avoid the mistakes of the Treaty of Versailles.

John Kenneth Galbraith, then a member of the U.S. military's economic team, recalled in his memoirs that more coal and less money in circulation was needed to jump start a German economy where the preferred currency was cigarettes. The German debt was 400 percent of production.[2] What was most urgently needed was to feed the population and get the economy started. And that required a monetary reform that was devised by two imaginative U.S. economists, Raymond W. Goldsmith and Gerhard Colm, both Jews who had escaped Nazi Germany. Joseph M. Dodge, a banker, was added to the team by the military governor, Gen. Lucius D. Clay. The result was the Colm-Dodge-Goldsmith Plan, which history has credited to Ludwig Erhard.

Under the plan, a new currency was secretly printed in the United States and named the Deutsche Mark, instead of the devalued Reichsmark. It was transported to Germany by ship in 23,000 boxes and distributed on June 20, 1948 to launch the currency reform. Shelves in western Germany immediately filled with goods, for sale with a valued currency. That's how the so-called German Economic Miracle started, with the added push of the renegotiation of the German debt in London.

The difference with the Paris Conference in 1919, which led Keynes to resign and write his prophetic condemnation of "the economic consequences of the peace," could not be more stark. The Deutsche Mark was born in the United States of German parents and was an immediate success, in a devastated country that had become an empire in the nineteenth century based on its internal market, single currency, and the iron fist of Bismarck. In 70 years it had lived through two world wars, hyperinflation, massive labor strikes, and a debt that could not be paid. A federal government structure, an independent constitutional tribunal and central bank, breaking up the powerful Konzern and a system for industrial relationships—those are the founding factors of the Federal Republic of Germany. The Allied governments helped to shape them, and from the start they helped to inspire the construction of the European Union.

The culture of economic stability that Professor Lorca-Susino mentions in her book contributed to the creation of the monetary union but did not come about overnight. In fact, while stable employment, prices, and balanced budgets can reduce the uncertainties that make economic activity more difficult, they also can generate social insecurities and drops in income levels. Economic stability requires avoiding crises, high inflation, and excessive volatility in the financial markets. The culture of stability is important in a democratic system, where the challenge for political leaders is to reduce instability to the lowest level possible without undermining the capacity of the economy to improve living standards through increased productivity, efficiency, and employment.

The essential characteristics of a monetary union were set out in the Werner Report of 1969, in which the then Prime Minister of Luxembourg proposed a 10-year plan, with several stages, to achieve full economic and monetary union. In the following decade, the duo made up of French President Giscard d'Estaing and German Chancellor Helmut Schmidt played a decisive role in the creation of the monetary snake and the European Currency Unit as well as European Council, the G7, and the establishments of direct elections to the European Parliament. Both argued the European community's untenable situation during a debate at the European Central Bank. D'Estaing started the debate:

> Every six months there were new headlines. The French Franc dropped. The Lira dropped. The Mark rose. In the long-run, that was an absolute contradiction. We said, "we cannot have a common market like this." Finally, we came to the conclusion that the only way to achieve a common market was to have a single currency. That idea was very hard to sell because all the central bankers were against it.

Schmidt argued that if there was no common currency, speculators would be playing ball with our currencies.

European Commission President Jacques Delors, who had devalued the French Franc when he was Finance and Budget Minister in the early 1980s, renewed the push for the common market as a domestic market, adding to it a social dimension and pushing for a monetary union as the first step toward an economic union and later a political union. He also directed the Delors Commission, in which 12 central bankers from the European community prepared the plan for a Monetary Union.

The fall of the Berlin Wall and the end of the Cold War disrupted this strategy of advancing small step by small step. As Vaclav Havel said, "the world, people, and history move at their own pace, which we can no doubt affect but which no one can completely control."

The problem is that at the Maastricht conference it was decided to move toward a monetary union without a matching move toward an economic union, with the member countries retaining sovereignty over economic and fiscal policies. That's why it was complemented with the Stability and Growth Pact, because there was concern that the countries in the so-called "Club Med" were not mature enough for a monetary union. But a monetary union is a political and not just technical decision, as shown by Chancellor Kohl's decision to change the Deutsche Mark for the euro, despite the opposition of a majority of the German people. Time has shown that this decision was endorsed by public opinion around Europe, and especially in Greece. The reason for this, without a doubt, is the instinct for survival, which requires trust and solidarity.

The main challenges remaining are examined in Part 4 (Chapter 11). Two observations here: The European construct is an exercise in voluntarily pooled sovereignty, based on shared values and interests totally opposed to those of the USSR from Stalin to Brezhnev; the second is that the three statistics that best reflect today's Europe—7 percent of the world population, 23 percent of its production and commerce, and 50 percent of its social spending—are not a challenge for Europe alone. For Europeans, their challenge is to maintain their social and welfare models. For others—like China, Brazil, other emerging countries, and even the United States—the challenge is to build a social model inspired by similar principles.

To the challenges that Professor Lorca-Susino points out, I would add one: where is the European version of the Hamilton who created the U.S. Treasury? Can we push our Great Plan forward with a collective Hamilton, step by step? This question is outlined in the European institutions' Five Presidents Report.

I wish Professor Lorca-Susino success in her continued research on these ongoing challenges.

Enrique Barón Crespo

Notes

1 Global Jean Monnet Conference. 2011. European Economic Governance in an international context, Comisión Europea, 24–25 de noviembre 2011.
2 John K. Galbraith. 1982. *A life in our times*. New York: Ballantine Books, 250–253.

Acknowledgments

This book has been many years in the making. In fact, since I finished my previous book, *The euro in the 21st century* I knew I was going to write it. To this end, I have been reading and thinking about the future challenges of the European Union and the euro.

This book has been written while the EU was experiencing the most dramatic economic and social events of its history, events such as the Greek financial crisis, the drafting of the TTIP, and the refugee emergency that will definitely shape its future forever.

In the preparation of this book, I have benefited greatly from the support and assistance of many institutions and individuals. My most important debt is to the University of Miami Business School and to the European Union Center at the University of Miami. I also owe my gratitude to many academic colleagues and professional experts who have enlightened and shaped my thoughts with their research, studies, and innovative points of view. Special thanks are due to Juan Tamayo for his professional editing and to the publishers and editors at Ashgate Publishing for their patience with missed deadlines.

This book is dedicated to everyone who has believed in me, once more, especially to my family and in particular to Victoria. Thank you all for your patience and support through the twists and turns in the making of this book. God bless you all.

Part I
Historical and theoretical introduction to the EU

1 The European Union and the Eurozone

United we stand, divided we fall

> Never was so much owed by so many to so few.
> (Winston Churchill)[1]

Introduction

The European Union (EU) and the Eurozone have been the regional integration example to follow, mainly because the political and economic behavior exercised by the bloc have never been identified as hegemonic, contrary to the image projected by the United States and China in recent years. But now the euro area is facing its first economic crisis since the euro was introduced on January 1, 1999 as a common currency and the whole European project is being called into question.

This book explains that the current crisis is not the result of a number of disconnected financial and economic imbalances, but that the imbalances are rooted in the political, social, religious and even ethnic structures of the EU's member nations.

The winner of the Nobel Memorial Prize in Economic Sciences, Milton Friedman, predicted that the passion for the euro would disappear with the first great crisis and economic difficulty. While in 2007 the world was confronted with what has been called the "Great Recession of the century," the first signs of the crisis began to be felt in the EU and the Eurozone on April 23, 2010, when Greece requested financial assistance. The crisis deepened when Ireland asked for help on November 21, 2010, expanded when Portugal sought assistance on April 6, 2011, and peaked in the summer of 2012 when Spain was offered access to credit and financial support. These events raised the possibility not only of the end of the single currency but also the collapse of the European Union. Since 2010, the governments of the Eurozone have allocated millions of euros to control another severe economic crisis with political and social implications, and have made efforts to close the economic gap between countries of the EU.

The difference between the European Union and the Eurozone

The European Union (EU) is understood as a single political bloc. But from an economic perspective, the EU is a fragmented union. The EU consists of 28 countries that have entered the European club over the years. The EU was born on May 9, 1950 when the French finance minister Robert Schuman laid the foundations for the creation of the European Coal and Steel Community (ECSC),[2] signed by six countries. The ECSC later transformed itself into today's European Union, governed by the Reform Treaty, also known as the Treaty of Lisbon.

To join the EU, countries must meet the conditions established by the Council of Europe—established during the 1993 Copenhagen Council—that make up the so-called Copenhagen Criteria and stipulate that countries must meet three criteria in order to be accepted as an EU member state. The first are political criteria that requires the institutions of the candidate country to guarantee democracy, the rule of law, respect for human rights and respect for and protection of minorities. The second requirement is an economic prerequisite that the candidate country must have a market economy that can cope with the competitive pressures of a free market economy. Finally, countries must have the ability to assume the obligations of EU membership, particularly to accept, respect and enforce the objectives embodied in a political, economic and monetary union.[3]

The accession process is a lengthy procedure because meeting the Copenhagen criteria requires time and effort. Since the ECSC was created with only six initial members, there has been a significant number of accession processes to bring the current membership to 28 countries. The two most significant accession took place on May 1, 2004—when "three former Soviet republics (Estonia, Latvia and Lithuania), four former satellites of the USSR (Poland, the Czech Republic, Hungary and Slovakia), a former Yugoslav republic (Slovenia) and two Mediterranean islands (Cyprus and Malta)"[4] joined, and in 2007, when Bulgaria and Romania joined, completing the European Union as it stands today.

Once a country is accepted into the EU, it can choose to adopt the euro as its currency. Of the 28 countries forming the European Union, nineteen[5] share the euro as a common currency and form what is called the Eurozone or euro area. The rest of the EU countries that do not have the euro still use their national currencies, although most of those countries are expected to adopt the euro in the future. The introduction of the euro as a common currency for EU member states has been an arduous process that has taken several years. Although the adoption of the euro is voluntary, once a country adopts the euro there are specific and very demanding obligations that must be respected.

The euro was born on January 1, 1999 as the common currency for eleven of the fifteen countries that formed the EU at that time: Austria, Belgium, Finland, France, Germany, Ireland, Italy, Luxembourg, Netherlands, Portugal and Spain. Later adopters were Greece on January 1, 2001, Slovenia on January 1, 2007, Malta and Cyprus on January 1, 2008, Slovakia on January 1, 2009, Estonia on January 1, 2011, Latvia on January 1, 2014 and Lithuania on January 1, 2015.

The failed European Constitution and the current Reform Treaty

The European Union is currently governed by the Reform Treaty signed in Lisbon on December 1, 2007 and commonly known as the Treaty of Lisbon. This treaty cannot be understood as a constitution like those of the United States and other democratic countries. It is a treaty in which EU member states agreed to the mechanics, structure and organization of the European Union, while at the same time agreeing to respect that each member country has its own national constitution.

There was one attempt to forge a treaty that could act as a true constitution of the European Union. It was agreed on June 18, 2003 and was signed in Rome by the Heads of State and Government of the member countries of the European Union on October 29, 2004. It was approved by the European Parliament on January 12, 2005 by a large majority—500 votes in favor, 137 against and 40 abstentions.

Once approved by the European Parliament, the treaty had to be approved by each member state by a parliamentary vote or national referendum. Although most countries approved it through their parliaments, France and the Netherlands submitted it to popular referendums. The proposal was rejected by voters in both countries, ending the attempt at what could have been the final level of EU integration: a political union. In addition, the rejections in France and the Netherlands caused a significant institutional crisis for the European project.

Opponents of the constitution claimed that the rejection was based on the voters' disapproval for four symbols that were embedded in the proposed text as a way to promote a common identity within the EU. These symbols were the Charter of Fundamental Rights, an official EU flag, an EU anthem, and the post of EU Foreign Minister. Critics believed that these four symbols would give more personality to the EU at the expense of national sovereignty and were seen as factors that strengthened and encouraged the construction of a social-cultural integration in Europe that could erode national identities. The rejections of the constitution in France and the Netherlands in fact turned out to be more a vote against the policies of the national governments of the day than against the creation of a European identity. Nevertheless, the rejections exposed the existence of a strong public discontent with the drafted constitution, viewed as distant and bureaucratic and highlighting the democratic deficit within the EU that many criticize.

To get out of this impasse, the EU began to work on what would be called the "Reform Treaty" and later the Lisbon Treaty because it was signed in Lisbon on December 13, 2007.[6] It entered into force on December 1, 2009, aimed at improving the functioning of the EU.

However, the Lisbon Treaty also faced uncertainty when Ireland rejected it in a national referendum on June 12, 2008. After the votes were tallied, 53.4% of those who voted did so against the treaty, and this once again delayed the EU's modernization project. Ireland was the only EU member nation that rejected the Lisbon Treaty by popular vote. The governments of France and Germany saw Ireland's rejection as especially deplorable because Ireland was one of the countries that had most benefited from its integration into the EU. Again, a thorough analysis of the Irish "no" showed that the rejection was due not to the contents of the Lisbon Treaty but to internal politics. The Irish later voted in favor of the treaty in a second referendum.

The Lisbon Treaty (2007) attempted to relaunch political integration and strengthen economic integration in the region and make the EU project an example of integration to follow and imitate. However, this treaty still has many detractors—mainly the so-called "Euro skeptics"—who want to delay any political integration to avoid what they see as the loss of national sovereignty and identity. The Reform Treaty was designed with two economic objectives in mind. First of all, to help member countries face competition from emerging giants like China, India and Brazil. The second objective was to prevent the deterioration of the European economy caused by the global geopolitical instability that could affect the economic growth of countries. Therefore, many defined the Reform Treaty as a project that would help the 28 member countries to work together to implement economic plans and political policies to better meet the new challenges caused by economic globalization and improved competitiveness.

Interestingly, one of the points of contention, and one of the reasons why the constitution was rejected, was the incorporation of a new EU objective. The failed constitution proposed that competition should be "free and undistorted." This objective was well discussed in France, and was one of the reasons the French voted against the draft constitution. French opponents argued that there was no need to state that competition should be free and undistorted since that was assumed to be a key principle of the EU's competition policy: to respect, promote and monitor competition. However, the Reform Treaty included a Protocol[7] which specifies that:

> THE HIGH CONTRACTING PARTIES
>
> CONSIDERING that the internal market as set out in Article 3 of the Treaty on European Union includes a system ensuring that competition is not distorted,
>
> HAVE AGREED that: to this end, the Union shall, if necessary, take action under the provisions of the Treaties, including under Article 352 of the Treaty on the Functioning of the European Union.
>
> This protocol shall be annexed to the Treaty on European Union and to the Treaty on the Functioning of the European Union.

Debate aside, EU member countries and companies are competing fiercely in a "zero-sum" game. Moreover, to improve the living standards of the region—achieved in part through the enjoyment of high quality products—competition is necessary to raise productivity and quality. Improving market competition promotes efficiency of production and prevents national governments from practicing protectionist policies that delay economic and political integration. Therefore, integration and competition to improve competitiveness are the answer, not the problem.

One debate arose when certain sectors of society blamed the euro—more specifically, the euro's appreciation against the U.S. dollar—because the common currency generated a loss of competitiveness by reducing exports. The French finance minister, Pierre Moscovici, said in early February of 2013 that the euro was too strong—one euro was trading above US$1.36 at the time—and was affecting European exports by making them less competitive. In fact, Moscovici added, a 10 cent rise in the value of the euro caused a loss of one billion euros for the aerospace giant EADS (Atlantico 2013).

The European Union as a successful example of regional integration to follow

Regional economic integration refers to a series of agreements that help a group of countries achieve greater regional coordination and that can range from a free trade area to a customs union, a common market, economic and monetary union and finally to a political union.

Economic integration is defined as the permanent abolition of discrimination between national economies, and political integration is reached when the maneuverability of some actors to impose their national interests on the decisions of European institutions is reduced (Nieminen 2005). However, each type of integration has well-defined phases aiming at obtaining a full union that can only be achieved with (1) the complete unification of the economies involved and (2) unified policies on a number of issues. Thus, the EU has experienced different forms of integration that involve not only political and economic agreements but social, cultural, and even linguistic and ethnic integration.

The EU has become an icon of successful regional integration. The Lisbon Treaty has achieved a high level of political integration among its members, and nineteen member states have reached economic and monetary union with the euro as their common currency. Despite this success, however, the integration process has had and still today has two different speeds. Economic integration has been rapid, stable and firm, but political integration has been low and sometimes demoralizing. This has been justified as the result of the idiosyncrasies and complicated structures of the countries that form the EU.

However, this complacency with the difficulties of integration has become dangerous because the EU is at a critical point. In fact, many voices say that the process of EU integration has come to an end. There have been problems implementing structural reforms, difficulties accepting and respecting economic and monetary requirements, failures in eliminating the rigidity of economic structures, and limitations of human capital. And some have tried to resolve the problems using national policies rather than EU institutions (Gross and Micossi 2008).

Currently, there is debate over whether economic integration helps integration policy or vice versa. Some argue that political decisions have been motivated by economic reasons (El-Agraa 1989) based on historical fluctuations in the economic integration process related to the economic dynamics behind policy decisions (Nieminen 2005). Others believe that political decisions are the drivers of regional integration and that political motives trigger the first step towards economic integration (Balassa 1961). Regardless of this debate, the euro has facilitated the process of regional integration not only among Eurozone member states but also in the European Union, since integration has helped the continent become a bloc admired as prosperous and diverse (Deppler 2007).

The European Union was born on May 9, 1950 when the French finance minister Robert Schuman—in a speech inspired by French economist Jean Monnet and Chancellor Konrad Adenauer of West Germany—first proposed the integration of the industries of coal and steel of Western Europe. The objective of this project is reflected in the following paragraph of a famous speech by Monnet on May 9, 1950.

> [The French Government] proposes that Franco-German production of coal and steel as a whole be placed under a common High Authority, within the framework of an organization open to the participation of the other countries of Europe. The pooling of coal and steel production should immediately provide for the setting up of common foundations for economic development as a first step in the federation of Europe, and will change the destinies of those regions which have long been devoted to the manufacture of munitions of war, of which they have been the most constant victims. The solidarity in production thus established will make it plain that any war between France and Germany becomes not merely unthinkable, but materially impossible.[8]

The result was that on April 18, 1951 the Treaty of Paris, agreed by Belgium, France, Germany, Italy, Luxembourg and the Netherlands, gave birth to the European Coal and Steel Community. This was the beginning of a process of political integration which continued on March 25, 1957 when the six signatory countries of the ECSC also signed in Rome the Treaty of the Economic Community, which led to the creation of the European Economic Community on January 1, 1958.

The EEC's main objective was the creation of the customs union within a maximum period of 12 years and the creation of a common market between the signatory countries that could bring about the free movement of capital, people, services and goods. It also introduced the Common Agricultural Policy (CAP) in order to establish the free movement of agricultural products within the member countries while establishing a common policy to protect farmers from competition from third countries. Thus, the customs union came into force on July 1, 1968 to facilitate the free movement of goods and eliminate all intra-Community tariffs but imposed a common tariffs for non-EU members.

The free movement of the three other sectors—capital, people and services—were not implemented until much later, when the Single European Act in 1986 was agreed. But the agreement sealed the beginning of the first truly unified market. Furthermore, the Single European Act served as seed for the Maastricht Treaty, signed on November 1, 1993, which transformed the project and gave it the name of the European Union. However, it was not until December 1, 2009, when the Treaty of Lisbon took effect, that the European Union assumed its current legal status. Article 2 of the Lisbon Treaty states:[9]

1   The Union's aim is to promote peace, its values and the well-being of its peoples.
2   The Union shall offer its citizens an area of freedom, security and justice without internal frontiers, in which the free movement of persons is ensured in conjunction with appropriate measures with respect to external border controls, asylum, immigration and the prevention and combating of crime.
3   The Union shall establish an internal market. It shall work for the sustainable development of Europe based on balanced economic growth and price stability, a highly competitive social market economy, aiming at full employment and social progress, and a high level of protection and improvement of the quality of the environment. It shall promote scientific and technological advance.

The fall of the Berlin Wall (November 9, 1989) became a turning point in the future of the European project. That historic moment on the one hand forced member states to accept the need and urgency to continue with the project of integration and, on the other hand, tested the European project's many declarations of the need for regional solidarity. The event therefore forced the European Community to consider the importance and necessity of further integration that could help absorb and assist former communist countries and the reunification of the two Germanys.

This new geopolitical reality generated many new dangers and opportunities. On May 29, 1990 the European Bank for Reconstruction and Development was created to assist all the countries that were no longer part of the suddenly extinct Soviet Union. And on January 1, 2004, the EU welcomed ten new member states, including eight from the Soviet Bloc which had now also disappeared: Cyprus, Czech Republic, Estonia, Hungary, Latvia, Lithuania, Malta, Poland, Slovakia, and Slovenia. And on January 1, 2007, the EU accepted the last two countries ever to enter the EU: Romania and Bulgaria.

The euro as a common currency in the Eurozone

A common currency is a currency shared by a number of countries that have agreed to give up their national currencies and adopt a common currency. The introduction of the euro in 1999 has promoted the integration of the economies of the Eurozone member states and has led to a reduction in transaction costs by helping economies become more competitive. Also, the euro has helped with political integration because the four fundamental freedoms that are required for membership in the European Union are enhanced by the use of a single currency in the countries of the Eurozone.

Nevertheless, the economic situation of some Eurozone members has generated doubts that the euro can be considered an optimal currency for the Eurozone. The theory of "optimum currency area" holds that a currency can be considered optimal for a group of countries if it helps maintain (1) full employment, (2) balance of international payments, and (3) stable prices.

Economic theory explains that the economic situation of a country is reflected in the strength of its currency. It is a fact that during the Pax Britannica the strength of sterling represented the global hegemonic power of Britain. However, due to the deregulation of currencies and financial markets and the effects of globalization, the strength of a currency may convey little information about the economic health of a country and almost nothing about the country's competitiveness in the world.

It is therefore important to analyze the current strength of the euro. It does not appear that the strong euro seen since 2001 was the result of strong economic fundamentals in the Eurozone. Instead, it appears to be the result of U.S. political and economic interests. U.S. authorities appear to have been interested in maintaining a weak U.S. dollar against the euro and other major currencies with several economic purposes in mind. Among these reasons are to help the U.S. export sector and reduce the huge trade deficit, lower the financial costs of the wars in Iraq and Afghanistan and devalue the debt issued by the U.S. Federal Reserve and now largely in the hands of countries such as China.

But if the U.S. trade deficit explained why the dollar was so weak, the current trade imbalances in the euro area cannot explain why the euro was so strong (Munchau 2007). In fact, the strength of the euro in recent years sparked harsh criticism from former French President Nicolas Sarkozy, who repeatedly asked for a common policy that would help lower the value of the euro. He argued that the euro exchange rate policy should be actively managed to ensure the competitiveness of products in the Eurozone, and deliberately advocated maintaining the euro at a level that would not affect the economic growth of the Eurozone. These words drew severe criticisms from Joaquín Almunia who was the EU's Commissioner for Economic and Monetary Affairs at the time. He declared that France should not blame the euro for the lack of French

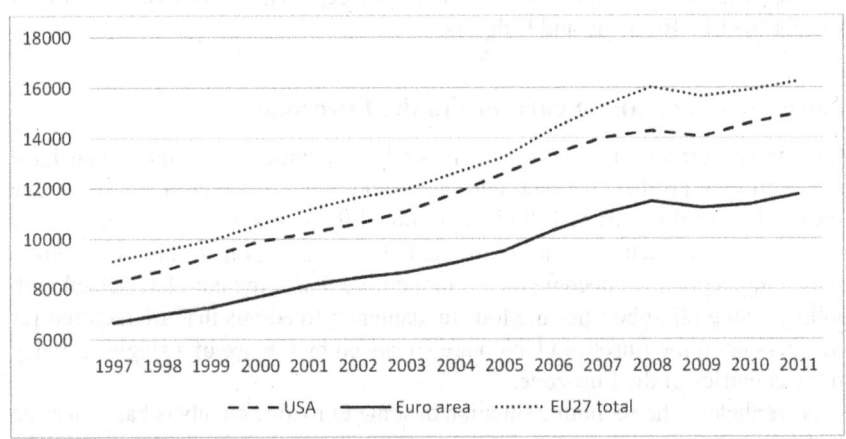

Figure 1.1 GDP in the USA and Europe, 1997–2011 (US$ billion).
Source: Based on data from OECD (2011).

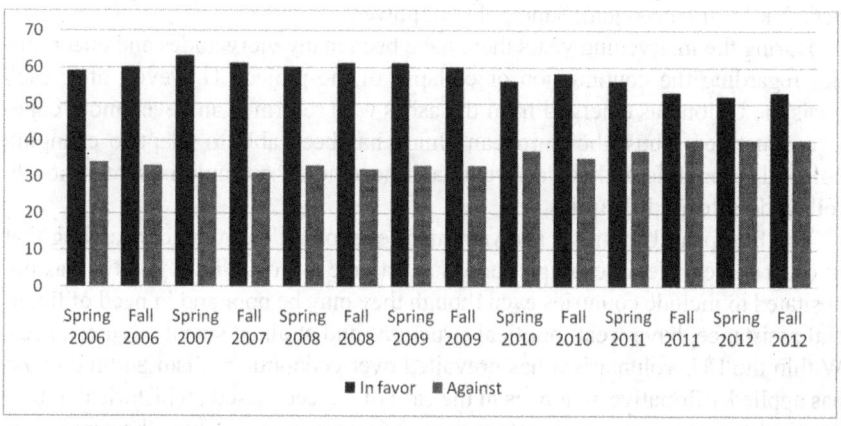

Figure 1.2 Public opinion on the euro, 2006–2012 (%).
Source: Based on data from the Eurobarometer 78.

competitiveness and the difficult economic situation of the country and should, rather, pay more attention to the evolution of the country's labor costs and productivity (Goldirova 2007).

It is noteworthy that the Eurozone's economic behavior directly influences the economic performance of the EU as a whole. Gross domestic product (GDP) is an economic indicator that shows the importance and economic weight of a country and in this case explains the economic importance of the euro area. The latest report of the Organization for Economic Cooperation and Development (OECD 2011–2012) showed that in 2012 the United States reported a GDP of US$14.991 billion while the EU reported a GDP of US$16.248 billion and the Eurozone US$11.748 billion. The GDP of euro area member states therefore accounted for more than 70% of the EU's total GDP and highlighted the importance of the euro area within the EU.

The current economic misfortunes of some countries are sparking questions of whether the euro has become a friend or an enemy. Some argue that the euro is the main cause of difficult economic times that some countries are suffering. The Eurobarometer survey No. 78,[10] published in December of 2012, showed that only 53% of EU citizens surveyed were in favor of the euro while 40% were against it. It is important to highlight that the euro held a 60% acceptance level between 2006 and 2009. The currency's approval rating has been declining since, however. The following graph shows the evolution of the euro's acceptance.

Final words

The creation of the European Union has been a long process that began after the Second World War, when a group of six countries agreed on the need to prevent further wars between France and Germany. Today, the EU is a group of 28 members that form an economic and political power.

During the intervening years there have been many vicissitudes and uncertainties regarding the continuation or collapse of the project. However, after each crisis the Union has emerged from the ashes with reformed and even more cohesive structures. Thus, the European Union has been able to adapt to changing political, economic and social events and become an example of integration to follow despite all difficulties.

The European Union has shown a high level of solidarity, understanding that in order to become an example, power must take a broad view. The EU has not hesitated to include countries even though they may be poor and in need of financial assistance, have weak political structures and strained social circumstances. Within the EU, voluntarism has prevailed over economic realism and the union has applied affirmative action, as in the case of Greece, based on historical, philosophical and political criteria rather than economic reasons. Thus, the project has had a demonstrably positive impact on member states and neighboring countries because there has been a systematic improvement of living standards of the citizens who become part of this club.

The introduction of the euro has also been an act of trust and cooperation because it means that those who leave their national currencies to adopt the euro rely on the economic maturity and solidarity of their new partners. The different aid packages granted to the countries of the Eurozone with economic problems have been costly samples of the solidarity spirit of the European Union.

Notes

1. Winston Churchill. www.creatinghistory.com/never-has-so-much-been-owed-to-so-few/.
2. France, West Germany, Italy, Belgium, Luxemburg and the Netherlands.
3. Europa. Accession criteria (Copenhagen criteria). europa.eu/legislation_summaries/glossary/accession_criteria_copenhague_en.htm.
4. Europa. The 2004 enlargement: the challenge of a 25-member EU. europa.eu/legislation_summaries/enlargement/2004_and_2007_enlargement/e50017_en.htm.
5. The Eurozone consists of Austria, Belgium, Cyprus, Estonia, Finland, France, Germany, Greece, Ireland, Italy, Latvia, Lithuania, Luxembourg, Malta, The Netherlands, Portugal, Slovakia, Slovenia and Spain.
6. Modifies the Treaty of the European Union (Maastricht Treaty) and the Treaty establishing the European Economic Community (Treaty of Rome).
7. The Lisbon Treaty, Protocol on the Internal Market and Competition. www.lisbon-treaty.org/wcm/the-lisbon-treaty/protocols-annexed-to-the-treaties/677-protocol-on-the-internal-market-and-competition.html.
8. European Union. Schuman Declaration, May 9, 1950. europa.eu/about-eu/basic-information/symbols/europe-day/schuman-declaration/index_en.htm.
9. Conference of the Representatives of the Governments of the Member States. Treaty of Lisbon amending the Treaty on European Union and the Treaty establishing the European Community, December 3, 2007. www.consilium.europa.eu/uedocs/cmsUpload/cg00014.en07.pdf.
10. European Commission. Public Opinion on the European Union, Standard Eurobarometer 78, Autumn 2012. ec.europa.eu/public_opinion/archives/eb/eb78/eb78_first_en.pdf.

2 The birth of the European Union and the Eurozone

History, myths, truths, and lies

> So much barbarism, however, still remains in the transactions of most civilized nations that almost all independent countries choose to assert their nationality by having, to their inconvenience and that of their neighbors, a peculiar currency of their own.
>
> (John Stuart Mill)[1]

Introduction

The twentieth century witnessed dramatic changes in the state and the nature of government and governance. In the first half of the century, humanity endured two World Wars, experienced a Cold War and suffered a Great Economic Depression. The second half of the century showed that cooperation is more productive than destruction, conflict and confrontation, which only bring social misery and economic pauperism. In particular, the end of the Cold War and the early stages of globalization helped a number of countries to understand that cooperation and the coordination of economic strategies can help to find synergies and generate more prosperity than a "zero-sum" game.

The devastation that the Second World War created in many nations required the implementation of a new economic and political system that began with the urgent need to correct dangerous imbalances in the monetary system—specifically, currency fluctuations to help trade flourish. Thus, the second half of the twentieth century saw the implementation of the Gold Standard and the Bretton Woods System, which was in force until President Richard Nixon ended it in 1971. The disappearance of this system was followed by a period of monetary instability, which helped European countries understand the need for a common currency that would do away with exchange rate fluctuations and transaction costs and help with price transparency.

The introduction of the euro has been considered the most dramatic change in the world's monetary systems since the adoption of the Gold Standard. The euro therefore has helped to integrate the various European economies, at a time when globalization has been wreaking havoc, into a united front to struggle efficiently in a multipolar world.

In 1954, Jean Monnet argued that European countries were very small compared to the United States, Russia or China and should unite to increase their strength and presence. The euro indeed has brought integration and prosperity, but also has many detractors such as U.S. economist Milton Friedman, who predicted that the euro would not be able to withstand a crisis because of the economic and political differences between those countries that adopted it.[2]

Before the introduction of the euro, officially on January 1, 1999 and physically two years later, each country had its own currency that represented the sovereignty of each nation and its people. When the common European currency was agreed, there were several disputes about what would be the format as well as the very essence of the common currency.

The original idea of a common European currency came from Robert Mundell, who won the Nobel Prize in Economics (1999). But while he is considered the intellectual father of the euro, it is important to note that he argued both sides of the issue on European monetary unification and the adoption of common monetary standards.

In some of his early studies, such as "A Theory of Optimum Currency Areas" published in 1961 in the *American Economic Review*, Mundell opposed a common monetary policy and argued in favor of making currency areas smaller rather than larger. However, at the 1970 Madrid conference on optimum currency areas he presented two innovative papers on the advantages of common currencies. In the first of these papers, "Uncommon Arguments for Common Currencies," (Mundell 1973b) he emphasized the forward-looking nature of the foreign exchange market. His second paper at the Madrid conference, titled "A Plan for a European Currency" (Mundell 1973a, 5), made clear his enthusiasm for the great European experiment:

> The only way to establish a unified money market is to kill the sporadic and unsettling speculation over currency prices that ravaged the European markets between 1967 and 1969 (. . .) Rather than moving toward more flexibility in exchange rates within Europe the economic arguments suggest less flexibility and a closer integration of capital markets. These economic arguments are supported by social arguments as well. On every occasion when a social disturbance leads to the threat of a strike, and the strike to an increase in wages unjustified by increases in productivity and thence to devaluation, the national currency becomes threatened. Long-run costs for the nation as a whole are bartered away by governments for what they presume to be short-run political benefits. If instead, the European currencies were bound together disturbances in the country would be cushioned, with the shock weakened by capital movements.

Indeed, in this work he explained the benefits of a common currency among European countries, which he named "europa." After the Madrid conference Lorenzo Bini-Smaghi, who was then a senior official of the European Monetary Institute (EMI), contacted Professor Mundell to delve more deeply into this novel idea. Bini-Smaghi wanted to know if Mundell himself had come up with the name for the currency. Mundell replied that he had not only come up with that name but also sensed that the popular use would shorten the name of the common currency to "euro" (Mundell 2002b). When Bini-Smaghi asked on how long it would take to introduce a common currency in Europe, Mundell replied it would be harder than expected, even if there were no political obstacles. Mundell expected it would take at least three weeks (Mundell 2002b). The introduction of the euro took three decades.

Although the euro physically entered circulation on January 1, 2002, production of banknotes and coins began in July 1999. A total of 15 mints spread across Europe were needed to print the first 14,900 million euro bills (equivalent to covering 15,000 football fields) of different denominations that were needed to launch the currency. Similarly, 16 mints were needed to strike a total of 52,000 million coins which weighed more 250,000 tons.[3] In mid-2011 there were 14,200 billion banknotes worth 847,000 million euros in circulation, and the European Central Bank reported that there were 95,600 million coins with a total value of 22,800 million euros. It was also reported that in the first half of 2011 a total of 295,553 counterfeit euro bills had been withdrawn from circulation.[4]

Since May of 2010, the EU and the Eurozone have faced a very difficult period that even suggested that the project and the integration process might come to an abrupt end. The reasons are twofold. The upward economic cycle, which brought with it an illusion of a new project, is over, and the economic crises now plaguing most countries in the Eurozone are putting into question all the mechanisms for economic and monetary controls and procedures. Second, with the addition of 12 new countries to the EU between 2004 and 2007 the European project seems complete. Consequently, the creation phase of the EU has come to an end and the process now lacks the dynamism and enthusiasm of the beginning.

Given this sense of an end of an era or a cycle, it may be that the Lisbon Treaty seems stalled mainly because there has been little progress toward integration in areas such as security, defense, immigration and social policies. Even the four freedoms—the movement of capital, services, goods and people across national borders—are still not fully implemented. All this has been exacerbated by the economic crises and financial turmoil that is causing some actors to wonder about the future of the EU and the euro.

The inception of the euro: past, present and future

The idea of having a monetary union among European countries has long existed in the region. In fact, throughout history there have been several unsuccessful attempts to create a monetary union. Bartel (1974) counted four major attempts: The Austro-German Monetary Union (1857–1866), the Latin Monetary Union (1865–1927), the Scandinavian Monetary Union between Denmark, Norway and Sweden (1875–1917), and one between Belgium and Luxembourg in 1921.

The creation of the Economic and Monetary Union required several political and economic efforts. The Werner Report was presented in 1969,[5] the European Monetary System and the ECU were launched in 1979 and 1989 saw the implementation of the so-called Delors Report (1989) proposed by Jacques Delors as a roadmap to facilitate the introduction of the single currency in three stages.

There is an important difference between those earlier and unsuccessful attempts at monetary unions and the introduction of the euro. While the attempts in the nineteenth and early twentieth centuries based their growth on the availability and value of gold and silver, the euro area is based on two pillars:[6] an economic union and a monetary union. The monetary union is based on the existence of the euro as a common currency and on the implementation of a common monetary policy monitored by the European Central Bank (ECB), whose primary mandate is to maintain inflation under control. The economic union is based on the Stability and Growth Pact (SGP), designed to maintain fiscal stability by imposing specific requirements on member states of the euro area.

In April 1989, the Delors Report laid out the plan for entering the Economic and Monetary Union and the definitive introduction of the euro in three well-structured phases. The first stage was programmed to take place between July 1990 and December 1994, and introduced the first of the four freedoms that form the pillars of the EU: the liberalization of capital movements. It also completed the internal market and removed restrictions on further financial integration. The second stage (1994–1999) involved the establishment of a series of economic and fiscal standards that countries aspiring to be part of the economic and monetary union must adhere to before they could adopt the euro. These requirements forced countries to achieve the same levels and standards on economic and fiscal policies. These requirements were called the Convergence Criteria, and were included in the Maastricht Treaty. They also established the European Monetary Institute to strengthen central bank cooperation and prepare for the European System of Central Banks (ESCB). This second stage planned the transition to the euro and defined the future governance of the Eurozone (the Stability and Growth Pact). Finally, in the third stage (1999 onward) exchange rates were fixed and the euro was launched.

The Maastricht Treaty, which was signed in 1992 and entered into force in November 1993, established a number of economic convergence criteria for adopting the euro that member countries had to follow on the issues of inflation,[7] public debt and deficit accounts,[8] interest rates[9] and exchange rates.[10] Member states of the European Union wishing to adopt the euro as a common currency in the third phase of the Delors Plan were obliged to meet these requirements. The ECB set the conversion rates between the euro and the national currencies of the 11 participating countries.

Finally, at the European Council meeting held in Amsterdam in 1997, the so-called Stability and Growth Pact forced compliance once countries in the Eurozone had adopted the single currency. The SGP can be understood as a gentleman's agreement in which Eurozone countries pledge to honor economic performance and budgetary disciplines designed to ensure the stability of the common currency. Most states have not respected this covenant and have not revealed their true financial and economic standing, with the consequently negative impact for the Eurozone.

Fiscal policy was therefore left in the hands of governments but with clear limits on debt and deficit, and monetary policy stopped being national and was turned over to the European Central Bank with an explicit mandate to ensure the stability of prices.

In 1999, 11[11] of the 15 EU countries were able to meet the requirements for entering the third stage and adopt the euro, creating the so-called Eurozone or euro area. Denmark, Sweden and the UK decided not to adopt the euro and to date have not done so. The case of Greece is significant because Greece wanted to adopt the euro on January 1, 1999 but was not able to meet the economic targets set by the convergence criteria specified in the Maastricht Treaty. It was somehow able to meet the criteria in 2000 and was admitted to the euro club on January 1, 2001. Between 2004 and 2007 a total of 12 new countries joined the European Union, but only seven have met the Maastricht convergence criteria for adopting the euro so far. The other countries are still working on meeting the requirements.

The common currency and some social peculiarities: the new millionaires and Euroskeptics

The euro has become an international currency that helped strengthen the image of the Eurozone and the EU as a political bloc. According to the survey "Survey on the Use of Euro Cash Outside the EU" (European Commission 2004) the availability of euros abroad in banks and exchange offices has improved, helping to promote the image of the Eurozone as a powerful international actor.

The introduction of the euro has never been free of debate for several reasons. First, there are seven denominations of bills, with the 5 euro bill the smallest and the 500 euro bill the largest.[12] This high denomination has been highly criticized mainly because it is very uncomfortable for consumers yet very convenient for tax evasion. Second, the physical size of the banknotes varies, with the 5 euro banknote the smallest and the 500 euro bill the biggest. The 5 euro banknote is 12 cm long and 6 cm wide, a size that from the beginning drew comparisons to the money used in the Monopoly board game and made the euro banknote lose respect in the eyes of some of the users. The Monopoly banknotes measured about 10 cm by 6 cm wide.

Finally, at the street level the main problem with the introduction of the euro was a wide tendency to "round up" when setting prices in euros, leading to a general rise in prices that affected the rate of inflation in some countries. For example, in the case of Spain the exchange rate was established on December 31, 1998 at one euro to 166.386 pesetas. So if a price set at 100 pesetas became one euro that was an effective overnight price hike of 66%.

Furthermore, the euro created and destroyed millionaires indiscriminately. Technically, a millionaire is someone with at least one million of his nation's national currency, if that national currency can be trusted as a store of value. For example, in the German case a millionaire was someone with a million German marks. However, when Germany adopted the euro, the exchange was set at one euro equal to 1.95583 marks. This meant that to be a euro-millionaire in Germany it was necessary to have the equivalent of almost two million marks. In France,

Table 2.1 To be a euro-millionaire

In	1 euro is...	1 million...	1 million euros
Spain	186.386 pesetas	Pesetas = €6,000	= 166 million pesetas
Germany	1.95583 D-mark	D-mark = €511,291,881	= 1,9 million D-mark
France	6.55957 French francs	French francs = €152,671	= 6,5 million French francs

Source: Author's calculations.

the euro was pegged at 6.55957 French francs, so to be a euro-millionaire in that country required more than 6.5 million francs.

The design of the euro banknotes opened another political debate because the common currency was expected to show only nonexistent architectural images to prevent the appearance of favoring national preferences (Cowell, cited in Hymans n.d.). While some applauded this neutrality as a sign of respect and objectivity for the new period of European integration, others were reluctant to lose icons representative of their identity and sovereignty. They criticized the failure to show any national architectural references as meaning that some parts of European history would be lost. For Germans the Deutschmark symbolized the resurgence of the country from the ashes of the Second World War and the reunification of the "two Germanies" under one coin. In fact, it is estimated that nostalgic Germans still have more than 13 billion marks between paper money and coins at home, with an estimated value of roughly 6 billion euros (Fuhrmans 2011).

Due to this decision to avoid national references, in 2009 the EU asked its citizens to vote on the design of a 2-euro coin commemorating the tenth anniversary of the euro.[13] On Thursday May 2, 2013, a new 5 euro banknote was put into circulation with the image of Europa, the goddess in Greek mythology for whom the continent was named.

Euroskeptics have been predicting the fall of the euro since 1992. Euroskepticism is the term used to describe those who oppose or do not believe in the process of European integration. This group grew out of the UK when the country joined the European Economic Community (EEC) even though there was some domestic political opposition to this move. The UK has refused from the outset to adopt the euro for two main reasons. As Stuart Mill argued, a national currency is a politically powerful symbol of independence, freedom and sovereignty. And as Mundell noted, a country that has been a dominant hegemonic power usually rejects a new currency, particularly if the new currency represents a threat to the position of its own national currency on the global stage.

With the intensification of the integration process, Euroskepticism now encompasses all doubts or opposition to anything related to the EU, the euro, and the Eurozone. Euroskeptic voices are now present in the European Parliament, where the Seventh Parliament had to allow the formation of a multi-party group called "Europe of Freedom and Democracy."[14] This group consists of 34 elected members

Table 2.2 Europe of Freedom and Democracy

Individual parties	Members
Frank Vanhecke (Belgium)	1
National Front for the Salvation of Bulgaria	1
Danish People's Party (Denmark)	1
Finns Party (Finland)	1
Movement for France (France)	1
Popular Orthodox Rally (Greece)	2
Northern Italy & I Love Italy (Italy)	9 + 1
Order and Justice (Lithuania)	2
Reformed Political Party (Netherlands)	1
UK Independent Party (UKIP) (UK)	10
Slovak National Party (Slovakia)	1
United Poland (Poland)	4

Source: Europe of Freedom and Democracy.

from different political parties and different countries who share anti-integration beliefs and favor the absolute sovereign independence of European states.

Euroskeptics currently tend to focus on two main issues. Their biggest concern is the economy, including doubts on the feasibility of an economic and monetary union and the euro as a common currency. Their second concern is with the lack of accountability in the implementation of the SGP and the slow pace for resolving fundamental economic and structural problems. These two points, together with what Euroskeptics see as an insufficient and incomplete integration process, add up to what has been called "Euro-sclerosis."

Within the Euroskeptic group there are also those who believe that the EMU and the euro have a hidden agenda: that the euro was planned with the sole purpose of challenging the economic supremacy of the United States. Professor Mundell indeed argued that the introduction of the euro would generate economic benefits as well as a number of important geopolitical benefits. Mundell believed that the introduction of the euro would help unite European countries against a possible invasion by the Soviet Union, erase Franco-German enmity once and for all and unite Europe as one strong bloc that could face the United States in an increasingly globalized world (Mundell 2002a). However, most Euroskeptics believe the euro is destined to remain a distant second to the U.S. dollar (Cohen 2003) and will never challenge the dominant role of the dollar as an official currency reserve—even though by December 2006 there were more euros than U.S. dollars in physical circulation around the world (Atkins 2006).

Opinions on the EU, the Eurozone, the euro and the economic crisis of 2010

The current economic crises are threatening the European project. Different actors have raised questions and concerns about the integration process and the future of the euro. They question whether economic and monetary integration is still

20 *Introduction to the EU*

positive for the development of a nation. They doubt whether the EU is the best actor to defend the economic interests of nations hit by economic crisis. And those countries that have been (or are) in the midst of a severe economic downturn wonder if being part of the EU and the Eurozone is still in their best interests.

A thorough analysis of opinions in EU member states gathered by the Eurobarometer polling firm shows that due to the current economic and financial crisis, Europeans favor dismantling the EU and the euro, and in fact want to bring back the structures of the nation-state to support their political and economic interests. The 77th Eurobarometer (European Commission 2012) poll of EU citizens, taken May 12–17, 2012, shows EU institutions losing trust while national institutions are gaining it.

The following chart shows that those countries with greater economic problems reported more discontent with their evolution and handling of the economic situation. By contrast, northern countries with fiscal stability were less affected by the crisis and showed a less negative attitude towards the EU and the euro. The chart also shows that those countries which suffer the economic crisis and have received financial support from the Institutions reported more dissatisfaction with the current economic situation Again, northern European countries did not express high levels of dissatisfaction with their economies.

The loss of confidence in the institutions of the EU is reflected in the Special Eurobarometer report No. 379, which shows that the percentage of respondents happy with the unification project lost one point since February 2006. In addition,

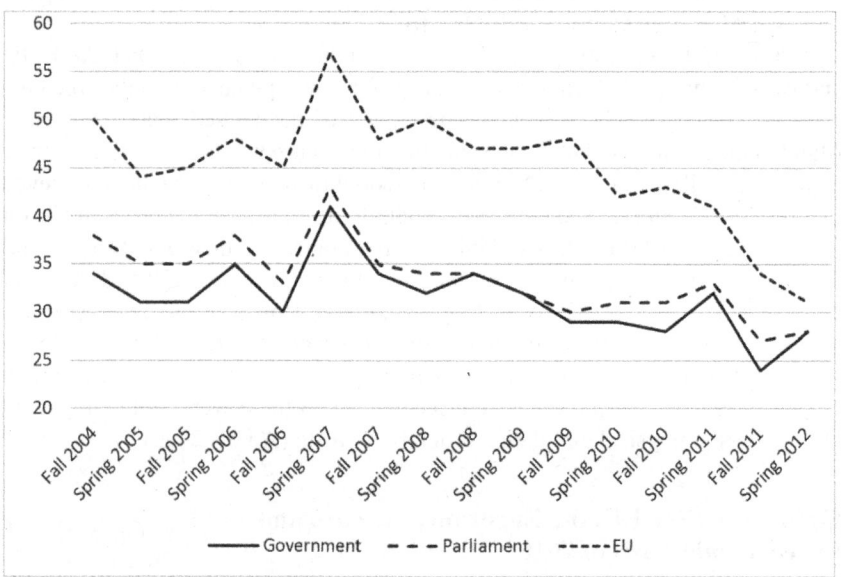

Figure 2.1 Levels of public trust in EU institutions, 2004–2012 (%).

Source: Based on data from the Eurobarometer No. 77.

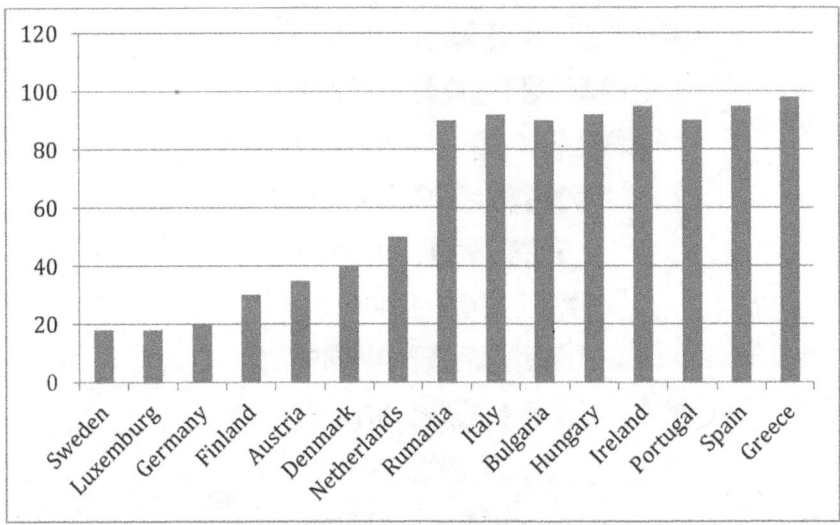

Figure 2.2 Levels of public discontent with the handling of the crisis and the economy, 2012.
Source: Based on data from the Eurobarometer No. 77.

this study showed that those who said they were dissatisfied with the project increased from 9% in 2006 to 11% in 2011, and that countries experiencing serious economic difficulties reported greater dissatisfaction and unhappiness with the living conditions in the EU, as reflected in the chart below.

Special Eurobarometer 379 also showed that respondents felt that the EU economy was better than the economies of India and Brazil but worse than the economies of the United States, China and Japan. As a result of the economic crises, popular support for economic and monetary union is losing ground, as evidenced in the following chart (European Commission 2012).

The surveys also showed a growing desire to reduce the speed of construction of the European project (Eurobarometer 64), which coincides with the fact that 55% believed the situation was going in the wrong direction in their country and 39% had doubts about the EU project (Special Eurobarometer No. 308). However, when citizens were asked whether the integration process should be delayed until all countries in the EU reached the same economic level—to avoid creating a two-speed Europe in which the countries of the north would be far more advanced than those in the south and east—the surveys revealed that 47% believed there should be no delay. Those who believed the process should be delayed, however, increased from 37% in the spring of 2007 to 40% in the December 2011 survey.

The economic crises clearly also influenced public opinion in Europe on the introduction of the euro. An IPSOS survey among member states published May 24, 2012 showed that 65% of respondents said that if there were a referendum on the euro they would vote for continuity, while 34% would vote to exit the euro zone.

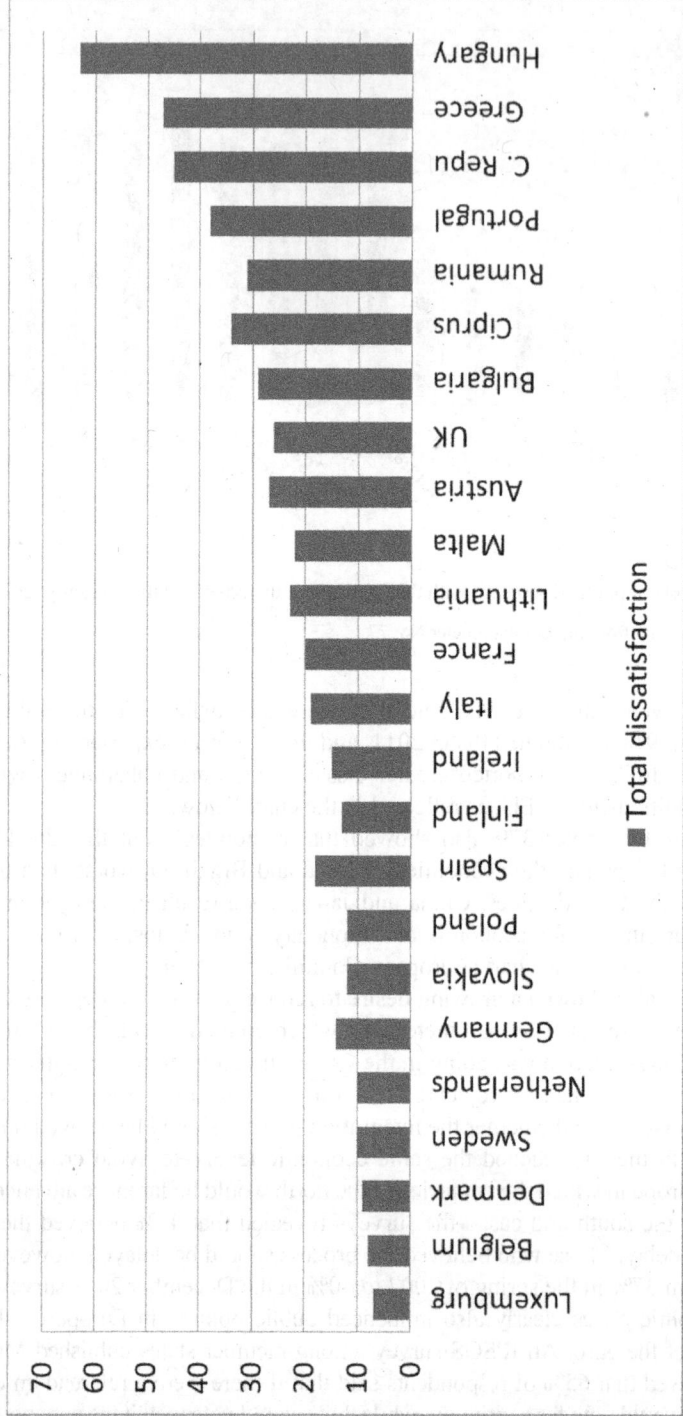

Figure 2.3 Levels of public dissatisfaction with the U.S. economy by state, 2012 (%).

Source: Based on data from the Special Eurobarometer 379.

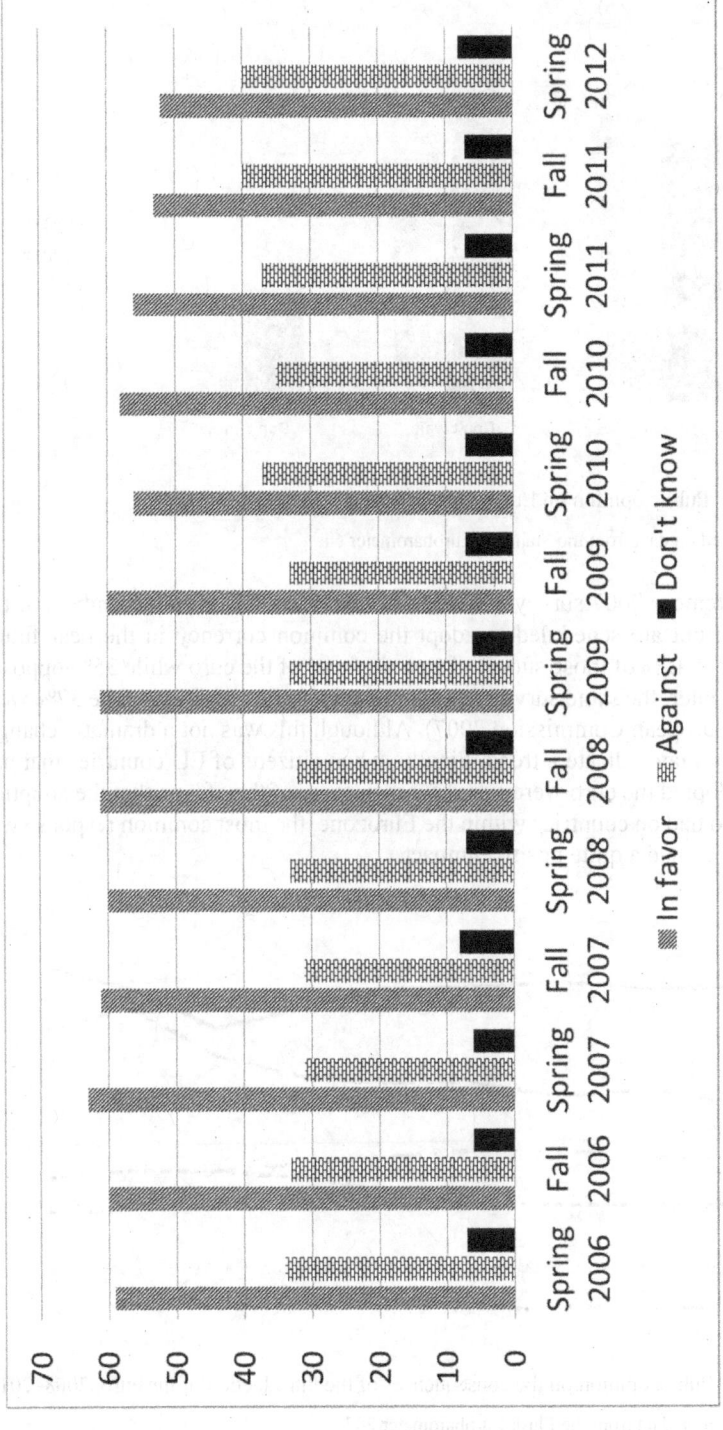

Figure 2.4 Public opinion on the EMU and the euro, 2006–2012.
Source: Based on data from the Special Eurobarometer 379.

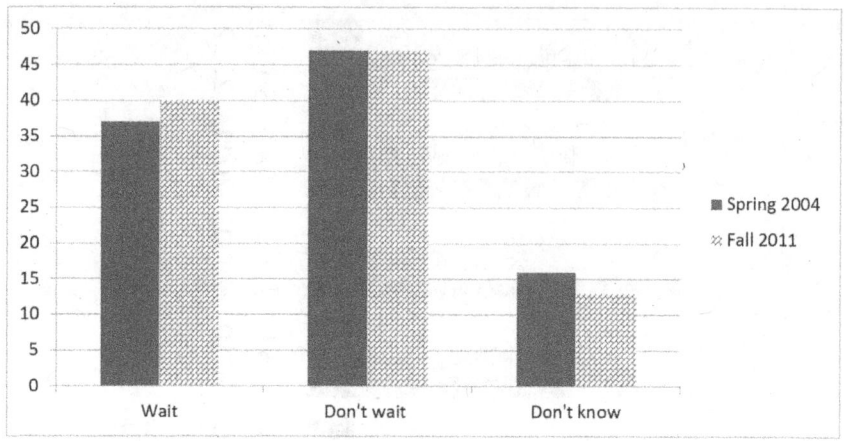

Figure 2.5 Public opinion on Europe at two speeds, 2004 and 2011.

Source: Based on data from the Standard Eurobarometer 64.

A September 2007 survey taken in EU countries that are not members of the euro zone but are scheduled to adopt the common currency in the near future showed that 45% of those surveyed were in favor of the euro while 35% opposed it. A year later, the same survey reported that 44% were in favor while 37% were against (European Commission 2007). Although this was not a dramatic change, it certainly may indicate a trend. Finally, when citizens of EU countries that had not yet adopted the euro were asked for their view of the effects that the adoption of the euro had on countries within the Eurozone, the most common response was that the euro had a quite positive impact.

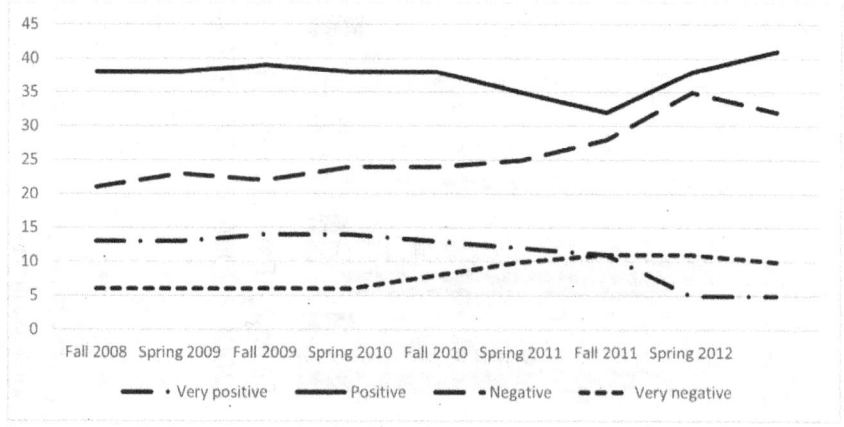

Figure 2.6 Public opinion on the consequences of the introduction of the euro, 2008–2012.

Source: Based on data from the Flash Eurobarometer 207.

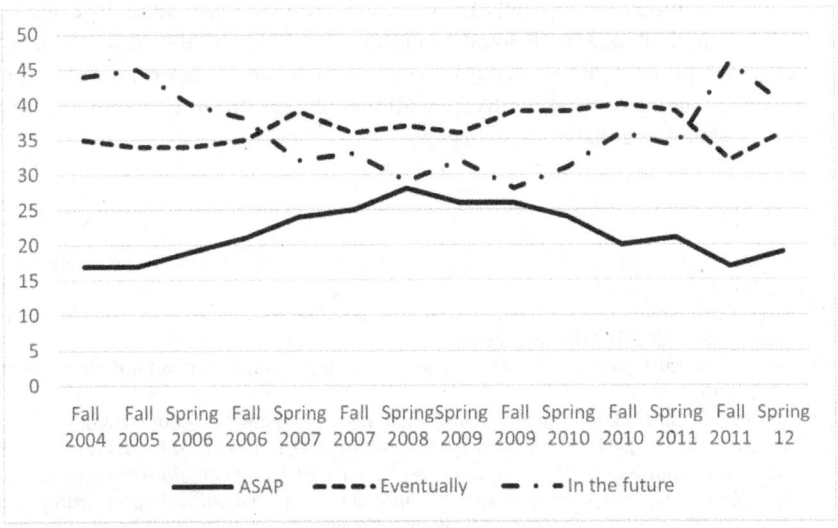

Figure 2.7 Public opinion on the best time to introduce the euro, 2004–2012.
Source: Based on data from the Flash Eurobarometer 207.

Final words

Euroskeptics did not expect that the Eurozone project could be a success. On the basis of previous failed attempts they assumed that the euro was only going to be another failure. However, all previous economic unions, including the Bretton Woods system, failed because the underlying economic growth was based on a commodity, a scarce resource that tied the economic growth of countries to the extraction and accumulation of that commodity. Gold became a tribal *totem* that limited the creation of value and wealth. The euro, however, is backed by productivity growth and most importantly the countries' investment capacity—unlimited resources that have intangible value.

If the Gold Standard was backed by supplies of gold, the euro is backed by the Stability and Growth Pact. Finally, the strong position of the euro is ensuring the reputation of the Eurozone as a major economic player, and the strength of the euro has helped the Eurozone achieve a prestigious position in the international political arena, strengthening its so-called, "soft power."

The integration of countries in the EU has forced them to join the secular business cycle. From its inception until the last membership expansion in 2007, the EU has enjoyed a period of economic growth. But due to the global crisis, the EU and the Eurozone zone have now entered a phase of political and economic stagnation. The problems of "Eurosclerosis" so highly criticized by Euroskeptics must now be overcome to help the bloc face the two major challenges of the twenty-first century. One is the economic challenge resulting from the deregulation of markets and institutions in countries like the United States, China and India, which forces the European bloc to completely restructure its production system. The second is an internal challenge, with some countries of the EU and the euro area lately developing a protectionist tendency as a defense mechanism against the effects of deregulation and globalization. Despite all this, the European Union must return to the understanding that *unity is strength*.

Notes

1. Robert C. Feenstra y Alan M. Taylor. *Macroeconomía internacional*, Barcelona, España: Editorial Reverte.
2. Milton Friedman. "Canada and flexible exchange rates." www.bankofcanada.ca/wp-content/uploads/2010/08/keynote.pdf.
3. Banco Central Europeo. "Initial changeover (2002)." www.ecb.int/euro/changeover/2002/html/index.en.html.
4. European Central Bank. "Biannual information on euro banknote counterfeiting." Press release, July 18, 2011. www.ecb.int/press/pr/date/2011/html/pr110718.en.html.
5. European Commission. 1970, *Report to the Council and the Commission on the realisation by stages of economic and monetary union in the Community*. http://ec.europa.eu/economy_finance/publications/publication6142_en.pdf.
6. Subdirección General de Asuntos Económicos y Financieros de la Unión Europea. "El Pacto de estabilidad y crecimiento," *Boletín Económico de ICE N. 2905*, del 16 al 28 de Febrero de 2007.
7. Inflation of no more than 1.5 percentage points above the average rate of the three EU member states with the lowest inflation over the previous year.
8. A national budget deficit at or below 3% of GDP and national public debt not exceeding 60% of GDP.
9. Long-term interest rates should be no more than two percentage points above the rate in the three EU countries with the lowest inflation over the previous year.
10. Applicant countries should not have devalued the central rate of their euro-pegged currency and should have maintained currency stability during the previous two years.
11. Belgium, Germany, Spain, France, Greece, Ireland, Italy, Luxembourg, Netherland, Austria, Portugal, Finland.
12. Banco Central Europeo. "Billetes." www.ecb.int/euro/banknotes/html/index.es.html.
13. Euobserver. "EU citizens to choose new euro coin design," *Euobserver.com*, February 7, 2008. euobserver.com/9/25623.
14. Europe of Freedom and Democracy. www.efdgroup.eu/.

Part II
The European Union and the economic crisis
The challenge

3 The economic crisis
Political and economic problems

> People do not understand what a great revenue economy is.
> (Marcus Tullius Cicero, 55 BC)[1]

Introduction

Despite the great success of the euro during its first decade of existence, several governments in the Eurozone faced a major crisis in 2010 and 2011 that put the euro project in question and the euro area on its knees before the world. The Eurozone countries must take responsibility and strengthen efforts to coordinate and reform the economic, monetary and social policies needed to maintain the positive performance of the project. Countries must adopt and carry out these reforms in order to avoid a painful result.

Greece has jeopardized all the past work because its continued lack of economic transparency has generated the Eurozone's first truly dangerous crisis of the last 20 years. Its concealment of the true state of its economic and political problems and its reluctance to upgrade and modernize its economy makes one wonder what happened to a Greek political class whose ancestors—Socrates, Plato and Aristotle—argued for the existence of a perfect state and government.

But Greece is not an isolated case, and there have been other countries which suffered a series of asymmetric shocks that led some to "think the unthinkable." The crisis appears to have increased the costs of participating in the Eurozone because of the dramatic events that resulted from the poor economic management and lack of political accountability in these countries. The Euroskeptics who predicted the inadequacy of a common monetary policy for certain countries indeed now seem to have been correct. What's more, leaving the euro club has become a possibility that is both imaginable and desirable, especially for those countries experiencing financial difficulties due to the level of government debt and the collapse of the national banking system that even sparked unprecedented civil unrest. However, abandoning the euro area is a complicated issue, both from a legal standpoint because it is not covered in any of the EU agreements, and from the economic point of view because the reintroduction of a national currency would be a difficult and painful process.

The solution to the crisis unleashed by the Greek tragedy requires a long-term approach that includes the introduction of mechanisms to help restructure and strengthen the social and economic fundamentals and policies that will help the project to emerge from its ashes, much like a phoenix.

The proper functioning of the Economic and Monetary Union (EMU) depends on the member states' adoption and enforcement of the required monetary and fiscal policies as well as the implementation of a series of structural reforms, especially in the labor market, to promote economic growth and the stability of the euro. However, the creation of the Eurozone was accompanied by an economic bubble, created by an increase in the monetary base available that led to a property boom in many countries.

Countries now must pay the piper, but there's little money to keep the euro area out of a crisis It is difficult to settle the excesses of the past when money is more urgently needed to restructure the economy. With the EU facing this dire situation, uncertainty about the future of the euro and the Union remains high.

The Eurozone crisis and the euro

The economic instability in certain countries of the Eurozone did not emerge spontaneously but was, rather, the result of the continuous mismanagement of their economies. The economic boom of the preceding years and the infatuation with the euro made some countries believe that it was not necessary to respect the criteria of the Stability and Growth Pact (SGP). They believed that their economic expansion would be eternal and would counteract all of their political and economic shortcomings.

The upswing of their economies created a mirage that suggested to politicians that they did not need to make any structural reforms in order to improve the economic health, competitiveness and productivity of their countries. The SGP required all countries adopting the euro to maintain their national debt below 60% of GDP and their budget deficit below 3% of GDP. It became clear in 2010, however, that most countries in the Eurozone did not meet either of the two requirements of the SGP, yet their possible "punishment" for failing to comply was never clearly stated nor much debated.

Although there was already an ongoing debate on the sustainability of public debt levels accumulated by certain countries before then, the critical moment came in late November 2009 when the holding company Dubai World announced that it would negotiate a rescheduling of the maturities of the company's debt, totaling approximately US$26 billion (Intereconomia 2009). At the same time, rating agencies and other financial institutions began to review the finances of some countries more closely.

This more thorough analysis brought to light that Greece had been hiding valuable information about the real situation of its budget and economic problems. As a result, in late 2009 the credit rating agency Fitch Ratings downgraded the sovereign debt of Greece, from 'A-' to 'BBB +' with a negative perspective, which opened the door to other cuts. The agency explained that the difficulties of the

Hellenic public finances, the "weak credibility" of its institutions, the medium-term expectations of the Greek government accounts and the uncertainty about a balanced and sustained recovery justified its drastic and sudden change of rating.

In early January 2010, Greece reported the true state of its public finances and confessed that the budget deficit in 2008 had not been the 5% of GDP that it had reported in April 2009 but rather 7.7% of GDP (European Commission 2010a). Furthermore, it was discovered that 2009 had closed with a deficit of more than 12% of GDP and not the 3.7% deficit promised in April 2009 (European Commission 2010a). By early 2010, the Greek public debt amounted to 113% of GDP, compared to the limit of 60% of GDP in the Stability and Growth Pact.

The Greek crisis required member states of the Eurozone to consider two tough options: to help or not to help the country. If financial assistance was not provided, Greece would collapse and drag down many other countries and institutions. Yet that fall would also show the need to respect the SGP. Moreover, it would also send a clear signal to other countries that any unwillingness to undertake vigorous economic, financial and political reforms would not be rewarded with economic aid, and that countries lacking financial discipline had no place in the euro club.

On the other hand, providing the funds needed to save the country would not only carry a high cost for all of the region's taxpayers but would highlight the possibility that the Eurozone had a problem of adverse selection—that countries might join the euro club in order to benefit from guarantees of financial protection in case of emergencies. Saving Greece would also increase the possibility that other countries would have fewer moral incentives to take care of their finances and might therefore engage in riskier economic and financial behavior because they expected that member states would be ready to help in case of economic or fiscal problems.

Greece continued to face an unmanageable government debt after 2010 that has now brought the nation to the brink of bankruptcy. Eurozone states continue to help, fearing a crisis that had eventually spread to other countries like Portugal, Ireland and peaked with Spain's problems beginning in the summer of 2012. Eurostat, the statistical branch of the European Commission, has reported that several countries remain unable to keep their deficits and debts under control and estimated debt compared to GDP at about 87% for the entire Eurozone, 66% for Spain, 87% for Germany, 85% for France and a chilling 159% for Greece.[2]

Legal conundrum on how to provide economic help

The EU and the Eurozone found themselves at a crossroads on how to solve their financial problems in part because the legal framework of the Lisbon Treaty (2007) does not provide the necessary tools to solve these types of financial problems.

The treaty makes it clear that countries are not required to provide financial assistance to other nations facing economic difficulties. The so-called no bail-out rule included in Article 125[3] notes that:

The Union shall not be liable for or assume the commitments of central governments, regional, local or other public authorities, other bodies governed by public law, or public undertakings of any Member State, without prejudice to mutual financial guarantees for the joint execution of a specific project. A Member State shall not be liable for or assume the commitments of central governments, regional, local or other public authorities, other bodies governed by public law, or public undertakings of another Member State, without prejudice to mutual financial guarantees for the joint execution of a specific project.

Article 125 was included in the treaty at the request of Germany in an attempt to force sound budgetary management on Eurozone countries. However, the Eurozone has financially assisted not only Greece but also Portugal, Ireland, Cyprus and Spain and even created several mechanisms for temporary and permanent relief in case of economic and financial difficulties. For starters, financial aid could be approved under Article 122(2),[4] which notes:

Where a Member State is in difficulties or is seriously threatened with severe difficulties caused by natural disasters or exceptional occurrences beyond its control, the Council, on a proposal from the Commission, may grant, under certain conditions, Union financial assistance to the Member State concerned. The President of the Council shall inform the European Parliament of the decision taken.

There has been some debate on whether the current debt crisis faced by many countries can qualify as an "exceptional occurrence," because these countries did not comply with the provisions of the Stability and Growth Pact. The Council of the European Union nevertheless enacted Regulation No. 407/2010[5] creating the European Financial Stabilization Mechanism (EFSM).

Secondly, although Article 50 of the Treaty of Lisbon[6] contemplates the possibility of a country exiting the EU, it does not contemplate the possibility of a country leaving the Eurozone but staying in the European Union and returning to a national currency in order to put its finances in order. Article 50 notes:

1 Any Member State may decide to withdraw from the Union in accordance with its own constitutional requirements.
2 A Member State which decides to withdraw shall notify the European Council of its intention. In the light of the guidelines provided by the European Council, the Union shall negotiate and conclude an agreement with that State, setting out the arrangements for its withdrawal, taking account of the framework for its future relationship with the Union. That agreement shall be negotiated in accordance with Article 218(3) of the Treaty on the Functioning of the European Union. It shall be concluded on behalf of the Union by the Council, acting by a qualified majority, after obtaining the consent of the European Parliament.

3   The Treaties shall cease to apply to the State in question from the date of entry into force of the withdrawal agreement or, failing that, two years after the notification referred to in paragraph 2, unless the European Council, in agreement with the Member State concerned, unanimously decides to extend this period.
4   For the purposes of paragraphs 2 and 3, the member of the European Council or of the Council representing the withdrawing Member State shall not participate in the discussions of the European Council or Council or in decisions concerning it. A qualified majority shall be defined in accordance with Article 238(3)(b) of the Treaty on the Functioning of the European Union.
5   If a State which has withdrawn from the Union asks to rejoin, its request shall be subject to the procedure referred to in Article 49.

The argument that a voluntary withdrawal from the Eurozone is impossible is based on the letter and spirit of various articles and especially Article 140 which directly mentions the "irrevocable fixing" of exchange rates and the irreversibility of the voluntary process for adopting the euro.[7] Therefore, participation in the Economic and Monetary Union becomes a legal obligation due to the irreversibility of the agreement and the irreversibility of the process of monetary union. Leaving the EMU and staying in the European Union is thus impossible. The only option is to leave the EU.

There are a number of reasons why a provision to facilitate the exit from the Eurozone was not incorporated into the treaty. First, the goal was to portray the adoption of the euro as a voluntary and closed agreement in which the member states share a total commitment to the Union. Second, the possibility of an expulsion or voluntary withdrawal clearly would have increased the risks of adverse selection and moral hazard. In addition, not having properly established procedures would increase the uncertainty of what might be the economic and political consequences if a country decided to leave the euro club. Finally, this crisis has shown that pacts and treaties can always be interpreted in different ways and that the Latin aphorism *pacta sunt servanda*—agreements must be kept—has been repeatedly violated by member countries.

The economic crisis and financial aid: coordination or break-up of the project

There is no doubt that the Greek crisis, caused by government mismanagement and misrepresentation of the true state of the economy, put the whole European unification project at risk. In addition, the European structures suffer from what has been called a "democratic deficit" because citizens have no channels for demanding information from the huge plethora of EU representatives and institutions or be part of their decision-making process. EU authorities therefore have been held responsible for this situation of generalized crisis affecting most EU countries. What's more, despite the many rules, regulations, meetings, and press releases, the bloc has been unable to function properly, mainly because the economic behavior of certain countries has not been properly supervised and no steps have been taken to rectify the problems. As a result, the EU as a whole has been forced to deal with the economic problems of some members of the Eurozone.

The crisis in the Eurozone has opened up a debate that at least has been refreshing compared to the EU's usually monotonous routine of meetings and assemblies. The economic situation in Greece and the political-economic debate that followed it required member states to think carefully and seriously about the future of the EU and the Eurozone project. They are well aware that the Eurozone is in the European Union and what affects one country affects the whole of the Union, regardless of the legal situation.

The difficult economic, financial and legal problems sparked fears that this would be the end of the unification project. However, Eurozone member countries began to coordinate with the International Monetary Fund (IMF), the European Commission (EC) and the European Central Bank (ECB)—what has been called the Troika—on economic and political efforts to help countries through their difficulties. There has been much speculation about the reasons for such economic efforts, and criticisms that behind the coordination was a drive to merely manage the crisis and limit the damage.

Many financial aid projects have been implemented since January 2010. These programs come with some specifications and requirements, such as how the funds must be distributed, who provides the finances and what is expected in return. But the financial assistance provided by the Troika has also brought a lot of controversy, difficulties and gray areas.

Although the IMF has been involved in many economic rescue operations around the world, its role in the EU crisis has been blurry for two key reasons. First, there was an agreement that financial aid packages would be proposed by the EC and the ECB, which left little room for the IMF to decide on its actions. Secondly, there have been questions as to whether the IMF could legally help to rescue Greece because its financial assistance would go to cover a budget deficit caused by financial and economic malpractice: a task that does not correspond to any of the three mandates that the institution mentions on its web page:

> The work of the IMF is of three main types. Surveillance involves the monitoring of economic and financial developments, and the provision of policy advice, aimed especially at crisis-prevention. The IMF also lends to countries with balance of payments difficulties, to provide temporary financing and to support policies aimed at correcting the underlying problems; loans to low-income countries are also aimed especially at poverty reduction. Third, the IMF provides countries with technical assistance and training in its areas of expertise.[8]

The effort to obtain the IMF's help with the Greek crisis has not been without controversy. Some critics saw Greece as an internal EU crisis that had to be addressed by member states without the help of an outside institution. However, the assistance of the IMF was necessary because member states had proved incapable of providing the supervision that was required.

Finally, a decision had to be made on the amount of financial aid and support mechanisms needed to assist the countries in difficulty, especially Greece. One of the support mechanisms adopted was an emergency system of bilateral loans to ensure the availability of funds. In the case of Greece, the euro group agreed, on May 2, 2010, to provide bilateral loans pooled by the European Commission (the so-called "Greek Loan Facility" or GLF)[9]—as the first economic adjustment program for a total of 80 billion euros to be disbursed from May 2010 through June 2013. (This amount was eventually reduced by 2.7 billion euros because Slovakia decided not to participate in the Greek Loan Facility Agreement and Ireland and Portugal exited the facility when they requested financial assistance for themselves.) This GLF currently consists of bilateral loans to Greece from 14 Euro area countries with an amount disbursed as of January 1, 2015 of about 53 billion euros.[10] The table below shows the approximate contributions of major member states.[11]

On March 14, 2012, Eurozone finance ministers approved a Second Economic Adjustment Program for Greece. Member states and the IMF committed again to the undisbursed part of the Greek Loan Facility, plus an additional 130 billion euros for the years 2012–2014. While the financing of the GLF was based on bilateral loans, the second program was to be financed by the EFSF, which had been fully operational since August 2010. In total, the second program estimated the Greek needs at about 164.5 billion euros in financial assistance through the end of 2014. Of this amount, the euro area commitment is expected to be around 144.7 billion euros, to be provided via the EFSF.[12]

In addition to these two economic adjustment programs for Greece, and since other Eurozone countries were also experiencing severe financing problems, the EU moved quickly to set up two temporary funds, the European Financial Stabilization Mechanism and the European Financial Stability Facility (EFSF). In July 2013, a new permanent crisis mechanism, the European Stability Mechanism (ESM), was launched to replace the two temporary funds.

The European Financial Stability Facility[13] is a corporation created June 7, 2010 under Luxembourg law with a mandate to provide temporary financial

Table 3.1 The Greek Loan Facility or First Economic Adjustment Programmme

Member states	Loans in € bn
Germany	15,165
France	11,389
Austria	3,194
Spain	6,650
Italy	10,008
Netherlands	3,194
Other countries	3,300
Total	52,900

Source: European Commission.

Table 3.2 The Second Economic Adjustment Programme for Greece financed by the European Financial Stability Facility (€ billion)

Disbursement	Date	ESFS	IMF
The first installment (in 7 tranches)	March to June 2012w	74	1.6
The second installment	December 2012 to May 2013	49.1	3.24
The Third installment	May to June 2013	7.5	1.74
The fourth installment	July to December 2013	3	1.8
The fifth installment	April to July 2014	2	
	TOTAL	135.6	8.38

Source: European Commission.

assistance until the permanent European Stability Mechanism came into force. The Eurozone countries are the shareholders of the EFSF, which was launched with guaranteed commitments totaling 724.5 billion euros from Eurozone countries and an immediate lending capacity of 440 billion euros. As of January 1, 2015 the amount distributed by this facility stood at about 185.5 billion euros, with Ireland receiving a total of 17.7 billion euros, Portugal getting 26 billion euros and Greece receiving a staggering 141.8 billion euros.[14]

In order to qualify for this financial aid, member states must submit to the European Commission a request explaining the need for aid and a proposal for an adjustment program. The final agreements between the member states requesting assistance and the European Commission are set in what are called Memorandums of Understanding. The EC, IMF and ECB oversee compliance with the Memorandum of Understanding to make sure the country is carrying out the necessary adjustments and can continue to receive financial aid. The EFSF not only lends the funds to the member state but also manages the loan. These funds are obtained by the EFSF on the capital markets at a lower interest rate because the funds are guaranteed by the Eurozone countries. The EFSF is not providing financial assistance to any additional countries, although the EFSF assistance program for Greece has been extended to June 30, 2015. After this date, the EFSF will merely continue to receive loan repayments from beneficiary countries and make interest and principal payments to holders of the EFSF bonds.

The second temporary mechanism is the European Financial Stabilization Mechanism. Under EFSM, the European Commission is allowed to borrow up to

Table 3.3 EFSF aid to Ireland, Portugal and Greece

EFSF	€ bn
Ireland (concluded Dec 8, 2013)	17.7
Portugal (concluded May 18, 2014)	26
Greece – 2nd Programme (due to end on Dec 31, 2014 but extended until June 30, 2015)	130.9

Source: European Financial Stability Facility.

a total of 60 billion euros in financial markets on behalf of the Union under the implicit guarantee of the EU budget. The EC then lends the money to member states in need of financial aid. This particular lending arrangement implies that there is no debt-servicing cost for the Union, and all interest and loan principal is repaid by the beneficiary member states via the Commission. The EFSM and the EFSF assistance can only be activated after a request for help is made by a member state that has agreed with the EC and ECB to implement a macroeconomic adjustment program with strict conditionality.

The EFSM was activated for Ireland and Portugal for a total amount up to 48.5 billion euros, of which 22.5 billion went to Ireland and about 26 billion to Portugal from 2011 to 2014. Loan disbursements to both countries concluded in 2014. It is important to note that EU member states outside the Eurozone are also eligible for assistance under in this program.

On July 11, 2013 finance ministers of the 17 Eurozone countries signed the Treaty establishing the European Stability Mechanism.[15] The pact followed the European Council's decision of March 25, 2011 and builds on an amendment to Article 136 of the Treaty on the Functioning of the European Union (TFEU). The ESM assumed the tasks previously fulfilled by the European Financial Stability Facility and the European Financial Stabilization Mechanism. Although the Treaty was signed by the 17 Eurozone countries, EU countries outside the Eurozone may participate in financial assistance operations, as represented in the next table.

The ESM is an intergovernmental institution under international law that can provide financial assistance to member states following a mutual agreement and under strict conditions. The ESM will only provide financial assistance if it is

Table 3.4 Capital subscriptions by member states to the European Stability Mechanism

Country	ESM key %	Capital subscription (€ bn)
Germany	27.146	190.02
France	20.386	142.7
Italy	17.914	125.39
Spain	11.904	83.32
Netherlands	5.717	40.02
Belgium	3.477	24.34
Greece	2.817	19.71
Austria	2.783	1.48
Portugal	2.509	17.56
Finland	1.797	12.58
Ireland	1.592	11.14
Slovakia	0.824	5.77
Slovenia	0.428	2.99
Luxembourg	0.25	1.75
Cyprus	0.196	1.37
Estonia	0.186	1.3
Malta	0.073	0.51
TOTAL	**100%**	**€700 bn**

Source: European Financial Stability Facility.

considered necessary to ensure the financial stability of the euro area as a whole. If a member state receives assistance, the country is required to implement a strict macro-economic adjustment program and a rigorous analysis of public-debt sustainability. The ESM so far has provided loans to Spain and Cyprus.

The agreement to bail out Greece and other countries therefore has become a financial burden on the already battered economies of the countries of the Eurozone. These countries are not only helping Greece, Portugal, Ireland and others but also have been injecting money into their own economies through "stimulus packages" designed to counter the effect of the economic crisis of 2008.

Notes

1. Marcus Tullius Cicero. BrainyQuote.com, Xplore Inc, 2015. http://www.brainyquote.com/quotes/quotes/m/marcustull165871.html (accessed May 21, 2015).
2. Eurostat. *Manual on government deficit and debt*, 2013 Edition. http://epp.eurostat.ec.europa.eu/cache/ITY_OFFPUB/KS-RA-13-001/EN/KS-RA-13-001-EN.PDF.
3. The Lisbon Treaty, Art 125. http://www.lisbon-treaty.org/wcm/the-lisbon-treaty/treaty-on-the-functioning-of-the-european-union-and-comments/part-3-union-policies-and-internal-actions/title-viii-economic-and-monetary-policy/chapter-1-economic-policy/393-article-125.html.
4. The Lisbon Treaty, Art 122.2. http://www.lisbon-treaty.org/wcm/the-lisbon-treaty/treaty-on-the-functioning-of-the-european-union-and-comments/part-3-union-policies-and-internal-actions/title-viii-economic-and-monetary-policy/chapter-1-economic-policy/390-article-122.html.
5. European Commission. "European Financial Stabilization Mechanism (EFSM)," Economic and Financial Affairs. http://ec.europa.eu/economy_finance/eu_borrower/efsm/index_en.htm.
6. The Lisbon Treaty, Art 50. http://www.lisbon-treaty.org/wcm/the-lisbon-treaty/treaty-on-european-union-and-comments/title-6-final-provisions/137-article-50.html.
7. The Lisbon Treaty, Art. 140.3.3. http://www.lisbon-treaty.org/wcm/the-lisbon-treaty/treaty-on-the-functioning-of-the-european-union-and-comments/part-3-union-policies-and-internal-actions/title-viii-economic-and-monetary-policy/chapter-5-transitional-provisions/408-article-140.html.
8. International Monetary Fund. "What the IMF does." Washington 2004. http://www.imf.org/external/work.htm.
9. European Commission. "Financial assistance to Greece," Economic and Financial Affairs. http://ec.europa.eu/economy_finance/assistance_eu_ms/greek_loan_facility/index_en.htm.
10. European Commission. "Financial assistance to Greece," Economic and Financial Affairs. http://ec.europa.eu/economy_finance/assistance_eu_ms/greek_loan_facility/index_en.htm.
11. Algemene Rekenkamer. "Greek loan facility." http://www.rekenkamer.nl/english/Publications/Topics/EU_governance_to_combat_the_economic_and_financial_crisis/Financial_stability_instruments/Financial_instruments/Greek_loan_facility.
12. European Commission. "European Financial Stability Facility (EFSF)." http://ec.europa.eu/economy_finance/european_stabilisation_actions/efsf/index_en.htm.
13. European Financial Stability Facility. "Key figures." http://www.efsf.europa.eu/about/key-figures/index.htm.
14. European Financial Stability Facility. http://www.efsf.europa.eu/about/index.htm.
15. European Commission. "Treaty establishing the European Stability Mechanism (ESM) signed." http://ec.europa.eu/economy_finance/articles/financial_operations/2011-07-11-esm-treaty_en.htm.

4 Fiscal austerity or government spending

> If Europe represents only 7% of the world's population,
> produces 25% of global GDP and must finance 50% of the overall social spending,
> then obviously Europeans have to work very hard to maintain their way of life.
> (Angela Merkel)[1]

Introduction

The Great Recession of the twenty-first century that began with the economic crisis in the United States in 2007 reached its most dramatic point in the EU when Greece announced its imminent bankruptcy. Since then, countries on both sides of the Atlantic have tried to implement political and economic measures to help other countries out of the crisis. Historically, the Keynesian dogma has been the recipe used by governments in economic recoveries.

An analysis of government spending patterns during the years preceding the 2007 crisis has shown that governments did not take advantage of the prosperous economic years to save their profits and get their finances in order. Instead they continued public spending until their debt reached unreasonable and unmanageable levels. Thus, when the economic crisis erupted and governments had to intervene, public spending increased significantly and pushed both public deficits and debts in many countries to unsustainable levels.

The debate centers on how to combat the crisis and reactivate the economies. On one hand, some believe that injecting public funds into an economy to help increase consumption through demand is the right approach. On the other hand, some argue that the economy should follow a strict spending pattern to shore up its main pillars, reorganize itself and achieve progress in the short term.

Demand-side policy argues for injecting money into the economy so that citizens can maintain or even increase consumption. Consumers have money to spend regardless of the type and quality of the products available. Supply-side policies, however, argue that a high-quality supply of goods and services creates its own demand—that if products are competitively priced and of high quality, demand will be created. Thus, supply-side policy requires far more variables to move the economy than just injecting money into it.

The EU's Stability and Growth Pact (SGP) states that member countries, particularly those using the euro, must keep their public debt below 60% of GDP. However, not only have most Eurozone member states never maintained their debt below that benchmark, but since 2008 their debt has soared. Among the countries with the largest debt/GDP ratio in 2011 were Greece (170%), Spain (69%), Italy (120%) and Portugal (108%). Curiously, those countries with lower rates of public debt were mostly in the Nordic region, such as Finland (49%), Denmark (46%), Norway (29%), and Sweden (38%).[2]

Economic austerity vs government spending: economic and political debate

The current economic crisis is testing all theories on how to solve a recession quickly and without mortgaging the future of generations to come. The Great Recession of the twenty-first century consistently reduced consumption and private investment, and forced governments to take on the responsibility of spending and investing in order to maintain a stable GDP and prevent a further economic slowdown.

Before the crisis erupted, demand-side policies and public spending policies prevailed in certain countries of southern Europe, including France after the change to a Socialist government. During the crisis, these countries spent money that they had to borrow in an attempt to overcome the crisis. Thus, southern European countries never truly fixed their finances. Instead, they have been spending borrowed money and incurring debts that future generations will have to pay off. This is politically irresponsible and economically unsupportable. Since the crisis began in 2007, public deficits and government debts have been increasing. Today, virtually no country in the Eurozone enjoys economic security or a balanced budget, much less a budget surplus. The problem is that this situation, with public debt levels that exceed 80% of GDP, is challenging the political credibility and economic reliability of many countries. Above all, it is jeopardizing the ability of governments to continue high levels of public spending in the hope of lifting their nations out of their economic crisis.

The reality is that since the Second World War, high levels of spending have become an addiction in countries like Japan, the United States and parts of Europe. The negative effect of over-indebtedness is not just economic stagnation, but high levels of unemployment and a worsening of the national debt rating, which brings with it an increase in borrowing costs. While the negative effects are clear, the most appropriate policy for reducing debt levels are much less clear. While some call for fiscal austerity to slow down spending and motivate savings, others believe that austerity is counterproductive because it shrinks the economy. This group argues that in an economic crisis, it is more important to revive the economy, through a stimulus, than to fix the imbalances. All this amounts to a debate whose summary is: austerity or spending?

Government debt is reduced when the budget deficit is decreased by using austerity measures. A deficit results when the government does not collect sufficient funds to meet expenses. Austerity can be achieved by (1) reducing costs, (2) raising taxes, or (3) a combination of the above two measures. Deciding how austerity will be implemented, however, is tough for politicians, economists and social agents. In summary, while some believe that taxes should go up, others require spending reductions. Still others believe that the sensible approach is a combination of the two, but always accompanied by structural reforms of public finances. Whatever approach is used, the reality is that countries must control their deficits and debts. The International Monetary Fund, in its *World Economic Outlook* (International Monetary Fund 2012) has stated that countries whose national debt exceeded 100% of their GDP have suffered deep economic stagnation and failed to reverse the trend.

If the decision is taken to raise taxes in order to collect more funds, the debate centers on whether direct or indirect taxes, or both, should be raised. Indirect taxes such as the value added tax (VAT), which taxes consumption, help to control spending and therefore have a direct effect on the savings rate. Direct taxes are those paid on wages, wealth and other forms of income. Studies have shown that an increase in direct taxation affects the middle class, influencing its purchasing power and in turn all industrial activity. An increase in direct taxation therefore increases unemployment by reducing consumption, and discourages investment and productivity.

Finally, governments must account for the Laffer Curve, which explains that although tax increases help to collect more revenue for the government, there is a point where any further tax increase will discourage people from working because the diminishing disposable income that workers will have left over after paying taxes will make working unattractive. Based on this theory, some believe that tax reductions are therefore the best possible way to stimulate the economy, cut the deficit and trim the public debt.

Public expenditure is defined as the amount of financial resources that governments spend on public services and other societal needs. This spending is understood as the way a government redistributes the economic resources of society that it receives through the tax system. Thus, public spending is an important instrument of economic policy because the government can use or abuse it to influence the levels of consumption, investment, employment—and win votes at election time. Those who advocate spending cuts argue that their policies have less negative effects on the economy in the long run than tax increases.

The reduction of public expenditure should not have a significant negative impact on an economy. It is important to clarify that reducing expenses refers in essence to the reduction of unnecessary government spending. What becomes problematic and debatable is where to draw the line between necessary and wasteful spending. The first reduction in public spending should be achieved by reducing the size of government, mainly by limiting or even decreasing public employment. During economic recessions, some countries counterbalance the decrease in private employment with a significant increase in public employment that becomes disproportionately expensive to maintain.

How governments organize public expenditures explains their political and economic orientation, which is usually in line with their ideological thinking. There are economists who believe that public spending should only maintain national and foreign policies and administer justice. Some people believe it should also help create productive infrastructure, education and basic health services. Finally, it is also argued that public money should be used to stimulate economic activity, create jobs and maintain the welfare system, or even to reduce inequalities in income distribution.

Reports by the European Commission in 2010[3] and 2011,[4] and a 2011 publication by the International Monetary Fund (Devries et al. 2011) show that while an economic adjustment via spending reduction might have a short-term negative impact by lowering GDP, the long-term impact has been much more positive. These studies also prove that tax increases have little effect on the production of goods and services in the short term, and that their effect is more persistent over time.

Fiscal pact and the debt ceiling: rules for a balanced budget

The Treaty on Stability, Coordination and Governance, informally called the Fiscal Pact, agreed on March 2, 2012. It was signed by 25 of the (then) 27 EU member states and went into effect on January 1, 2013. Britain and the Czech Republic refrained from signing this agreement, a position that was about to break the unity of the EU.

This treaty introduces the so-called "golden rule" that all EU countries must meet in order to achieve a balanced budget, but it has a bigger impact on the countries that use the euro. This golden rule was introduced due to the lack of implementation and respect shown by most of the countries of the Eurozone for the SGP. The rule specifies that fines will be imposed on countries that do not meet the financial stability requirements, and requires that the fines collected will either be paid into the European Stability Mechanism (ESM) or go to help the budget of the European Union. Most significantly, however, the pact requires that starting March 1, 2013, any economic assistance (bail-out program) should be conditioned on the recipient country's ratification of the treaty (RTVE 2011). The requirement reflects the belief that all countries that have ratified the fiscal pact will improve their economies and help to reduce overall risk premiums and market concerns.

This golden rule "forces" countries to introduce a clause in their constitutions mandating balanced budgets and debt limits. The novelty of this rule is that member states that already have given up their monetary policies by adopting the euro are now required to surrender their fiscal policy as well. In Germany, the constitution already includes the requirement of a balanced budget, and parliament (the Bundestag) ratified by a large majority the European Fiscal Pact with 604 MPs present in the room: 490 voted in favor, 111 against and 6 deputies abstained (RTVE 2012). In fact, Germany had been promoting this rule under Angela Merkel, who after the failures of the SGP sought to enshrine economic austerity and fiscal stability laws that transforms the EU as a union of stability (Palop 2012). On December 7, 2011, Spain approved an amendment to the constitution that limits the annual public structural deficit to 0.40%, including the deficit of the central, regional and municipal governments (Viñas 2011a). In France, there is no need to change the constitution to adopt the golden rule. The highest constitutional authority, consulted on July 13, 2010 by President Hollande, explained that there was no need to change the constitution to include a provision which specifies that the structural deficit should not exceed 0.5% of GDP per year because it can be adopted as an organic law (EuroEFE 2012). In Italy, in April 2012, the Senate passed by 235 votes in favor, 11 against, and 24 abstentions, a constitutional amendment that accepted the "golden rule" (APF 2012).

In the United States, the problem of government spending is relatively solved. When the Treasury Department does not collect enough taxes to cover the needs of government spending, the government faces a budget deficit. To cover this deficit, Congress can authorize the Treasury to go into debt in order to cover the deficit. However, to control the debt, the U.S. Congress in 1917 established a limit on the amount the government is allowed to borrow. Since it was established, the United States has had to increase the ceiling on numerous occasions: Bill Clinton increased it eight times in eight years, George W. Bush did so seven times during his two terms, and President Obama had increased it three times from the time he took office on January 20, 2009 until the summer of 2011.

To increase the debt ceiling, the Treasury Department must ask Congress for a change in legislation and the president must sign it into law. Each increase in the debt ceiling brings along a great political debate on whether the government should keep borrowing to finance its spending or if the government should adopt austerity measures to reduce the budget deficit and government debt.

Fiscal adjustments: punishing the government

In view of the economic problems facing most EU countries, and especially those in the Eurozone, a debate has begun on what may be the most appropriate approaches and measures to combat the crisis, reduce unemployment and improve economic growth. While there are a group of economists, political figures and parts of society who advocate higher taxes in order to increase government spending, others have argued that the right prescription is to cut spending and lower taxes. The effects of a tax increase, a decrease in expenditures or a combination of any of these two would affect the economy depending on whether the economy is in an expansionary or recessionary phase of the business cycle. There has been a misunderstanding in this debate, however, because productive and efficient public spending should not be confused with unnecessary and irresponsible spending such as political boondoggles.

There have been a number of countries in the Eurozone that have required financial assistance, such as Portugal, Ireland and Greece. In return, these countries have promised to cut government spending, reduce budget deficits and improve debt levels—that is, to implement austerity measures. However, due to the poor economic conditions facing these countries, there has been a debate regarding the suitability of austerity packages—if a country already suffering zero or negative economic growth is forced to cut government spending, the economic slowdown is very likely to worsen.

The problem is that these countries already have a debt problem and have lost economic credibility with investors and the market. Credibility would only be recovered when a country begins to implement the changes necessary to put its fiscal house in order. In addition, these problematic countries cannot wait and must act swiftly to put debts and deficits on the path to recovery. In fact, since the Second World War countries had not faced deficits and debt as high and dangerous as the current ones. The incentive for countries in economic difficulties and with high public debt to apply recovery measures is preceded by the need to present to financial markets some policy actions that would help them regain their lost economic credibility. The question is how to define the level of debt and deficit that would help restore credibility, trust and economic growth. In the Eurozone, countries will recover credibility when they meet the limits set out in the SGP.

In February 26, 2013 the President of the European Commission José Manuel Barroso asked EU countries and especially Eurozone member states that had received financial aid to maintain spending cuts and limit unnecessary spending to help improve competitiveness and economic growth. His statement was backed up by the success experienced by countries that implemented austerity measures, like Latvia, Portugal and Ireland (Baker and Stott 2013).

Ireland

On February 25, 2011 Ireland elected 166 deputies to the lower House of Parliament for the next five years. The results showed that citizens had turned against the ruling party, Fianna Fáil, for negotiating a bail-out package with the so-called "Troika"—the European Commission, European Central Bank and International Monetary Fund—valued at 85 billion euros (EFE 2010). The rescue package had been agreed by the government on December 15, 2010 and was ratified by the Irish Parliament (Dáil). Fianna Fáil went from winning 47% of the votes in the 2007 election to receiving just 17% in 2011 (EFE 2011). The winner of that year's election was the main opposition party, the conservative Fine Gael (FG). The rescue plan was heavily criticized by Fine Gael for two reasons. On the one hand, the opposition criticized the interest rate charged on the bail-out funds, estimated at 5.8% and viewed as too high. The opposition also accused the government of making a serious mistake when the executive branch decided to rescue the national banking system with public money, which in turn increased the deficit and public debt. In fact, Ireland at the time was considered a country to imitate because it was enjoying sound economic stability with a high level of employment, low inflation and a balanced government budget or even surplus. But the rescue mission meant that the government assumed responsibility for more than 35 billion euros in debt that banks had on their books.

This debt acquisition raised the government deficit to more than 32% of GDP. The Troika offered assistance in return for Ireland's implementation of an adjustment plan to reduce the public deficit to 3% of GDP in 2014. By 2007 Ireland's government deficit had reached levels of 30% and since 2010 it had been improving.

Portugal

In Portugal, the Social Democratic Party (PSD) led by Pedro Passos Coelho defeated the ruling Socialist party of Prime Minister José Sócrates, in parliamentary elections held on June 5, 2011. The PSD received 40% of the votes, while the Socialists received only 28.5%. This election reflected another dramatic shift in the political scenario of an economically troubled country, with voters punishing the Socialists and taking a turn to the right. More problems came in May 2011, when Portugal announced to the world that it was in need of a bail-out. In exchange for this aid, Portugal had to undertake a set of measures that would help economic growth, competitiveness and job creation, especially among young people. Second, the country was asked to undertake fiscal reforms to reduce public debt and deficits. Finally, the assistance was accompanied by a set of measures to ensure the stability of the financial sector (Agencias 2011). Thus, in May of 2011, Portugal became the third Eurozone country, after Greece and Ireland, to obtain foreign aid.

The year 2013 began on bittersweet notes for Portugal. On January 22, 2013 Portugal announced a deficit of less than 5% of GDP. The next day, it returned to the long-term debt market for the first time since it received the bail-out and met with strong international demand. This confirmed that the country had implemented measures that helped it to regain the confidence of markets and investors. On February 20, 2013, however, the government announced that the economy would suffer a decline in growth of 2%, which was more than expected. In addition, on February 13, 2013 it was announced that the unemployment rate in the fourth quarter of 2012 had reached a record high of 16.9%, compared to 14% in the same period in 2011.

Spain

Spain is another country that was heavily affected by the economic crisis and witnessed a change in political orientation after the general elections of November 20, 2011, when the conservative Popular Party (PP) led by Mariano Rajoy won 46% of the vote and formed a government with control of 186 seats in the 350-member parliament.

With the change of government, new policies were announced and fiscal adjustments followed. As it was in the case of Greece, when the new Rajoy government audited the national accounts of the outgoing socialist government led by José Luis Rodriguez Zapatero, the debt and deficit figures found did not coincide with the figures announced by the outgoing administration. When Cristóbal Montoro became the Minister of Finance and Public Administrations he pledged to reduce the deficit left by the outgoing government, estimated at 8% and not the 6% as had been announced by the Socialists. On December 23, 2011 the Rajoy government announced that based on the new figures, it would be impossible for the government to reduce the deficit to the 3% benchmark required by the Stability and Growth Pact (Pérez 2012).

The difference between the two deficit figures was so wide that the Commission believed that the incoming team had somehow manipulated the figures for political reasons. In February 2012, the independent audit confirmed that the true deficit of the country in 2011 was not 6% but a dangerous 8.5% of GDP. On March 5, 2012 after the confirmation of the discrepancy, Rajoy faced Angela Merkel who accepted that it was going to be difficult for Spain to cut its deficit to 4.4% by 2012—which was the promise Rajoy had made during the electoral campaign. Instead, a new target of 5.8% in 2012, still high, was agreed (González 2012). Finally, on April 23, 2012, the EU statistics office, Eurostat, confirmed that Spain's public deficit had reached 8.5% of GDP in 2011. In the "Debate on the State of the Nation" which was held on February 20, 2013, Rajoy announced that the government deficit in 2012 had reached 7% of GDP, which was higher than the 5.8% he had promised. What's more, if the financial aid granted to the Spanish banking sector in the summer of 2012 is taken into account to calculate the real deficit of the government, the level would be close to 10% (Pérez 2013).

Estonia and austerity measures: an example to follow

Estonia is a very interesting case because it has shown that austerity policies and measures can work. Estonia joined the EU on May 1, 2004, decided on July 13, 2004 that it had complied with all the requirements of the Maastricht Treaty and adopted the euro on January 1, 2011. Estonia, therefore, became the fifth country, along with Slovenia (2007), Slovakia (2009), Malta (2008) and Cyprus (2008) to adopt the euro as their national currency. The other seven countries in the region—Poland, Romania, Hungary, Czech Republic, Bulgaria, Lithuania and Latvia—are still working to meet the Maastricht requirements.

For Estonia, the adoption of the euro was considered a positive factor for its economy because the common currency would help its commerce, where 50% of its exports are directed to countries of the euro area. Estonia understands that compliance with fiscal and monetary requirements was needed not only to adopt the euro, but also to embark on a long road to stability. Thus, since Estonia became part of the Eurozone it has followed public debt and budget adjustment requirements, set by the SGP, which have helped its economic growth, job creation and inflation stability.

This small country, with an economy of only 19 billion euros compared to more than 13 trillion euros for the overall Eurozone, has become an example that "living within one's means" can be very rewarding. Before Estonia adopted the euro in 2011, its currency and economy faced challenges that hinted the country would not be able to adopt the euro on schedule. While the Estonian government decided to implement tough fiscal adjustments based on spending cuts, in May of 2009 the U.S. government approved a stimulus package of nearly US$800 million for the country. Estonia introduced harsh austerity measures, even though it was one of the countries hardest hit by the economic crisis of 2007 as its economy contracted by 20%—a far better contraction than Greece experienced at the peak of its own crisis.

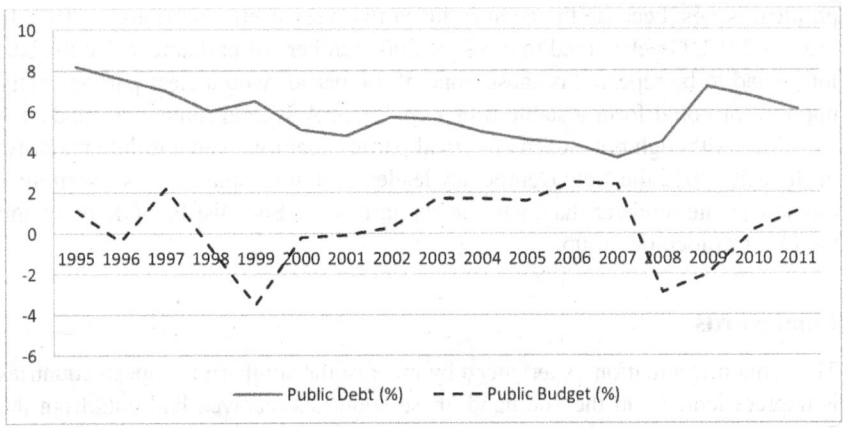

Figure 4.1 Estonian public debt and budget, 1995–2011.
Source: ECB Statistics.

Greece

Greece's current problems go back to when it adopted the euro in 2001. When Greece applied to join the euro, its public debt already exceeded 100% of GDP, but authorities agreed to these levels because the country had already reduced its debt level significantly. Greece also faced a budget deficit that exceeded 5%, which is well above the required 3% limit. Greece therefore joined the Eurozone with government debt and deficit levels that, already, were breaking the benchmarks required for much-needed fiscal stability. The current economic situation of Greece should not be a surprise for anyone. In fact, it has been "the chronicle of a death foretold."

In May 2010, Greece announced to the world that its debt would exceed 350 billion euros in 2014 because it had not complied with the requirements of the SGP. It later became clear that during the two terms in power of Konstantinos Karamanlis the figures reported on the deficit and debt were not the real ones. After the victory of the socialist candidate George Papandreou in the 2009 elections the new government performed an audit of the public accounts that revealed the deficit was not the 4% of GDP reported by the outgoing government of Karamanlis, but almost 13% of GDP (EFE 2013).

The difference between a 4% and a 13% of GDP can be explained by the way the debt was calculated. Greece had issued national debt using a complex financial structure provided by Goldman Sachs, which has helped to issue debt in currencies other than the euro. Since these debts were denominated in other currencies, they did not have to be reported because countries in the Eurozone do not have to report to Brussels these kinds of financial products (EFE 2010).

The Greek tragicomedy highlighted not only economic problems but also political issues, because the country faced two very costly elections in 2012. In May of 2012, Greeks voted to elect the 300 members of parliament, but the balloting had to be repeated because none of the parties won a clear parliamentary majority or could form a stable ruling coalition. A second round was held June 17, 2012. Although none of the political parties again won an absolute majority, on June 20, 2012 the New Democracy leader, Antonis Samaras, was sworn in as the new prime minister thanks to the support of the Socialist PASOK party and the Left Democratic group.

Final words

The economic situation experienced by most of the southern European countries is unprecedented. On the one hand, these countries received bail-outs from the Troika to overcome their mismanagement of public finances. These governments had to give up their monetary and fiscal independence because the financial aid was tied to fiscal adjustments that their citizens had not been willing to endure.

It is paradoxical that most of the new governments have criticized the austerity measures imposed by Brussels. However, they had no other option but to obey and implement the program. In fact, all of the countries that received financial aid are carrying out those measures, even though they have lost part of their sovereignty and ended up abiding by programs imposed by Brussels that had very significant political costs.

Explaining why most of the Eurozone states are facing the current bout of economic distress is not difficult. In these countries, the political power structures are very rigid and not open to civil society. Therefore, a party in power can implement the wrong fiscal policies and ruin the country. As a result, at election time the electorate votes for the opposition in what becomes a punishing vote for the party that ruined the country due to the lack of opportunities for candidates and other political parties.

Estonia, with an economy hit hard by the crisis, implemented policies that helped it adopt the euro on schedule and achieve financial stability in a very short period of time. But while Estonia's implementation of its austerity plans paid off after just three years, this is not the recipe that southern European countries want to implement.

Finally, while spending cuts caused widespread strikes and social upheavals in countries like Greece and Ireland, Estonia endured its cuts with fortitude and without street disturbances. Its voters even re-elected the politicians who imposed the austerity measures. Estonia also cut the salaries of cabinet ministers by 20% and laid off 10% of all public employees, whose average monthly pay stands at roughly 700 euros per month—the lowest in the Eurozone. In addition, among the many measures implemented to help the country exit the recession, Estonia established a very favorable business environment by reducing and simplifying its tax system. Since the adoption of the euro, Estonia's economy has been on an upswing, growing by more than 7% per year while most of the countries of the Eurozone were growing at less than 1.5%. Additionally, Estonia has been the only country that has enjoyed a budget surplus. Thus, Estonia has become the example to follow on how to emerge from economic misery.

Notes

1 Rafael Poch. "Merkel suaviza los impulsos antieuropeístas de Cameron," *La Vanguardia*, January 29, 2013. http://www.lavanguardia.com/internacional/20130129/54363211574/merkel-suaviza-los-impulsos-antieuropeistas-de-cameron.html.
2 Datos Macro. "Deuda Pública". http://www.datosmacro.com/deuda.
3 European Commission. "Public finances in EMU 2010." European Economy No 4/2010 Brussels: European Commission.
4 European Commission. "Public finances in EMU 2011." European Economy No 4/2011 Brussels: European Commission.

5 The Transatlantic Trade and Investment Partnership in times of crisis
The euro and the price of crude oil

> It is safe to say that the U.S.–EU transatlantic partnership is as important a relationship as there is.
> (John Kerry)[1]

Introduction

Beginning in mid-2009, the world experienced a feeble economic recovery, held back by an increase in oil prices. History has taught us that nations developed thanks to major industrial revolutions which in turn fostered economic growth. The first industrial revolution took place in the nineteenth century when engineers started using refined coal as a source of efficient energy. The second major economic revolution came in the twentieth century with the development of the petroleum industry, with fuel oil and gasoline as key sources of energy. The world's industrial performance and economic growth so far in the twenty-first century is still dependent on fuel oil and gasoline—limited resources that have become a source of political and economic instability.

The U.S. National Bureau of Economic Research (NBER) announced on September 20, 2010 that the Business Cycle Dating Committee had determined "that a trough in business activity occurred in the U.S. economy in June 2009,"[2] marking the technical end of the recession that had begun in December 2007[3] and the beginning of an expansionary phase of the business cycle. This recession had lasted 18 months, making it the longest since the Second World War. The Federal Reserve has estimated that it would take the U.S. economy "12 years to recover the previous level of employment."[4] That is why this can be labeled as the Great Recession of the twenty-first century.

The following graph shows that since January 2009, real GDP has been growing in the United States. It is important to note that the NBER declares expansion when there has been two consecutive quarters of GDP growth. By the same token, it declares a recession when the economy suffers two consecutive quarters of GDP decline.

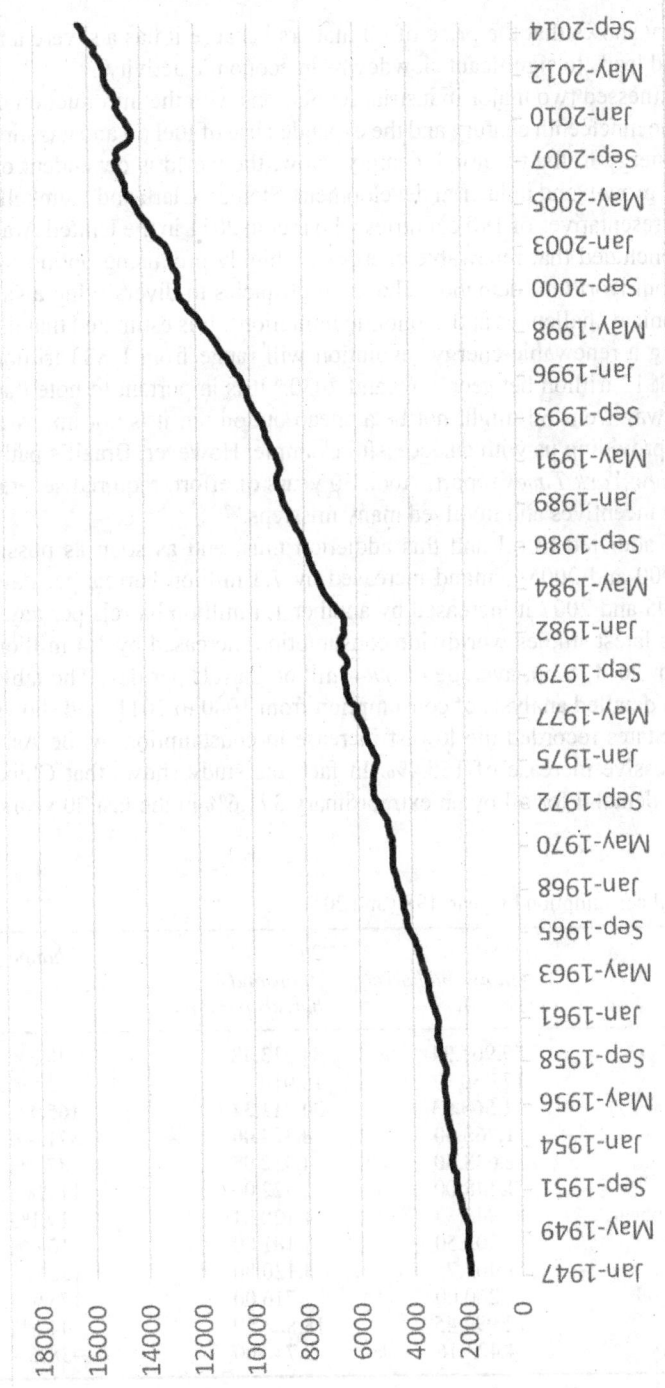

Figure 5.1 U.S. GDP, chained (2009) dollars, 1947–2014 (US $ billion, seasonally adjusted, four monthly, at annual rates).

Source: Economagic.

The geopolitical significance of oil: past, present and future

Economic history shows that the price of oil matters because it has a severe and direct impact and leads to significant slowdowns in economic activity.

The world witnessed two major industrial revolutions with the introduction of refined coal in the nineteenth century and the expanded use of fuel oil and gasoline as a source of energy in the twentieth century. Now, the world is dependent on oil for economic growth and industrial development. Steiner, Clark and Yumkella reported that representatives of 190 countries who met in 2011 in the United Arab Emirates had concluded that renewable energy is a highly promising option for breaking free from world oil demand.[5] The main obstacles to diversifying away from oil are technical challenges and economic limitations. It is estimated that the cost of triggering a renewable-energy revolution will range from US$3 trillion to more than US$12 trillion between now and 2030.[6] It is important to note that diversification away from oil might not be a cheap option but it is not impossible, with Brazil providing us with a successful example. However, Brazil's path, according to a *New York Times* report, "took 30 years of effort, required several billion dollars in incentives and involved many missteps."[7]

The world is addicted to oil and this addiction must end as soon as possible. Between 2000 and 2005 demand increased by 7.3 million barrels per day, and between 2005 and 2007 it increased by another 1.4 million barrels per day.[8] According to the latest studies worldwide consumption increased by 1.4 million barrels per day in 2011, to an average of 89.4 million barrels per day. The table below contains a detailed analysis of consumption from 1980 to 2011[9] and shows that the United States recorded the lowest increase in consumption, while Asia showed an impressive increase of 165.4%. In fact, the study shows that China has increased its demand for oil by an extraordinary 371.6% in the last 20 years,

Table 5.1 Crude oil consumption by year, 1980 and 2011

Country	1980 (thousand barrels per day)	2011 (thousand barrels per day)	Change
WORLD	59,901.24	84,213.48	40.5%
USA	17,056	18,010	5.59%
Asia	**11,568.63**	**30,712.34**	**165.4%**
China	**1,765.00**	**8,324.00**	**371.6%**
South America	2,633.50	4,932.95	87.7%
Brazil	1,148.00	2,522.00	119%
C. America & Caribbean	945.33	1,128.84	19.1%
Cuba	202.50	181.00	10.6%
Africa	1,402.75	3,120.80	122%
Egypt	260.00	716.00	175%
Europe	12,994.45	18,823.59	44.5%
Russian Federation	4,423.16	2,740.00	−38%

Source: Index Mundi.

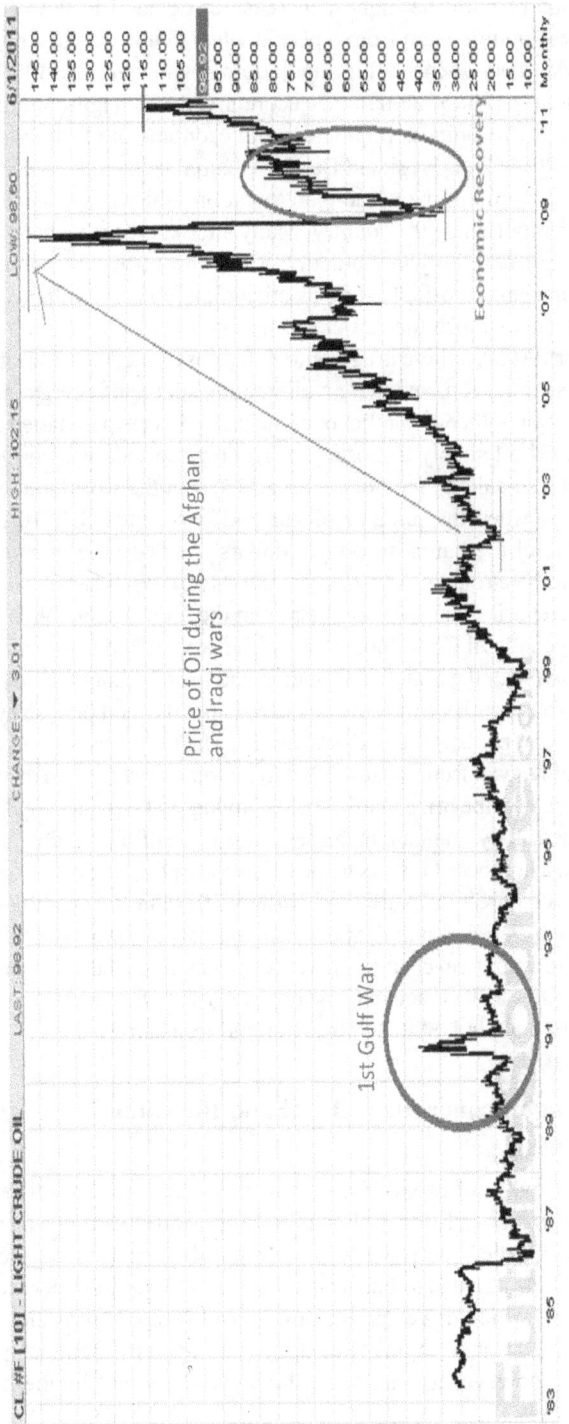

Figure 5.2 Price of Light Crude, 1983–2011 (US$ per barrel).

Source: Futuresource.com.

making it the country with the highest increase in demand in the entire world. What's more, these numbers are from a period when China was just beginning to join the free market and when its full population—estimated at 1.3 billion—was still not fully integrated into the nation's economy. Just imagine the increase in demand when the entire Chinese population and economy are fully integrated.

On March 31, 2011, U.S. President Barack Obama declared the need to reduce U.S. oil demand and proposed a broad plan to cut one-third of the 10 million barrels of oil per day imported by the country. Many alternatives have been discussed, but no option has been put fully into practice. There have been talks about increasing the use of renewable bio-fuels such as ethanol, decreasing reliance on oil by making cars and trucks more fuel-efficient and even investing in high-speed rail and mass transport. At least there is agreement that fossil fuels are a limited natural resource that cause pollution, and that an alternative source of energy is needed.

Every single major bellicose conflict over the past 75 years has started as a political dispute that used oil supply as hostage.[10] The first episode was in October 17, 1973 and led to the so-called First Oil Crisis, which sent the world into a profound economic recession when the price of oil jumped from under US$10 a barrel to about US$40 a barrel measured in today's dollars. At that time, members of the Organization of Arab Petroleum Exporting Countries (OAPEC) decided to stop shipping oil to those countries that supported Israel in the Yom Kippur War with Syria and Egypt. The Second Oil Crisis took place in January 1979 due to political unrest in Iran, which ended with the Shah's resignation and led to a reduction in production from 6 million barrels per day to 1.5 million barrels per day and prices skyrocketing from US$40 to US$80 per barrel in today's dollars. The third episode was during the Iraqi occupation of Kuwait from August 1990 to February 1991, when the world suffered another increase in the price of oil. The beginning of the Afghan and Iraqi wars also were accompanied by dramatic increases in the price of oil. Further, in 2011 the world experienced a number of revolts in the Middle East that negatively affected the price of oil. The civil unrest in Tunisia in February 2011 spilled over to other countries in the area such as Egypt and Libya, where civil society was asking repressive governments to allow political change. Governments in most of these countries once again used oil supplies as leverage and, as a consequence, the price of oil spiked in just two months from about US$84 to close to US$115 a barrel.

The economic significance of crude oil and the value of the U.S. dollar

The main problem with oil production is that it is a limited natural resource as well as the basis for social and political stability and economic performance around the world. Further, the price of oil is not only closely linked to political and bellicose conflicts but also to business cycles. In a recession, there tends to be less demand for oil, which drives prices down. And when there is an expansion, demand increases and prices go up. Thus there is an inverse relationship between demand and price: however it is managed by a cartel and not by the free forces of demand and supply.

In this case, a cartel is a group of oil-producing countries that get together to set prices and quotas which may or may not satisfy demand. In general terms, in the United States cartels of any sort are illegal. Yet internationally, there are no limitations to cartel formation. The Organization of Petroleum Exporting Countries (OPEC), which supplies about 40% of global oil, has always been the top beneficiary of high oil prices when they repeatedly soar due to political turmoil in those same countries.

In the international petroleum industry, crude oil products are traded on various oil bourses based on (1) established chemical profiles, (2) delivery locations and (3) financial terms.[11] The three most quoted oil products are North America's West Texas Intermediate Crude (WTI), North Sea Brent Crude and the UAE's Dubai Crude.

There are 46 oil exporting countries but the prices of these three oil products are used as a barometer for the entire petroleum industry. Historically, all three have traded closely but Brent Crude is typically priced at about US$2 over the WTI Spot price, which in turn is typically priced US$5 to US$6 above the OPEC Basket prices as shown in the graph below.

The following graph, with more detail on the evolution of spot prices for WTI, Brent and Dubai/Oman, shows that the price of each one has dropped significantly while the spread has almost disappeared, both anomalies in this market.

WTI, also known as Texas light sweet, is a grade of crude oil used as a benchmark in oil pricing. Brent Crude is also a major trading classification of sweet light crude oil that serves as a major benchmark price for purchases of oil worldwide. Brent Crude is extracted from the North Sea and is comprised of Brent Blend, Forties Blend, Oseberg and Ekofisk crudes.[12] Brent is the leading global price benchmark for Atlantic basin crude oils. It is used to price two-thirds of the world's internationally traded crude oil supplies.

The OPEC Reference Basket (ORB), also known as the OPEC Basket, is a weighted average of prices for petroleum blends produced by OPEC countries. It is used as an important benchmark for crude oil prices.[13] On June 15, 2005, the OPEC basket was changed. The Reference Basket currently consists of a weighted average of the following blends: Saharan Blend from Algeria, Ecuador, Iran Heavy from the Islamic Republic of Iran, Basra Light from Iraq, Kuwait Export from Kuwait, Es Sider from Libya, Bonny Light from Nigeria, Qatar Marine from Qatar, Arab Light from Saudi Arabia, Murban from UAE, BCF 17 from Venezuela and Girassol from Angola.[14]

In the case of the United States, it is estimated that the impact of the price of crude on the economy amounts to a 0.25% drop in GDP for every US$10 increase in the price of crude.[15] The graph below shows that when the price of WTI was stable from 1990 to 2007, the real U.S. GDP recorded a significant upward swing. But when the price of energy spiked to all-time highs in 2007, the country's GDP suffered a significant drop and it began to recover only as the price of oil dropped in mid-2008.

It is important to note that when high oil prices hold back an economy, there is a secondary effect on the transportation sector that is reflected in the Dow Jones Transportation Average. The DJTA

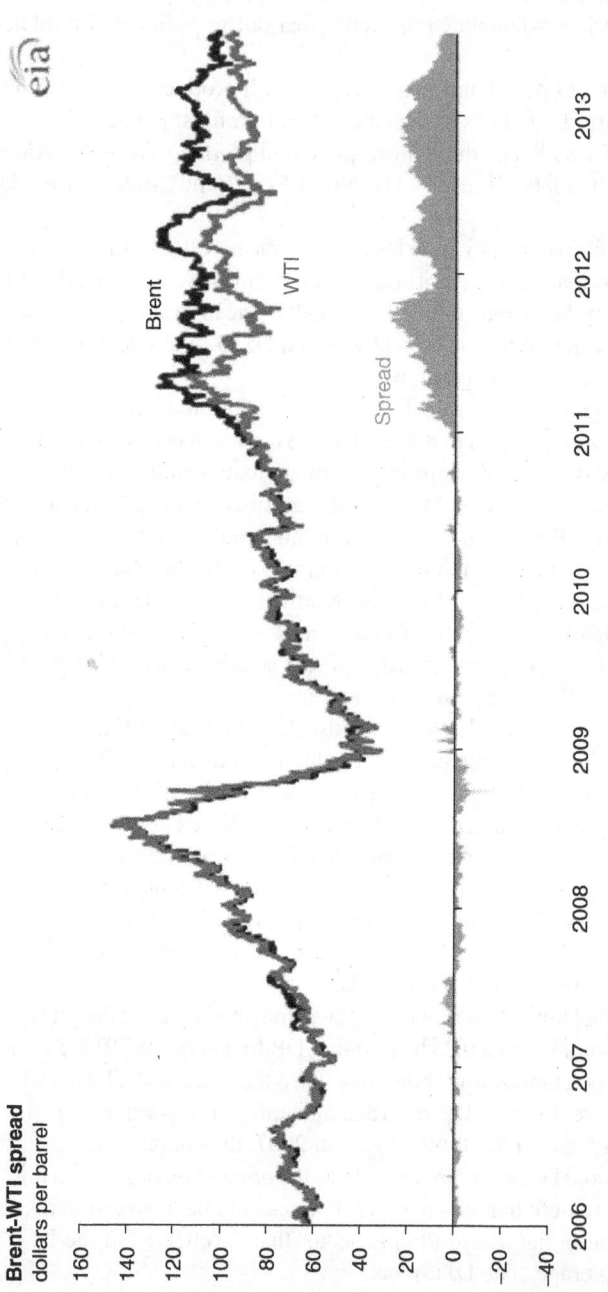

Figure 5.3 Brent–WTI spread, 2006–2013 (US$ per barrel).

Source: U.S. Energy Information Administration, Price difference between Brent and WTI crude oil narrowing. http://www.eia.gov/todayinenergy/detail.cfm?id=11891, June 28, 2013.

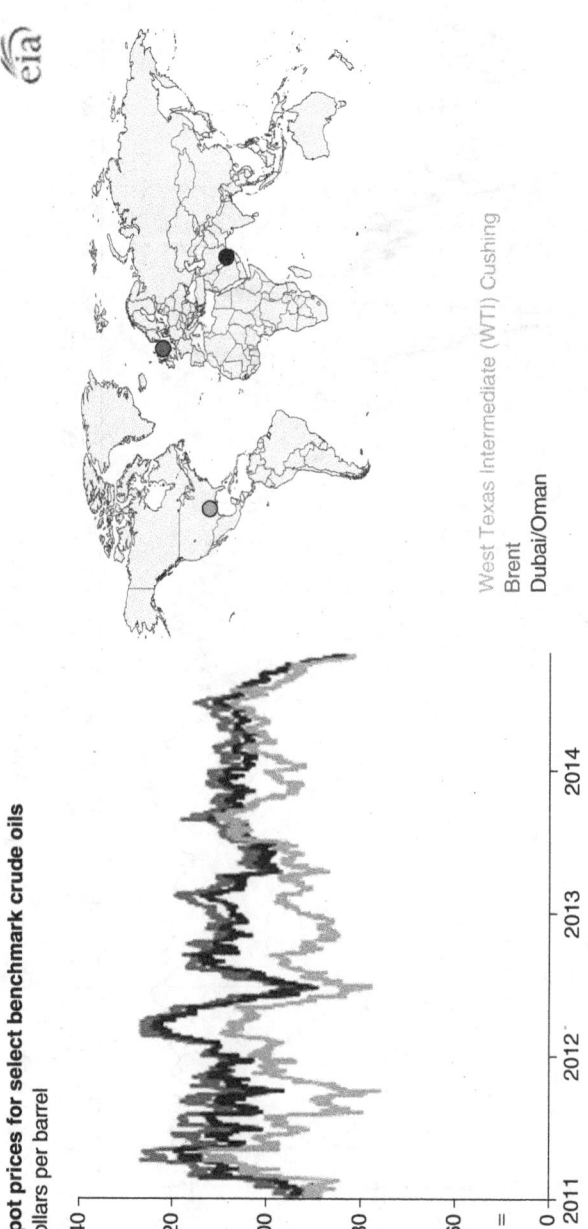

Figure 5.4 Spot prices for selected benchmark crude oils, 2011–2014 (US$ per barrel).

Source: U.S. Energy Information Administration, Benchmarks play an important role in pricing crude oil, http://www.eia.gov/todayinenergy/detail.cfm?id=18571, October 28, 2014.

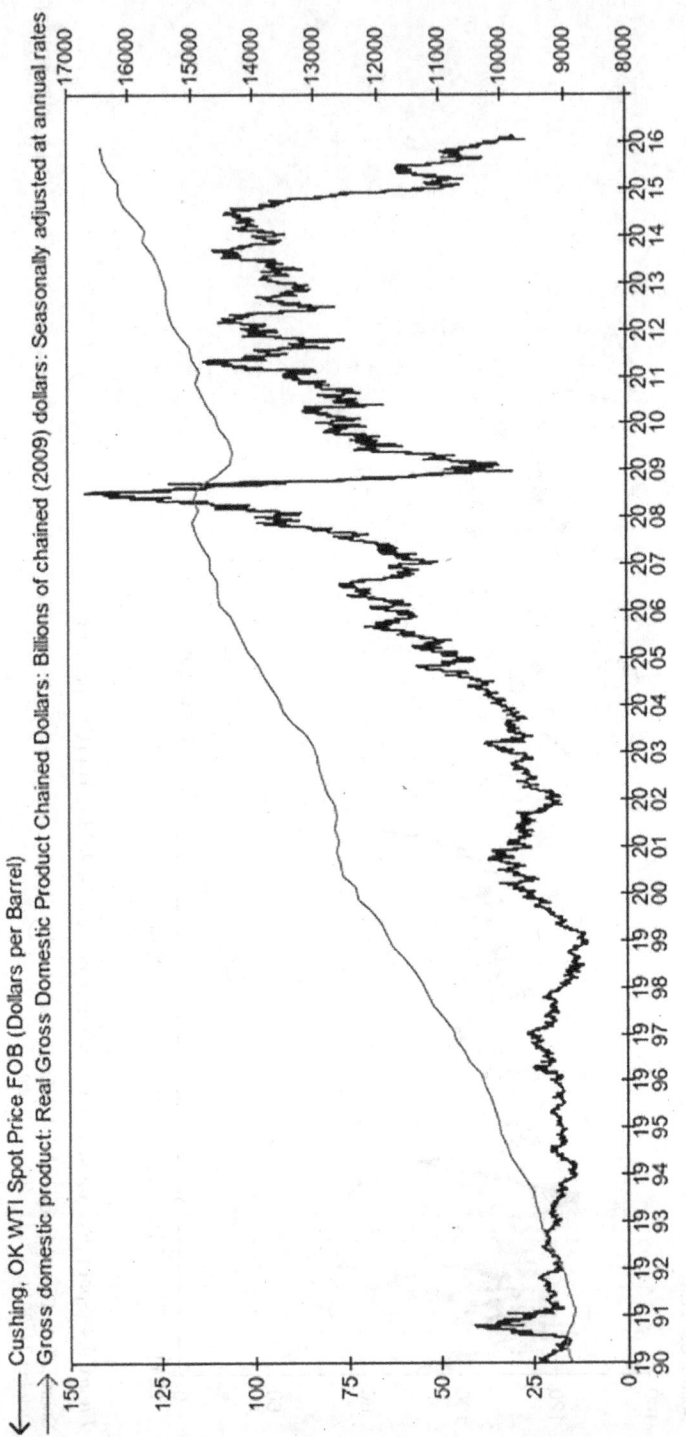

Figure 5.5 Real GDP and WTI crude spot price, 1990–2016 (US$ per barrel).

Source: Economagic.

The euro and the price of crude oil 59

is the most widely recognized gauge of the transportation sector. It is also the oldest index used today, even older than its more famous brother, the Dow Jones Industrials (DJIA). The Transportation Average was the first stock index developed by Charles Dow in 1884.[16]

The graph below shows the evolution of the DJTA from 2008 to June 2011, which demonstrates that when oil prices decrease, it is cheaper to drive trucks or fly planes and as a consequence, all 20 components of the DJTA trade higher.[17]

Since 2012, the United States and most countries in the Eurozone and the (EU) have been seeking a way out of the economic crisis brought on by the Great Recession. Furthermore, the United States has learned that it must work hard towards energy independence in order to break the link between high oil prices and economic recession. For this reason, the United States has been looking for ways to be energy self-sufficient, and between 2005 and 2010 the country's shale-gas industry grew by 45% per year. But while the United States is working towards energy independence, most countries in the Eurozone remain heavily dependent on oil and gas. The geopolitical controversy with Russia over Crimea has become a destabilizing issue for the EU, deepened by the cancellation of the South Stream pipeline project on December 1, 2014, which was to supply gas to the EU. Russia selected Turkey as its preferred partner for the alternative route, which will supply natural gas to Bulgaria and Serbia, and then Bosnia-Herzegovina and Croatia.

The United States and the EU are about to finalize the Transatlantic Trade and Investment Partnership, which Secretary of State John Kerry has said would

> reinforce our common effort to counter violent extremism, support the sovereignty of Ukraine, build energy security and independence for many nations in Europe that currently have to rely on one source—Russia, and also it will help us address such global problems, such as nuclear proliferation and climate change. That's what comes out of this kind of cooperative effort and the growth that it will spur.[18]

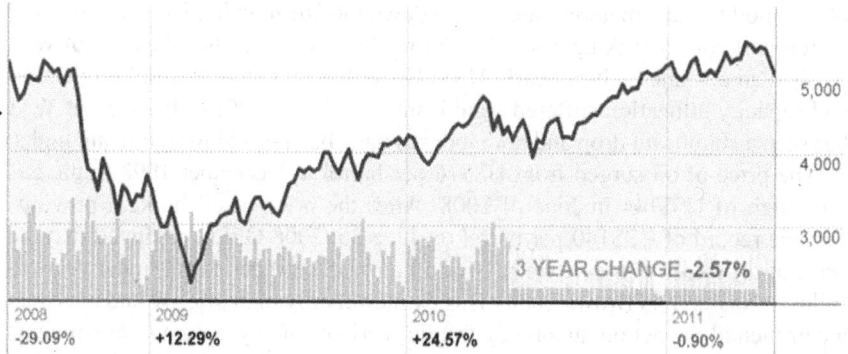

Figure 5.6 Dow Jones Industrial Average, 2008–2011.
Source: CNN Money 2009.

The price of crude oil and the U.S. dollar: the impact of energy prices for the TTIP

The economic performance of the United States and the EU, particularly the Eurozone member states, will be largely determined by the price of crude oil and the price of the U.S. dollar.

Energy prices can have powerful and deep impacts on a country's economy. To begin with, energy prices affect the final price of most goods and services due to transport, electricity, and fuel costs. Thus, if these rise faster than wages, consumers have less disposable income. This in turn would have a deep impact on consumer confidence and result in less consumer spending and business activity and hiring.

While the United States has recovered more strongly from the 2008 crisis than Europe, which is still in the throes of the Great Depression, the recoveries of both the United States and the EU remain relatively weak as of mid-2015. In the United States, stock prices have reached all-time highs but unemployment is still weak and capacity utilization remains below its 2008 level. The Federal Reserve Board constructs estimates of capacity utilization for industries in manufacturing, mining, and electric and gas utilities.[19] For a given industry, the capacity utilization rate is equal to an output index (seasonally adjusted) divided by a capacity index. This indicator is displayed as a percentage that points to the overall slack in the economy or a company at a given point in time. If a company is running at a 70% capacity utilization rate, it has room to increase production up to a 100% utilization rate without incurring the expensive costs of building a new plant or facility. In the United States, industrial production figures are based on the raw volume of goods produced monthly by industrial firms. The industrial production and related capacity utilization figures are considered coincident indicators because changes in the levels of these indicators usually reflect similar changes in overall economic activity that affect GDP. The Federal Reserve watches industrial production very closely because it believes that inflation shows itself first at the industrial level, particularly when supplies of basic materials become tight and the increases in the cost of commodities and materials are passed down the line to individual consumers.

It is particularly striking to see that during the recession, when the price of WTI reached an all-time high of nearly US$140 per barrel, both industrial production and capacity utilization suffered significant drops. Since 2014, the price of WTI has seen a significant drop and both indexes have been reaching significant highs.

The price of oil surged from US$16 per barrel in December 1998 to the all-time high of US$144 in June of 2008. After the price of oil broke a previous all-time record of US$140 per barrel on June 26, 2008 OPEC predicted that the price of oil would range between US$150 and US$170 per barrel in the years to follow. (Nasseri and Brown 2008) This extraordinarily high price would have had a detrimental impact on an already fragile world economy, forcing governments to work desperately to find ways to reduce the high energy bills for their economies and people. In fact, these efforts resulted in an important drop in the price of energy in the United States and a positive impact on the U.S. economy.

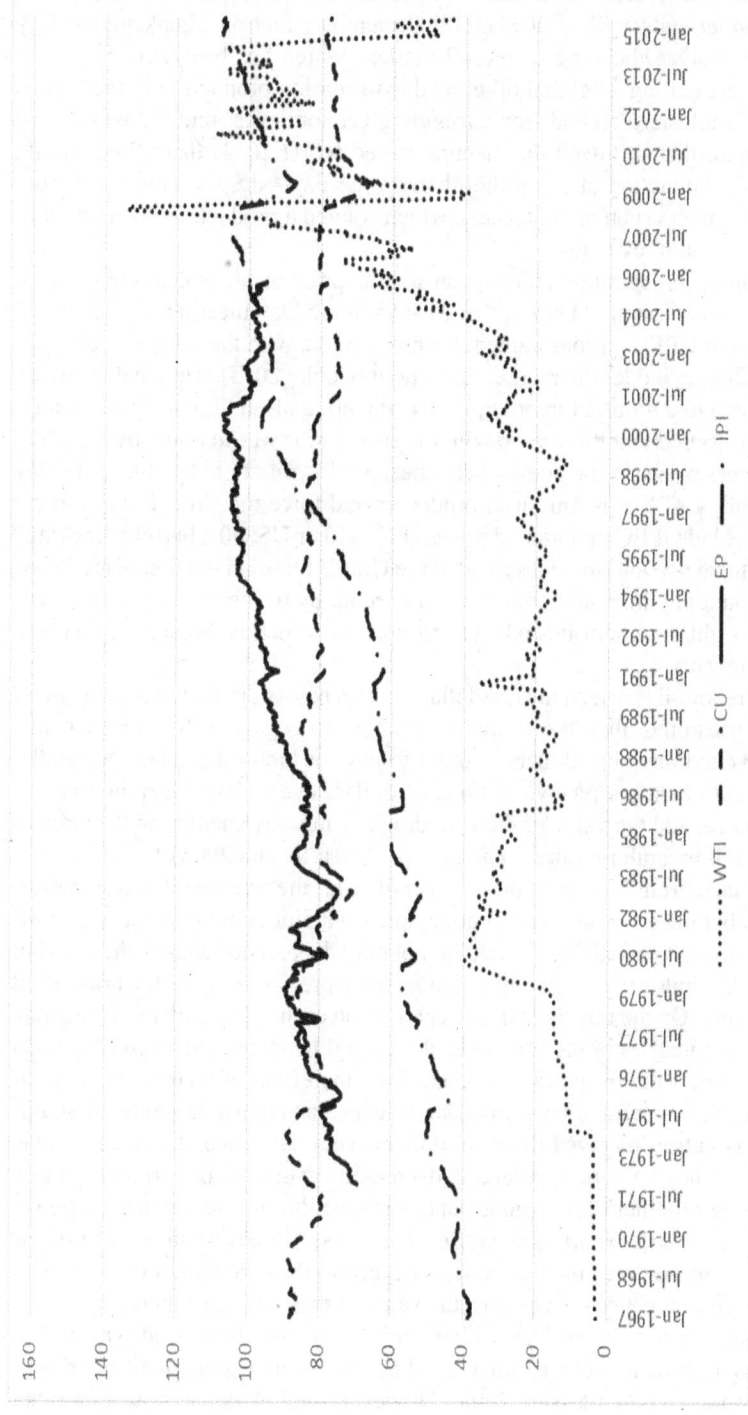

Figure 5.7 Economic indicators for the U.S. economy, 1967–2015.
Source: Economagic.

Since June 2014, crude oil prices have plunged 30% and sparked alarm among OPEC member states (Zhou 2014). OPEC members met on Thanksgiving Day of 2014 to analyze the state of the oil market, which has been suffering from what some are calling a "global oil glut" due to soaring production in the United States and lackluster demand from struggling economies around the world. The announcement that followed the meeting stated (Hirst 2014) that OPEC would maintain oil production at 30 million barrels per day—despite objections from desperate members such as Venezuela, which wanted a production cut in order to increase prices and revenues.

This announcement automatically caused the price of oil around the globe to spiral into a steep plunge. During that Thanksgiving Day meeting in Vienna, oil ministers from OPEC nations agreed, for now, to live with the effects of the U.S. "fracking" boom and let the markets sort it out (Cooke 2015). They believed that if OPEC were to cut output in order to raise the price of oil, it would lose market share. They argued that the way to win this energy war was to allow overproduction to depress prices to the point where cheap OPEC oil might be able to destroy the profitability of North American producers and force the United States to cut production. Had OPEC maintained prices at US$40 or US$50 a barrel, "fracking" would not have become so widespread in the United States in the first place. Now, OPEC is changing this traditional *modus operandi* by trying to depress oil prices in order to fight the boom in shale gas production, which is threatening to make OPEC irrelevant.

The barrel of oil is priced in U.S. dollars, which has a number of consequences. First, countries other than the United States have to engage in foreign exchange transactions and buy U.S. dollars in order to pay for their oil imports. Secondly, oil-producing countries receive billions of dollars every day, depending on the price per barrel and the value of the U.S. dollar. Thus, any changes in the price of oil will be felt by both producers and buyers (Lorca-Susino 2008).

For instance, from 2001 until the summer of 2011, the price of oil was extraordinarily high but the value of the U.S. dollar against major currencies was very low. In fact, during this period, the U.S. dollar not only depreciated against the euro but the U.S. dollar index was suffering a significant depreciation while the price of oil was increasing. On the buyers' side, a depreciation of the U.S. dollar will help pay the oil bill in countries of the Eurozone, the United Kingdom and even China. On the sellers' side—the oil-producing countries—the effect of a cheap U.S. dollar and a high price of crude oil has what can be called a "bipolar" reading. First, oil-producing countries receive billions of dollars every day. Second, since the value of the dollars they have been receiving decreased against major currencies, those dollars would buy them fewer goods and services; that is, the purchasing power of oil-producing and exporting countries decreases. Moreover, since most of the producing countries have their currencies pegged to the U.S. dollar, the weakness of the U.S. currency also drove down the value of their own currencies.

This depreciation of the U.S. dollar during this specific period was at first regarded as a strategic move by the United States to gain export share and reactivate its economy (Lorca-Susino 2008). However, the low dollar strategy did not

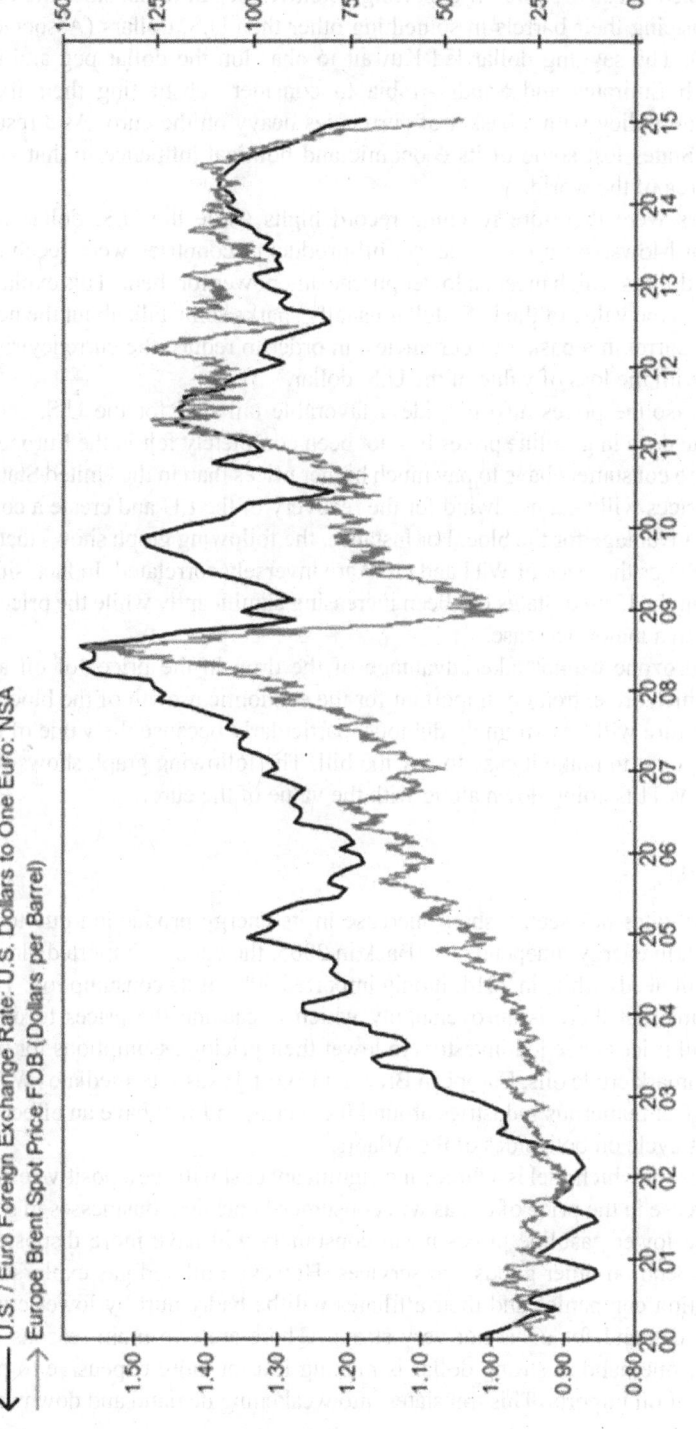

Figure 5.8 The relationship between the U S dollar and the European Brent Spot Price.
Source: Economagic.

totally succeed because some oil-exporting countries began to consider the possibility of pricing their barrels in something other than U.S. dollars (Associated Press 2007). The sagging dollar led Kuwait to abandon the dollar peg and the United Arab Emirates and Saudi Arabia to consider substituting their fixed exchange rate policy with a basket of currencies heavy on the euro. As a result, the United States lost some of its economic and political influence in that very important area of the world.

Oil prices were therefore reaching record highs while the U.S. dollar was testing record lows. As a consequence, oil-producing countries were receiving "devalued" dollars which meant a lower purchasing power for them. This explains why a drop in the value of the U.S. dollar usually sparks some talk about the need to price the barrel in a basket of currencies, in order to reduce the currency risks associated with the loss of value of the U.S. dollar.

Falling gasoline prices also provide a favorable tailwind for the U.S. economy. But the drop in gasoline prices has not been completely felt in the European Union, where consumers have to pay much higher prices than in the United States. Thus, gas prices will be a headwind for the recovery of the EU and create a comparative disadvantage for the bloc. For instance, the following graph shows that in the United States the price of WTI and GDP are inversely correlated. In fact, since 2014 GDP in the United States has been increasing significantly while the price of WTI has seen a major decrease.

If the Eurozone cannot take advantage of the drop in the prices of oil and gasoline, which are extremely important for the economic growth of the bloc, its economic future will be extremely dubious, particularly because the value of the euro is not going to make it easy to pay the bill. The following graph shows that the price of WTI is going down along with the value of the euro.

Final words

The United States has seen a sharp increase in its energy production due to its desire to obtain energy independence. Back in 2005, the country imported almost 60% of its oil needs while in 2014, it only imported 30% of its consumption. This clearly means that there is an oversupply which is causing the prices to drop. Tumbling oil prices have led investors to lower their pricing assumptions for two of the benchmark crude oils, European Brent and West Texas Intermediate (WTI). This will affect numerous industries around the world, and will have an effect on the business cycle on both sides of the Atlantic.

Industries for which fuel is a direct and significant cost will see a positive effect from a decrease in the price of oil, as will consumer-dependent businesses in general because lower gasoline prices mean consumers will have more disposable income to spend on other goods and services. However, oil and gas exploration and production companies and their affiliates will be badly hurt by lower crude prices. The demand for oil is not very strong. There are two main reasons for that. On the one hand, a strong dollar is making it a lot more expensive to pay for the cost of oil imports. This translates into weakening demand and downward pressure on oil prices. Of particular interest is the case of the Eurozone. First, most of the countries that use the euro are still facing the challenges of the economic recession. Second, if the Eurozone continues to face a significant drop in the price of the euro, this will make oil prices even more expensive. Therefore, the Transatlantic Trade and Investment Partnership will be heavily affected by the future changes in the price of this commodity.

Notes

1. John Kerry. "Remarks with EU High Representative Federica Mogherini following their working lunch," U.S. Department of State, December 3, 2014. http://www.state.gov/secretary/remarks/2014/12/234646.htm.
2. National Bureau of Economic Research. http://www.nber.org/cycles/sept2010.html.
3. National Bureau of Economic Research. http://www.nber.org/cycles/sept2010.html.
4. National Bureau of Economic Research. http://www.nber.org/cycles/sept2010.html.
5. Akim Steiner, Helen Clark, and Kandem H. Yumella. "The renewable future," May 9, 2011. Project Syndicate. http://www.project-syndicate.org/commentary/asteiner12/English.
6. Akim Steiner, Helen Clark, and Kandem H. Yumella. "The renewable future," May 9, 2011. Project Syndicate. http://www.project-syndicate.org/commentary/asteiner12/English.
7. Larry Rohter. "In Brazil, fuel of future has already arrived," April 10, 2011. http://www.nytimes.com/2006/04/10/world/americas/10iht-ethanol.html.
8. Econobrowser. "Lower oil prices'" May 8, 2011. http://www.econbrowser.com/archives/2011/05/lower_oil_price.html.
9. Index Mundi. "Crude oil consumption by year." http://www.indexmundi.com/energy.aspx?region=eu&product=oil&graph=consumption.
10. It is not the purpose of this particular work to elaborate on the nuts and bolts of the relationship between conflict, oil price and economic slowdown per se. That might be the topic of a future article.
11. For a detailed guide on the many different types of crude oil visit www.oilprice.com, accessed at: http://oilprice.com/Energy/Crude-Oil/A-Detailed-Guide-on-the-Many-Different-Types-of-Crude-Oil.html.
12. Vantage Point. "Brent crude trading", Trader Tech, accessed at http://www.tradertech.com/trading/brentcrude.
13. Organization of the Petroleum Exporting Countries. "OPEC basket price", accessed at http://www.opec.org/opec_web/en/data_graphs/40.htm.
14. Organization of the Petroleum Exporting Countries. "Member countries", accessed at http://www.opec.org/opec_web/en/about_us/25.htm.
15. VIX and More. "Chart of the week." http://vixandmore.blogspot.com/2011/04/chart-of-week-crude-oil-and-transports.html.
16. Investing Answers. "Dow Jones Transportation Average." http://www.investinganswers.com/term/dow-jones-transportation-average-djta-1302.
17. CNN Money. http://money.cnn.com/data/markets/dowtrans/.
18. John F. Kerry. "Remarks at the Atlantic Council's Conference on Trade and National Security: Renewing U.S. leadership through economic strength," Atlantic Council. U.S. Department of State. April 23, 2015. http://www.state.gov/secretary/remarks/2015/04/241019.htm.
19. Federal Reserve Board. "Industrial capacity and capacity utilization", accessed at: http://www.federalreserve.gov/releases/g17/current/default.htm.

Part III
EU countries
Different political, social, and cultural idiosyncrasies

6 Germany
The big brother of the European Union

> If you want to know your past, then look at your present for it's the outcome.
> If you want to know your future look at your present which is the cause.
> (The Buddha)

Introduction

Germany is the hand that rocks the cradle of the European Union. Neither the EU nor the euro would exist today if Germany had not agreed to the terms and conditions that created the regional bloc and introduced the new currency, which have always been favorable to Germany and have been accepted by the other member states. Germany has become the big brother of the project, and when Germany speaks, the EU listens.

Germany also enjoys international respect and has become the most influential member state in the EU because of its economic orthodoxy and political trustworthiness. Germany enjoys an enviable economic health based on a historically controlled inflation, low unemployment and high productivity. These factors made it the number one exporter in the world until 2009, when the country was overtaken by China.

With these credentials, Germany is undoubtedly the economic engine of Europe and the leader in the Eurozone. But what prompted Germany to believe in the EU, to accept the euro and to help countries in trouble such as Greece, Portugal, Spain and Ireland?

Germany and its economic rectitude: its attitude towards the current crisis

Germany was politically forged in the nineteenth century through the efforts of Otto Von Bismarck, who created the German Confederation and gave rise to the "German Empire." The country's economic power began with the introduction of the Reichsmark as currency in 1924 and since then, the Germans have seen how their national currency reflected the political and economic power of their country. Accepting the euro on January 1, 1999 was not an easy task for Germany.

Germany may seem to be a phoenix, constantly reborn from its ashes. From a political standpoint, it went from being an empire under Bismarck to participating in two world wars that totally destroyed the country's infrastructure, led it to political disintegration and a dramatic division of the country into two entities: East Germany and West Germany. From an economic point of view, no other developed country has suffered from such devastating hyperinflation and paid the cost of the destruction of two world wars—the so-called "reparation payments." The only other country that has faced reparation payments has been Japan.

The period of hyperinflation in the Weimar Republic after the Second World War and the global recession of the 1930s forged the economic character of the country. These two events are considered to be the economic factors which triggered the advent of Nazism and the Second World War. This period of hyperinflation in Germany lasted only a few years (1920–1923) but has become the saddest episode in the history of the country and is still one of the most studied monetary catastrophes in economic history because of its military, social and policy implications.

On May 5, 1921, British Prime Minister David Lloyd George delivered the so-called "London Ultimatum" to the German ambassador in London. The ultimatum demanded the German Reich paid war reparations for the astronomical amount of 132 billion gold marks in 66 annual payments (Germany in fact paid reparations each year from 1930 to 1988, with the last payment coinciding with reunification of East and West Germany). The ultimatum also required the demilitarization of Germany, as required by the Versailles Peace Treaty of 1919. In the absence of German cooperation, the allies threatened to occupy the Ruhr District but on May 11, 1921, the government of Reich Chancellor Joseph Wirth and the Reichstag unconditionally agreed to the demands.

The episode of hyperinflation was the result of the costs and expenses of the First World War. In order to make the required payments, German monetary authorities decided to print money, which decreased the value of the currency even as the prices of goods and services increased. With rising prices, more money was needed to maintain the standard of living in the country, so more money was printed and the government entered into a diabolical cycle that could not be broken. In fact, the Reichsbank at one point boasted of the efficiency of its paper mills in producing paper money.

Hyperinflation has never been forgotten in Germany, and it is still an economic lesson taught in German schools. But the hyperinflation episode was not the only trigger for the rise of Nazism and the Second World War. The behavior of the Allies also played an important role in those developments. In January of 1923, French and Belgian troops occupied the Ruhr because Germany had delayed the war reparation payments. This occupation resulted in months of protest strikes, which increased unemployment, slowed the economy and fueled a vicious cycle: a national economy strangled by the debts imposed on Germany to reconstruct Europe for the military devastation it had caused. At that time, the German government was a fragile political coalition, which after the invasion of the Ruhr lost the support and respect of elite army leaders and fueled dangerous nationalist sentiments.

Since that time, Germany has been obsessed with maintaining the Stabiltätspolitik based on keeping inflation under control and maintaining a stable and democratic political system. Maintaining price stability to preserve political stability remains the top priority for the Bundesbank (German Central Bank). Monetary rectitude and Bundesbank anti-inflationary policies have been the envy of most European countries, which have occasionally tried to imitate them without much success. As a result, the Bundesbank had mixed feelings during the talks on the introduction of the euro and the establishment of the Economic and Monetary Union. The Bundesbank was not only concerned over the disappearance of the German mark and its own sovereignty but most importantly it did not want to be part of a club of countries that did not understand the critical importance and implications of price stability.

Historically, the Bundesbank's commitment to keeping inflation under control has been so strong that it has never hesitated to put into practice rather radical monetary policies that could lead to economic recessions or even changes of government. Since it was founded, the Bundesbank has enjoyed a true political independence that enabled it to implement the necessary monetary policies without political constraints. By contrast, those central banks that are not clearly independent from their government have tended to obey and comply with government wishes, using monetary policy to help governments finance social policies that help win re-election.

The project for the Eurozone became a reality only when Germany was certain that requirements for maintaining economic and monetary stability were included in the Stability and Growth Pact (SGP). However, it has been shown that the lack of respect for these requirements was clearly the cause of the current EU crisis and the financial difficulties of some member countries.

Germany has been instrumental in developing a plan for financial support for countries in difficulty like Greece and others, which ultimately were rescued by German taxpayers even though it was widely assumed that Germany would be reluctant to lend money to countries in difficulty. The latest survey published by the *Financial Times* showed that 60% of Germans opposed helping Greece (Atkins and Peel 2010).

Despite the support of Germany for countries in economic and financial difficulties, Chancellor Angela Merkel has stressed that these countries were responsible for their own problems because they did not put their finances in order, lacked government accountability and were guilty of political complacency. In addition, Germany is fully aware that the problem will not go away just by helping a particular country, but that the country must learn and implement economic and financial discipline.

Germany is not interested in dismantling the Eurozone or fracturing the European Union, yet it also does not want its disciplined and hard-working taxpayers to bear the burden of the lack of financial and economic responsibility of other countries.

Germany and its economic, political and social restructuring: renew or die

Germany has been unfairly treated by history at times. Its efforts to leave behind its sad past and become a prosperous democratic nation throughout the twentieth century have not been recognized and have even been mocked. Germany has also shown great generosity, especially after the fall of the Berlin Wall in 1989 and German reunification the following year. Reunification caused an almost immediate monetary, economic and social crunch for West Germany as it tried to help East Germany rise to the levels of the West.

In 1989 East Germany—officially the German Democratic Republic or GDR—had to begin to modernize its obsolete economy and production systems and rapidly adjust to the new demands of innovative technology and highly trained human capital. In fact, over 55% of the industrial equipment of the GDR was more than 10 years old and almost 50% of the economy was based on agriculture and mining, while the service industry was almost nonexistent (Wunsch 2005). Products manufactured by the Communist-ruled GDR were mainly sold to countries under the Soviet Union's influence and their quality did not match Western standards because those products had never been exposed to free market competition. Moreover, the labor market of the GDR was based on a workforce of about 10 million people and zero unemployment, at least according to government claims that few outsiders believed (Wunsch 2005).

On the other hand, West Germany—officially the Federal Republic of Germany or FRG—enjoyed an industrial infrastructure that had the latest generation machinery, operated with maximum efficiency and was exposed to the pressures of a market economy. In the late 1980s, however, the FRG was beginning to suffer the effects of globalization and the country's unemployment rate rose to 8% of the estimated 28 million workers.

At the time of reunification in July 1990, the GDR adopted the tax laws and social security system of the FRG. The FRG in turn created the Treuhandanstalt as a public body in charge of the intense process of privatizing companies, real estate and all other assets owned by the GDR government. The main objective of the Treuhandanstalt was to avoid what had happened in other former communist countries, where such assets wound up in the hands of former regime officials or were given away to foreign investors for ridiculous prices (Zschiesche Sánchez 2003). The one dark episode of this reunification was the conversion at parity of the GDR Mark (Ostmark) to the FRG Deutschmark. Overnight, East Germans saw their purchasing power increased significantly and began to demand and consume the products manufactured by the West, while avoiding products produced in the East that were low-quality and expensive. Therefore, industrial production in the former GDR declined significantly. This decline had a negative impact on the labor market in East Germany, with production slowdowns creating 3 million unemployed between 1989 and 1991. However, the generous workfare and retirement plans offered by the FRG helped to soften the blow. In short, unemployment in the former GDR quickly exceeded 10% in just two years. On the other hand, the demand for goods and services helped increase production in the FRG, and the unemployment rate in that part of unified Germany fell to 5% in 1990. Economic growth also was fueled by the need to spend billions equalizing the infrastructure in the newly unified nation, including transportation and communications.

The equalization of wages in the newly unified Germany posed another problem because of the lower productivity of the former GDR. East German citizens were characterized as having high levels of education that unfortunately were of little use in the globalized economy they had just joined. To prevent a mass migration from East to West which would have undermined the labor market of the East and collapsed the labor market in the West, the FRG decided to maintain relatively high wages in the East and implement a full restructuring of the education system to increase worker productivity. Thus, the problem was not the low productivity of workers in the former GDR but the wrong type of human capital for the times. These GDR workers had great knowledge in the social sciences but their industrial skills were outdated for the production of goods and services. Despite this gap between wages and productivity, the FRG government preferred to maintain high salaries in the East while focusing on improving productivity through education to avoid a more massive labor migration from East to West that was already starting to affect the labor and real estate markets in the FRG.

Unified Germany grew 2% in 2004 but with an uneven rate of unemployment. In the former GDR, unemployment hit 20% while in the West it was about 10%—a situation that the FRG government understood to be unsustainable and unbearable. In August 2002, a panel of experts led by the Director of Volkswagen, Peter Hartz, proposed to the political coalition that was ruling Germany at that time—the Social Democratic Party and the Green Party, led by Chancellor Gerhard Schröder—a project to improve the labor market and promote industrial competitiveness. This project was called the Hartz Reform and became part of Agenda 2010, which the German government implemented as part of an effort to reform the entire social system and labor market in order to stimulate economic growth and reduce the high unemployment rate.

Schröder presented the foundations for this reform in a speech to the German Parliament in March 2003, explaining that it was necessary to reorganize the system and that the aim of Agenda 2010 was to improve the economy, the social security system and the position of Germany in the global market. Agenda 2010 served as the foundation for what would become the failed Lisbon Strategy 2010, put forward by the EU itself to improve the productivity and competitiveness of the bloc. The EU effort was quickly forgotten and never implemented. The German Agenda 2010 was criticized by some leftist political parties, trade unions, media and even industry leaders and certain sectors of the population, who argued that the Hartz Plan required the largest cuts in social benefits and the welfare system introduced in Germany since the Second World War.

Schröder was also criticized by his own party, which forced him to leave the party presidency in February 2004. Yet, his tenacity and patriotism remained intact and he implemented Agenda 2010 resulting in a dramatic reduction in unemployment. Despite the success, the reforms continued to be criticized by Schröder's own party to the point that he lost the regional elections in 2005 and was forced to call early national elections in autumn of that year. The mobilization of the German left against reforms that had achieved a high level of economic and social success helped Angela Merkel to win the elections and still keep the Agenda 2010 implemented by Schröder.

Germany and the euro: advantages and disadvantages

After Greece and other countries publicly admitted the chaotic state of their finances due to economic mismanagement and political indulgence, German citizens became highly critical. In January 2011, a survey published by the German newspaper *Bild* indicated that 49% of German respondents did not want to continue in the Eurozone and preferred reverting to the Deutsche Mark as their currency (Bild 2010).

This frustration could be explained by the Germans' disappointment with the failures of their troubled EU partners. Still, Germany did not want to see the end of the European Union, the Eurozone or the disappearance of the euro. For Germany, the euro has always been regarded as a positive factor for its own economy.

The introduction of the euro and the disappearance of the German mark nevertheless became a widely debated issue. The German mark was a symbol of the power of a great nation that had a well-structured monetary system independent from political power. Money was simply not available for possible electoral or political manipulation because monetary policy was not in the hands of politicians. Germany also saw the introduction of the euro as a way to maintain control over a group of countries that had systematically carried out devaluations of their national currencies in order to gain unfair competitive advantages over Germany which they could not achieve through their own hard work. In addition, the introduction of a common currency brought price transparency and lowered transaction costs, which indirectly helped Germany increase its export markets.

On the cost side, the introduction of the euro meant that Germany would have to give up its national currency. The German mark had become the national symbol and pride of a country with an incredibly successful monetary, political, economic and social heritage. German Finance Minister Theo Waiger said in April 23, 1998 in a debate before the Bundestag (national parliament of the FRG) that Germany had not renounced the German mark, but rather had expanded its success story to European level.

German authorities nevertheless feared that the European Central Bank would not follow their country's two golden rules: political independence and price stability. Because of these doubts, Germany did not accept the introduction of the euro until it was clearly stipulated that the ECB would follow the German model. Forcing Eurozone countries to accept the ways and means of the Bundesbank as the model for the ECB was expected to guarantee its independence from the political process. Indeed, the independence of the ECB and its compliance with price stability is the sole reason that explains why the euro and the Eurozone are still a reality despite the economic crisis and mismanagement of some governments.

On the benefit side, the introduction of a common currency was to reduce the economic risk associated with currency speculation and competitive devaluations. Germany no longer had to deal with the devaluation of the Italian lira, the Spanish peseta, the French franc, and others. It would now be the euro that would have to face the cruelty of the currency market. Therefore, Germany would not have to spend reserves to maintain the price of the German mark in the face of attacks and devaluations by other European currencies, as it had been doing for many years. For example, in 1992, the Bundesbank had had to spend 44 billion marks of its national reserves to defend the pound sterling and the lira, and still could not prevent the attacks of speculators during the so-called Black Wednesday. Finally, the introduction of the euro helped Germany by spreading the cost of the reunification of the GDR and FRG. Germany had been helping European economies and their currencies since 1971 and it was time for these countries to support Germany in its reunification efforts and the sharing of expenses.

Ultimately, it was obvious to German authorities that the creation of a common market would require a common currency that would provide a more predictable environment for German exports and investments,

Competitive devaluations: all against Germany

Under the Bretton Woods System, German industry became the most efficient and competitive in Europe and the country's economy became the leader among European nations. The secret of this success was an industrial capacity that was so efficient it could easily take advantage of any increase in demand within its borders and in most European countries. Germany was a success story because it was able to maintain strong growth in productivity while keeping labor costs low despite increased competitiveness and export growth.

When the German trade surplus began to grow and remain high, other countries began to suffer from trade deficits and economic imbalances. Misalignments and trade deficits among European countries were based on profound differences in economic approaches. Germany used its surpluses for industrial innovation and modernization, which increased industrial capacity utilization and productivity. Other European nations chose not to use this surplus in the same way, so their industrial capacity and productivity always lagged behind Germany's.

Before the euro, Germany had to withstand competitive devaluations in other European countries while at the same time the mark faced the strength of the U.S. dollar by itself. This situation continued from Bretton Woods until the euro was adopted. When the U.S. dollar entered a devaluation phase because of multiple factors, the mark appreciated by the same amount. These two currencies are the two sides of the same coin, and no other currency in Europe could face the U.S. dollar or other monetary stress except the German mark. Meanwhile, other European countries eased their economic problems, sparked by their own lower competitiveness, by cheating with unfair devaluations of their currencies.

The competitive devaluations of the French franc and the Italian lira against the mark meant that German products became more expensive in France and Italy, which led consumers in those countries to buy domestically produced goods instead. Lost sales and market share in France and Italy in turn would impact the German economy because France and Italy account for more than 25% of total

German exports. Finally, the number and frequency of these unfair devaluations in the 1990s was such that countries with strong currencies asked the European Union to punish governments that devalued their national currencies solely in order to gain unfair competitive advantages and economic profits.

One of the strongest motives behind the founding of the EU and the introduction of the euro was to eliminate such competitive devaluations. So on March 13, 1979 the EU created the European Monetary System, also known as the "currency snake." The EMS was the first step toward unifying the various European currencies in a trading band under the control of the Exchange Rate Mechanism (ERM). Although the EMS was an important step in the right direction, it also had disadvantages. The upper and lower bands of the currency snake were signaling to the market, speculators and investors when each national central bank would have to defend its currency. This signal led to aggressive speculative attacks that resulted in the well-known exit of the pound sterling, three devaluations of the peseta and an agonizing period of economic instability until the euro was created on December 31, 1998 and member states pegged their currencies to the euro.

After the introduction of the euro, Germany's GDP remained the highest in the EU and the country became the largest trading partner of France and Italy. Today, Germany has placed its industry in a competitive niche as a result of the hard but continuous improvements of its productive factors as well as structural reforms to improve its workforce. What's more, although the euro was seen by Germany as a way to avoid competitive devaluations by its European neighbors, as of today a possible reintroduction of national currencies and the abandonment of the euro by some EU members would not harm the basic commercial structures of Germany.

Germany's industrial power has proven to be virtually immune to economic cycles. Its high technology and extremely diversified production of high-end products, ranging from food to pharmaceuticals, clothing, electronics and services, defy fluctuations in the value of the euro. That is, the demand for German products is virtually inelastic and independent of the value of the euro. According to a survey of the Fortune 500 list of best companies in the world, Germany has a total of 15 companies in the first 100, France has 10, Italy has five, Spain has three and Greece has none.[1]

Final words

Europe's turbulent history was the basis for the creation of the EU after the Second World War. But for most Europeans it was Germany that drove the issue because of the consequences of trying to pay reparations for the world wars. Today, Germany is, for many European citizens, a victim of its past and of its economic success. Germany introduced the famous Agenda 2010 and subsequently ceded the government to the conservative party to witness the evolution and success of the reforms they had initiated an example of political maturity that has not been followed by any other government on the continent.

These deep reforms implemented with Agenda 2010, even after assuming the enormous cost of integrating a practically bankrupt East Germany, have not been imitated in France, Italy or Spain. These three large European countries have opted to continue on a path of economic instability and political lobbying rather than make an effort to implement their own versions of the very much needed Agenda 2010 through a broad national consensus.

The European left sees German economic orthodoxy as an attempt to impose the German way upon the rest of the EU. And the conservative parties in the majority of European countries are either confused or do not have enough political vision to undertake the necessary reforms if it's going to cost them an election, as happened with Chancellor Schröder.

Note

1 CNN Money. "Fortune 500" http://money.cnn.com/magazines/fortune/fortune500/2008/employers/.

7 Spain
Before and after the euro

> It is much easier at all times to prevent an evil than to rectify mistakes.
> (George Washington)[1]

Introduction

The economic and financial troubles that unfolded in 2007 have negatively affected many countries around the world, becoming the first global crisis of the globalized world. Spain faced a difficult period as well, and after years of economic expansion the country went into a deep crisis. The competitive advantages that Spain enjoyed in the past have started to weaken.

Before adopting the euro, Spain would solve periods of economic difficulty by using unfair devaluations of the peseta to help improve the evolution of its GDP and labor market. As of mid-2015, Spain was still immersed in a mild recession, as the country suffered from high unemployment and economic stagnation that has persisted since 2007 because it can no longer devalue the peseta. As a consequence, the country is witnessing the emigration of highly skilled workers—a severe brain drain.

Throughout history, Spain has suffered from a persistent unemployment problem that improves or worsens depending on the economic cycle but since 1976 has effectively been the Achilles heel of the economy. The country had two great opportunities to restructure and modernize its production system to help improve the labor market and reduce the historically high unemployment rate.

The first opportunity came when Spain discovered America and became an empire where the sun never set. It received all kinds of riches from overseas that were not used to lay the foundations for an innovative industrial and commercial fabric. The second came when Spain joined the European Union and began to receive funds to modernize its production model. But it failed to take advantage of the opportunity and stuck to a model based primarily on income from tourism and construction industries.

By mid-2015, Spain faced unemployment levels similar to those recorded during the 1950s, which had led to a massive emigration to Latin America and Europe, mainly Germany, which needed to be rebuilt after the Second World War. And, as in the 1950s, the country experienced an exodus of labor.

Nevertheless, the integration of Spain into the EU and especially the adoption of the single currency brought the country remarkable economic benefits and political stability, mainly because the dangerous increases in oil prices would have been devastating for the economy without the umbrella of a strong euro. Therefore, in the current economic crisis the euro has been protecting a Spanish economy that otherwise could have been hit by record high inflation and political instability.

Without the ability to devalue and without a dynamic and modern production system, Spain is in need of a third "confiscation" to help raise the funds needed to improve the government coffers. In the first "confiscation" between 1835 and 1837, in the reign of Queen Isabel II, Juan Álvarez Mendizábal and Pascual Madoz seized and sold off monastic properties. President Jose Maria Aznar more recently privatized the "commanding heights" of the state economy in order to improve the country's outlook. The country should now carry out a third "confiscation" by reforming a state structure that has become too large, corrupt and expensive to maintain.

The beginning and end of an empire

Spain developed its identity as a nation when the Iberian Peninsula became part of the Roman Empire and with the fall of the empire, it entered a period of political, economic and social instability. In 1492, the Catholic kings succeeded in unifying the country after expelling the Arabs and endowed the new kingdom with a national identity rooted in Catholicism. In addition, with the discovery of the Americas and the incorporation of colonies and overseas territories, the country began to enjoy a golden era due to the great wealth arriving from this empire.

During the time of the empire, Spaniards enjoyed a high living standard but never expected that their colonial riches might one day disappear, as the colonies eventually sought and obtained their independence. Spain therefore did not use the wealth from its colonies to create a more modern production model.

The 1812 Constitution of Cadiz included some significant reforms such as equal rights, representation for the American territories and the integration of the overseas territories as provinces, meaning that the Crown lost the income from the entire American continent. Under the constitution the riches from the colonies were to go directly to the state administrative apparatus and not the monarch, establishing for the first time in history a substantial difference between the "finances of the nation" and the "finance of the monarch." King Fernando VII's later abolition of this constitution and Spain's return to absolutist monarchical rule were triggers for the eventual disintegration of the empire.

When Spain lost its last colonies in 1898, the country lost an important part of its national income, which meant that its people had to work harder to maintain their living standard. Spain had failed to foresee that this "manna" from its colonies could come to an end and had not looked for alternatives to the "import" of precious stones, gold, crafts and exotic crops from overseas. It had been living off international income and not off national labor.

The country's farmland was in the hands of a few rich families that exploited farmers and suffocated any industrial initiatives. With the collapse of its empire and without an efficient production system, Spain found itself on the road to becoming a failed state, which initiated a spiral of violent conflicts that culminated in the Civil War of 1936.

At the end of the Civil War Spain was bankrupt. Its abundant reserves of gold and silver had left the country, its working-age population had shrunk and public and private infrastructure had been destroyed. The little productive capacity that the country had managed to create after the fall of the empire was destroyed in the fighting. The dictatorship of General Francisco Franco was based on an economic autarchy that was a burden on an already shattered society until the late 1950s, when the country began to see an improvement after it joined the International Monetary Fund and the World Bank and began receiving much needed financial aid.

The peseta as an escape valve for low economic productivity

The peseta was born as the national currency of Spain in 1868 under the Latin Monetary Union (1868–1927) and died when Spain adopted the euro. But the peseta was not created as a symbol around which to create a national unity, as in the case of the pound sterling, but rather to end the multiplicity of currencies that existed at the time. When the peseta was born, it was pegged at 25.22 to the U.S. dollar (García Delgado and Serrano Sanz 2000) and when it disappeared it was worth 142.15 pesetas per U.S. dollar.[2]

Until its disappearance, the peseta suffered a number of devaluations, all geared to help the Spanish economy achieve an unfair advantage for its inefficient productive system, a burden that Spain had been dragging around for centuries. Spain, it seems, did not quite understand that competitiveness is achieved through professional excellence and entrepreneurship assisted by innovative human capital, and not through currency manipulations.

The incorporation of Spain into the Bretton Woods system in 1958 forced the government in Madrid to keep a parity of 60 pesetas per U.S. dollar. In 1964, Spain withdrew from the club and the peseta had to adapt to a flexible system. The years of Bretton Woods were very beneficial to the peseta, as explained by Jaime Caruana, general manager of the Bank for International Settlements, during the opening of the conference titled "Dollars, Debt and Deficits—60 years after Bretton Woods" (Caruana 2004). Under the Bretton Woods system, Caruana argued, Spain received financial aid and technical assistance from the International Monetary Fund (IMF) to help the country modernize its monetary system and the economy in general, assistance that helped the economy to take off immediately.

But just two years after the end of Bretton Woods, Spain carried out the first of a series of competitive devaluations. Under Bretton Woods, the country had been forced to open its borders to international trade, update its agricultural and industrial sectors and modernize production factors. Without the Bretton Woods rules and regulations, the country had no obligation to maintain a strict monetary policy and as a result experienced a deterioration in its already battered commercial balance. In the years after Bretton Woods, the Spanish government opted for an expansionary monetary policy that together with a high rate of imports of products and raw materials led Spain to a period of high inflation, low competitiveness and a worsening of the foreign trade sector. In this situation, Spain devalued the peseta in 1967, setting a new exchange rate of 70 pesetas per dollar. (Torrero Mañas 2008) Thanks to the competitive devaluations and a cabinet of technocrats, Spain achieved full employment for the first time in 1973.

When the world suffered the second oil crisis in 1976, which forced countries to adjust their economies to the new times and especially to modernize their productive systems, Spain was in the midst of a delicate political transition from dictatorship to democracy and could not undertake the necessary adjustments. In an attempt to stop a contagion effect and avert even worse economic difficulties and perhaps even social tensions, the government granted businesses and industries a series of subsidies. The costs of production, however, turned out to exceed the market price of the products subsidized. The public deficit then soared, nominal wages were affected—with a deep impact on household demand—and finally the country suffered a dramatic rise in the unemployment rate. In order to pull the economy out of this hole, the government again devalued the peseta in July 1977 by up to 24.87% against the U.S. dollar. Unfortunately, this option, whose sole purpose was to try to help the economy recover its lost competitiveness, did not work. The devaluation damaged the balance of payments and scared off foreign capital investments so badly needed for economic improvements. At that moment, the country slipped into a deep economic crisis and all the political parties, trying to avert social tensions, agreed in a display of patriotism to sign the so-called "Moncloa Pacts" in 1977.

This highly publicized pact only helped to shift from Franco's kind of vertical labor unionism led by Noel Zapico to a vertical control of unions led by communists like Marcelino Camacho and Nicolas Redondo. This change in the type and source of the union movement in Spain was the result of a political and economic environment in Spain characterized by a society with very limited political formation. The country was switching from a dictatorship to democracy, communism had not yet collapsed in Europe and the pro-Marxist constitution of Portugal was still in force. As a result, the governing structures developed under these circumstances proved to be unworkable and prone to corruption. Further, the victory of the socialist PSOE party in 1982, as a result of an intense and unproductive political fight among the center and right-wing parties, resulted in the creation of a government whose political and economic ideology overrode the needs of society. The new socialist government was unable to provide the economy with the necessary stability and flexibility, which meant that in 1980 and despite the much-needed drop in the price of oil Spain saw its GDP growth stall, unemployment reached over 20% and inflation soared. The government again chose to solve this dangerous economic, political and social situation by devaluing the peseta in 1982 (Arancibia 1982).

In 1986, Spain became part of the European Union and began a period of economic prosperity because of the arrival of fresh capital from the EU's Structural and Cohesion Funds, granted to Spain to help raise its infrastructure and services to European levels. Despite the arrival of this financial aid, the country did not restructure its labor market or its productive system. But at least EU membership helped Spain to improve its political stability and adopt several timid measures—highly controversial but necessary—to improve the labor market and ease the high unemployment.

Spain began a prosperous decade, from 1994 to 2006, not only because of the funds received from the EU but also because the U.S. economy had started a solid expansionary cycle in March of 1991. That helped Spain to emerge from the deep economic depression it had suffered since 1986, without having to do too much internal work.

With the help of the EU assistance funds, plus the favorable U.S. business cycle and a series of economic measures that were put in place in 1996, Spain finally passed the bar imposed by the EU in the Maastricht Criteria and, against all odds, was able to adopt the euro on time on January 1, 1999. The expansive economic cycle that came with EU membership also helped the country enter the European Monetary System (EMS) on June 19, 1989 which further helped to improve an extremely positive situation for the country. Membership of the EMS required the peseta to comply with the fluctuation bands of the European Exchange Rate Mechanism, also known as the "currency snake."

During the years of the European Monetary System and the Exchange Rate Mechanism, the peseta suffered a number of devaluations for two reasons: the difficult economic situation of the country and the continuing attacks on the currencies that were part of the currency snake. The peseta had a very difficult year in 1992, when it lost 5% of its value on September 16 and another 6% on November 21. In addition, in 1992 the country hosted both the Olympic Games held in Barcelona and the World Exhibition (Expo) in Seville, commemorating the 500th anniversary of the discovery of America. Ironies of history, 500 years after the discovery of America, Spain was still suffering a very delicate economic situation due to the lack of an efficient and competitive production model.

The costs incurred in the organization and preparation of these two international events caused the government to increase its deficit, while unemployment remained curiously high at 11%. In May 13, 1993, Spain had a deficit of 3%, inflation of 4.5% and unemployment of 24%. The economy entered a severe recession, and the government tried to fight it by implementing expansionary monetary measures which were quickly discounted by the market. The peseta then suffered another speculative attack and its defense cost the National Bank of Spain a staggering 3.2 billion pesetas. Still, there was no other choice but to devalue the currency by another 8% (El País 1993). Unfortunately, even this was not enough and Pedro Solbes, the Spanish Minister of Economy at the time, had no other options but to devalue yet another 7% on March 5, 1995 (Vidal-Folch and Carvajal 1995). This was the last devaluation of the peseta before it was replaced by the euro in 1999. The chart below shows the evolution of the peseta against the U.S. dollar.

The following table presents a number of key economic indicators that reveal the difficulties of the Spanish economy at the time of the many devaluations of the peseta.

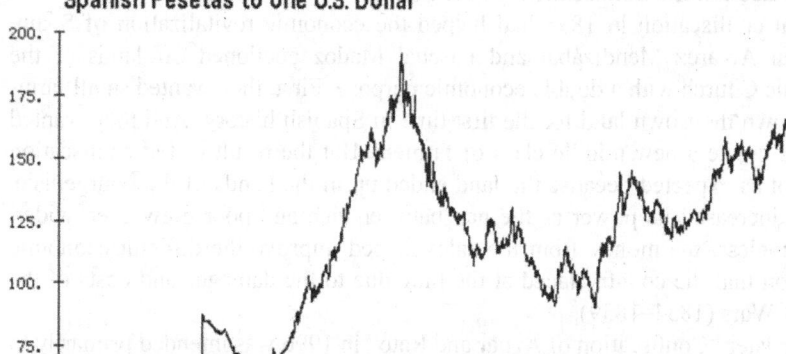

Figure 7.1 The peseta and the U.S. dollar, 1972–1999.
Source: Economagic.

Table 7.1 Spain, macroeconomic data, 1967–1995

Devaluation date	Budget deficit as % of GDP	Unemployment rate	Inflation
1967	n.a.	3%	3.39%
July 1977	>1%	24.54%	5.71%
Dec. 1982	5.5%	16.79%	5.34%
Sep. 1992	7%	20.06%	5.93%
Nov. 1992	7%	20.06%	5.93%
May 1993	6.3%	23.90%	4.57%
March 7, 1995	6.2%	22.77%	4.67%

Source: EFE 1995.

The euro and the need for a competitive devaluation: the third confiscation

The much-needed economic expansion that took place after 1996 was not only the result of the business cycle and changes in economic policies but also of the increased government revenues from what can be defined as a confiscation of wealth.

In 1996, the Spanish government began to privatize the nation's largest state enterprises that could be considered the commanding heights of the economy such as Endesa, Repsol, Indra, Tabacalera and Telefonica to try to fill the state coffers.

84 Political, social, cultural idiosyncrasies

This process might well be called the "Confiscation of Rato and Aznar," a reference to the "Ecclesiastic Confiscation" of 1835.

That confiscation in 1835 had helped the economic revitalization of Spain, as Juan Alvarez Mendizábal and Pascual Madoz auctioned off lands of the Catholic Church with a double economic purpose. First, they wanted small farmers to own their own land for the first time in Spanish history. And they wanted to help create a new middle class of farmers. But the result of the confiscation was not as expected because the land ended up in the hands of the bourgeoisie, which increased its power as the gap between rich and poor grew even wider. Nevertheless, the money from the sales helped improve the difficult economic situation that the country faced at the time due to the damages and costs of the Carlist Wars (1834–1839).

The later "Confiscation of Aznar and Rato" in 1996 was intended primarily to help small Spanish investors have access to a percentage of the privatized companies. In addition, this confiscation invited foreign investors to enter the country and participate in business opportunities and help with job creation. However, as in the case of Mendizábal and Madoz, most of the companies were acquired by a new bourgeoisie created around the political class that controlled the privatizations. Regardless of who got to buy pieces of these newly privatized companies, however, the government did manage to raise money and reduce the public deficit.

The economic expansion and the funds raised with the confiscation helped to revive the economy, which increased consumer confidence and private investment. In addition, a significant process of internationalization took place among the most significant national companies: market-leading Spanish companies went international, mainly in the countries with which Spain shares a cultural affinity and language, and invested nearly US$10 billion between 1993 and 2000.[3]

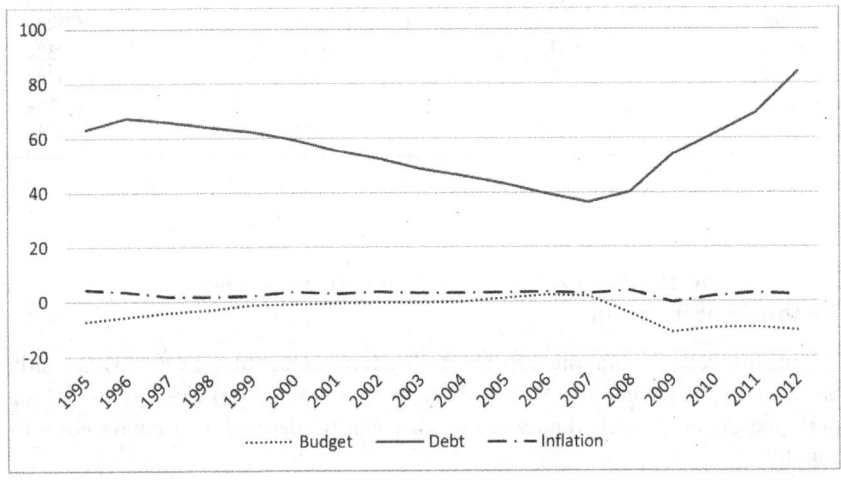

Figure 7.2 Public finances in Spain, 1995–2012.

Source: ECB Statistics.

This business expansion helped to reduce the extremely high unemployment rate, lower inflation, increase exports and improve the budget deficit, and Spain was able to adopt the euro in accordance with the EU's timetable. A study of the evolution of Spain's debt, deficit and inflation rate before 1999 shows that the country did not meet any of the requirements of Maastricht (Martínez 2003).

The Spanish business cycle and the economic recession of the twenty-first century

On January 1, 1999, Spain and 10 other European countries adopted the euro, and the peseta ceased to exist. Once in the Eurozone, with financial support from the EU and the implementation of draconian economic measures—much like those implemented in Spain by Ullastres with his stabilization programs in the 1960s—the country saw its economy grow more stable and it joined the IMF. According to the World Bank,[4] all these changes helped Spain become the world's tenth largest economy in 2007 in terms of nominal GDP. However, the global crisis that began that same year hit the country hard, and even in mid-2015 Spain was still suffering from a high budget deficit, low competitiveness and an unemployment rate above 20%—all factors presenting serious challenges to its future economic development.

With the adoption of the euro, Spain gave up its monetary policy autonomy and lost control and authority over the money supply, turning over its monetary fate to the mandates of the European Central Bank. This was a great challenge, as Spain was traditionally a country without any monetary discipline that used interest rates and competitive devaluations to gain competitiveness when its economy was stagnant.

When Spain adopted the euro, the country had its finances and economy in order for the first time in many years and had passed the test of the euro. With the advent of the euro, the European Central Bank implemented an expansionary monetary policy that affected all countries of the Eurozone. However, this expansionary policy was not what Spain needed at that time because it was receiving very high revenues from tourism and the EU funds. With low interest rates characteristic of any expansionary monetary policy, the ECB was shaping the conditions for the perfect economic storm: spending and domestic consumption soared and household savings rates dropped to their lowest levels in Spanish history. These two factors indeed created an economic bubble. While Germany, France and several Nordic countries used their own economic booms to modernize their industries and increase competitiveness, Spain squandered capital, maintained an inefficient production model, failed to recapitalize the national coffers, maintained a parasitic political caste and allowed widespread corruption around a construction sector bubble that will take decades to digest. When the construction bubble burst, it showed an overvaluation of real estate prices of more than 40% (Ramírez 2008).

From 2008 until mid-2015, Spain did not meet most of the Stability and Growth Pact (SGP) requirements for the proper functioning of the euro, highlighting the country's lack of economic and financial discipline. Spain might have been able to solve those problems if the government had carried out another competitive devaluation of its currency, but that was no longer possible with the euro.

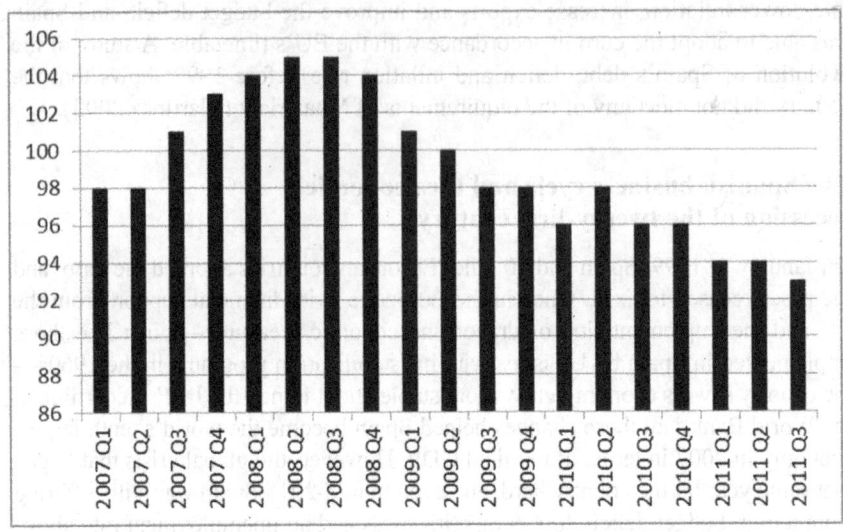

Figure 7.3 Spain: real estate price index, 2007–2011.
Source: ECB Statistics.

Taking into account the number of devaluations carried out by Spain in the last 50 years, and since neither its economic fundamentals nor its productivity have changed significantly, if Spain had kept the peseta it would already have depreciated the currency four times by mid-2015. Under the euro, the country's economy recorded negative growth from 2008 to 2014.

The Misery Index and the brain drain in Spain

The improvements of the Spanish economy during the expansionary phase of the business cycle unfortunately favored a postponement of the economic restructuring needed to modernize the productive system and do away finally with the problems that traditionally curtailed the Spanish economy for centuries. These weaknesses and problems were very well known, yet were not solved by any of the governments, including those in the past 40 years of democratic rule.

With the advent of the crisis in 2007, these traditional problems, mainly related to the rigid labor market structure on both the demand and supply sides, intensified and sparked a slowdown of the economy so dramatic that in September 2011 the IMF questioned the economic forecasts of the Spanish government. Since 2007, the country's unemployment rate had increased dramatically. In 2012 and 2013, the private sector recorded an unemployment rate of more than 20%, the highest in all of the EU. What's more, some reports predicted that the unemployment rate would not come down to levels close to 9% until 2026 (Viñas 2011b). Due to the high rate of private unemployment, it is not surprising that public employment has been seen as a refuge and therefore rose by more than 125% (Soriano 2012) between 1976 and 2006. Indeed, in 2006 the number of employees at the state, federal and national levels and public companies was 3,186,000, while the number of people working in the most important economic sectors of the country—retail, wholesale and hospitality—was about 3,134,000 million (Tejo 2011).

Due to the economic troubles the country experienced from 2007 to mid-2015, there has been a significant change in the labor market, with an increase in unemployment, a drop in labor market participation and a negative migration rate, all trends that have worsened the country's Misery Index. The Misery Index was created in the 1960s by Arthur Okun, economic advisor to President Lyndon Johnson, as a way to include unemployment and inflation in measurements of the U.S. economy. The Misery Index sheds light on how the evolution of the economy is affecting the purchasing power and living standards of society. In the United States, this index played a significant political and economic role when Jimmy Carter used it during his 1976 campaign against President Gerald Ford. During the months of the campaign, the index reached a devastating level of 13%. But after Carter won the election, the index continued to rise and eventually hit 22%, a level never before experienced in the country. As a result, Carter lost the election to Ronald Reagan, who then enjoyed the lowest Misery Index level in history.

Applying Okun's methodology to create a "Misery Index" for Spain, it is clear that the country faces a serious unemployment problem with a consequent increase in poverty levels and a deterioration in the standard of living and purchasing power. The index created for Spain shows that the historical maximum was reached in 1994 when it hit a staggering 30%. Since 1996, Spain has been adjusting its economy to adopt the euro and enjoyed an economic bonanza, two

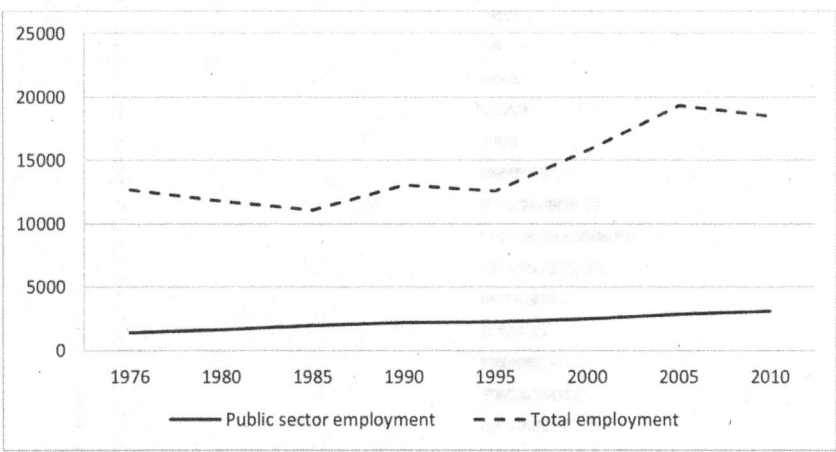

Figure 7.4 Spanish labor market, 1976–2010 (in millions).
Source: Instituto National de Estadística.

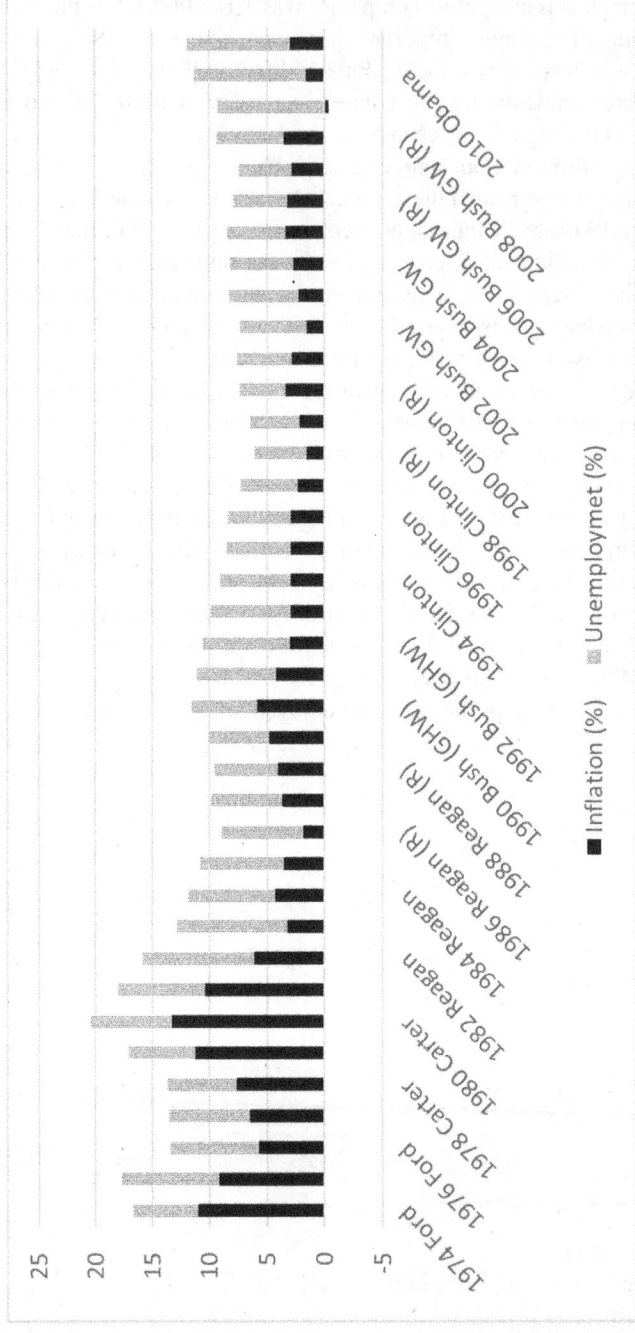

Figure 7.5 Misery Index under U.S. presidents, 1974–2011 (% of unemployment and inflation).

Source: MiseryIndex.com.

factors that helped to improve the index in 2003 to the lowest level in Spanish history. Between 2003 and 2007, the rate remained broadly stable between 12% and 13%. But beginning in 2007 it soared dramatically to levels close to those experienced in the 1990s. This increase was the result of a significant hike in the unemployment rate and not so much in the rate of inflation, which makes the problem even more dramatic.

A comparison of the Spanish index with misery indices for other euro area countries and the United Kingdom shows that Spain's numbers are much higher than any other country's. In 2007 the Spanish index also suffered the biggest increase compared to the others.

A detailed analysis of the components that make up the Misery Index—inflation and unemployment—for the Eurozone shows that the inflation rate remained moderately subdued at 2% between 1996 and 2007 due to the work of the European Central Bank. The inflation rate exceeded 3% in 2008 but dropped to about 1% in 2009 due to the economic crisis. An analysis of the unemployment component shows that stability also was the norm until 2010, when the rate began to increase.

Because of the expectations that unemployment will remain high until 2026 and the current limited economic growth in Spain, the country has experienced a higher than expected emigration rate. Indeed, in the first quarter of 2011 the country reported an exit of 14,109 residents and the entry of only 7,875 resident foreigners (Vega 2011).

Spain has been a country of emigrants for the past 500 years, and there have been times when the outflows even damaged the economy. The history of Spanish emigration dates back to 1492, when the *conquistadores* left for the New World in search of fortune and glory. A second wave of emigration took place during the Civil War (1936–1939), when many intellectuals and others left Spain to

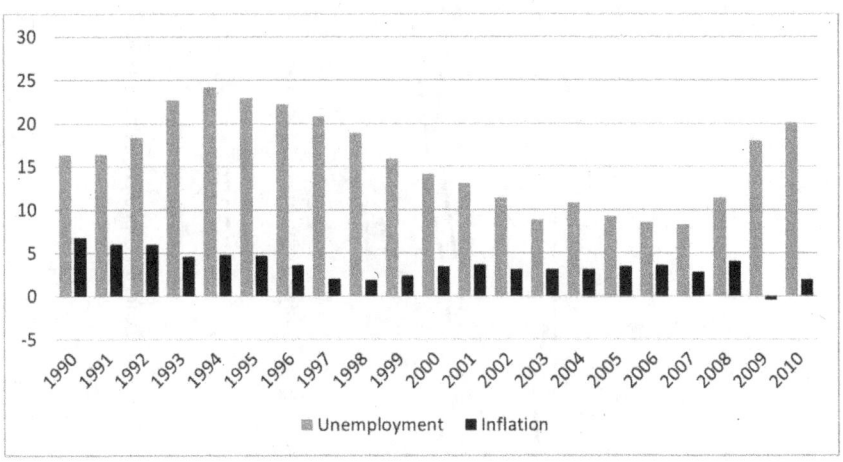

Figure 7.6 Misery Index for Spain, 1990–2010.

Source: ECB Statistics.

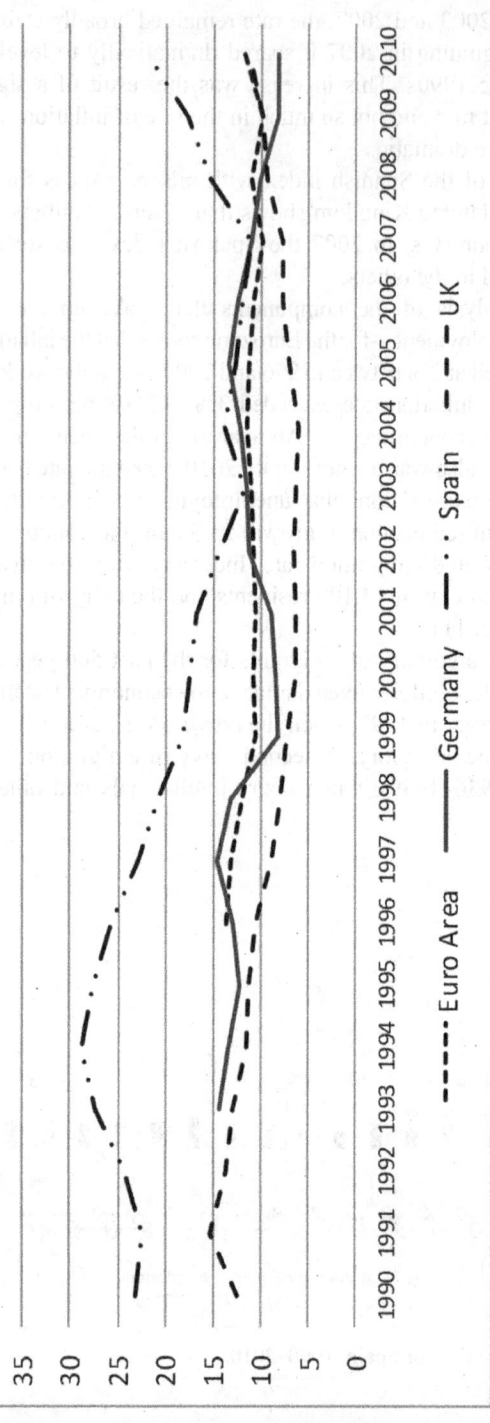

Figure 7.7 Misery Index for European countries, 1990–2010.
Source: ECB Statistics.

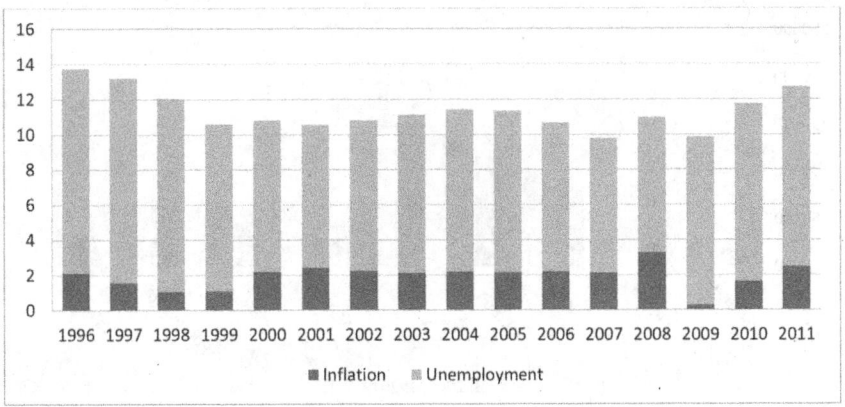

Figure 7.8 Misery Index for the Eurozone, 1996–2011.
Source: ECB Statistics.

settle down in the United States and several Latin American countries. A third major emigration wave took place in the 1950s, due to post-war economic difficulties. This wave was formed largely of young men with relatively low levels of education and almost no professional skills but eager to work and prosper. These workers went mostly to Latin America and northern Europe, particularly Germany, where immigration was structured and organized under an agreement between the Spanish and German governments that to this day remains a model for such labor arrangements.

The current migratory wave is reflected in the data of the Censo de Españoles Residentes en el Extranjero (CERE) (Census of Spaniards Resident Abroad).[5] In 2002, the CERE reported that 1 million Spaniards had taken up residence outside the country, but in 2010 this figure had risen to 1.4 million and in December of 2012 the number had increased even further to 1,516,646. The cities of Madrid, Barcelona and Coruña experienced the highest rates of emigration[6] between 2008 and 2010.

A detailed analysis of the most recent emigration flow shows that the main destination countries are not other European countries, as might be expected. Despite the free movement of people, capital, goods and services offered by the EU, most of the new wave of Spanish migrants have chosen the United States and Latin America as their new home rather than France and Germany.

The high levels of emigration since 2008 have unleashed a dramatic brain drain as highly skilled workers leave, impoverishing their homeland and putting their know-how to work for the benefit of their new countries.

In addition, the high value of the euro against most currencies in the past eight years has contributed to this migration trend because a strong euro makes it easier to resettle the migrants in their new country. Previous migration experiences have shown that once the workers put down roots in a new country there is no turning back, either because they really don't want to return or because

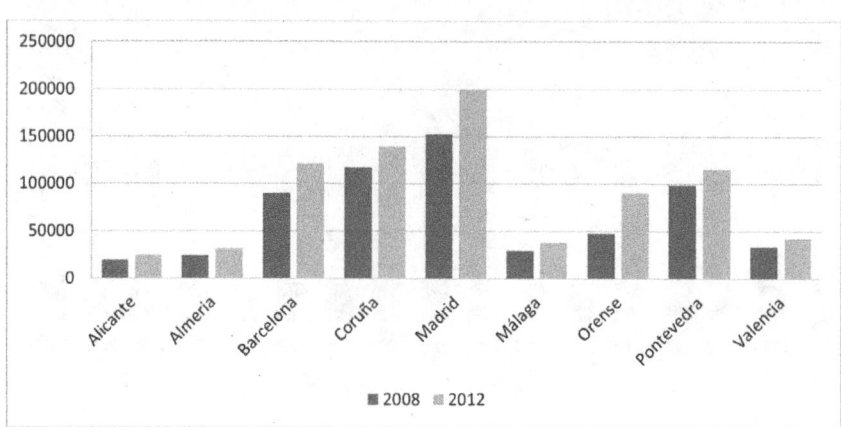

Figure 7.9 Census of Spaniards resident abroad by place of origin, 2008 and 2012.
Source: Instituto Nacional de Estadística.

they find it truly difficult to return. This is the unfortunate truth found in a 2005 study by the External Advisory Group (EAG) which concluded that only one in 1,188 professionals and academic researchers who leave the country actually return to Spain. (El Mundo 2005) In fact, the experience of the Plan Ramon y Cajal attracting academic researchers back to Spain does not seem to have had much success, since, of the 774 contracts offered, only 437 were accepted (El País 2006). Another problem was highlighted during the "Jornadas de jóvenes post-doc en el extranjero" organized by the Consejo Superior de Investigación Científica (CSIC) in Madrid in December 2010. Participants argued that even

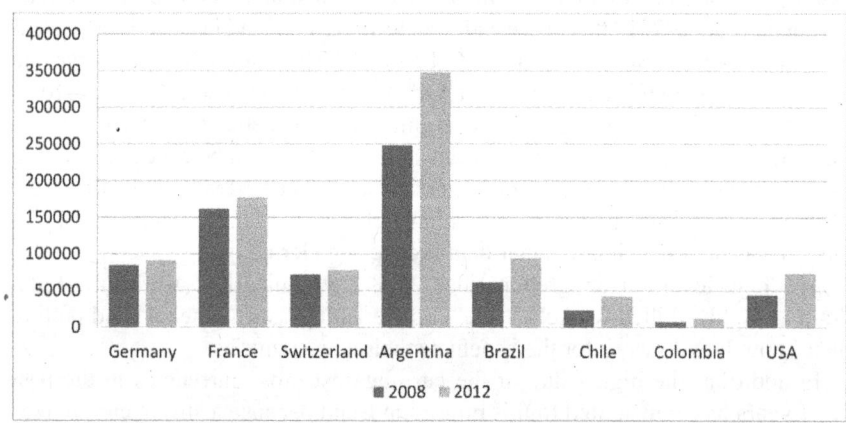

Figure 7.10 Census of Spaniards resident abroad by destination, 2008 and 2012.
Source: Instituto Nacional de Estadística.

those young Spanish scientists and researchers who spent time abroad and wanted to return to Spain were usually eligible only for junior research positions instead of being offered the opportunity to work on their own projects (Europa Press 2010).

Final words

The economic history of Spain is marked by lights and shadows that are constantly repeated in an economic cycle highlighted by high deficit, high unemployment and high levels of emigration—a very complicated situation for Spain to overcome (Almunia 2009).

The major difference between the current and previous crises is that with the euro, the country cannot devalue its currency. This shows more strongly than ever that Spain should have used the prosperous times brought on by various sources of revenue—the discovery of New World riches and its entry into the European Union—to restructure its economy and production model. Unfortunately, the economic good times were not used to reinvent the country and the government preferred to use uncompetitive relief valves to adjust the economy rather than making major structural reforms. Before the euro, the country used competitive devaluations of the peseta to adjust the economy. After the euro, this tactic could no longer be used and the country began to suffer from a high rate of unemployment, resulting in a painful brain drain that is now impoverishing the country.

Spain must now adjust to the modern times from a political and economic point of view. The country needs to not only reinvent and modernize its productive functions and model, but more importantly the government should be brave enough to carry out a third confiscation: the confiscation of the state. This is a pressing issue as the country needs to simplify a political structure that has become too large, too inefficient, and too expensive.

The first two "confiscations" in Spain helped raise the capital needed to get the country out of painful recessions and near-bankruptcy. The third confiscation is required not to sell the "commanding heights" of the economy but to reduce the inefficient, corrupt and expensive state structure and make it more viable and affordable for citizens who pay for it through very high taxes. This restructuring of the Spanish state should include a modernization of the constitution of 1978, written and approved under unique political, economic and social circumstances that do not resonate in the twenty-first century. Although this confiscation has an important economic rationale, it will be difficult to put into practice. And although politicians benefited directly and indirectly from the previous two confiscations, this third round would end many of the benefits obtained by politicians through the outdated and opaque state structures.

The economic crisis that is sweeping the country was not caused by the euro and bringing back a national currency such as the peseta will not solve the problem. It is the government which must help reinvent Spain and promote an excellent environment for economic and human activity, the appropriate formula for helping to produce innovative goods and services in the twenty-first century.

The government should also help to improve intangibles such as a modern and quality education and promote entrepreneurship and self-employment and the spirit of cooperation—instead of supporting public employment, bureaucracy and unproductive dead hands. It is important to step back and think about the phrase that Albert Einstein hung on the wall of his office at Princeton University: "Not everything that can be counted counts and not everything that counts can be counted."[7]

Notes

1 George Washington. Letter to James McHenry, Aug. 10, 1798. http://www.notable-quotes.com/m/mistakes_quotes.html#7LIIhE8dSMCFXeHX.99.
2 Economagic. "Spanish peseta to one U.S. dollar." http://sub0.economagic.com/em-cgi/data.exe/fedny/day-fxes2us.
3 The Economist. "A good bet?" April 30, 2009.
4 World Bank. "Gross domestic product." http://siteresources.worldbank.org/DATASTATISTICS/Resources/GDP.pdf.
5 Censo Electoral de Españoles Residentes en el Extranjero (CERE). http://www.ine.es/oficina_censo/cifras_electores.htm.
6 Censo Electoral de Españoles Residentes en el Extranjero (CERE). http://www.ine.es/oficina_censo/cifras_electores.htm.
7 Albert Einstein. http://thinkexist.com/quotation/not_everything_that_counts_can_be_cou-nted-and_not/15536.html.

8 Greece and the battle of ideas

> The future welfare of Greece and its citizens lies more
> than ever on the shoulders of the Greek politicians
> to keep their part of the solidarity pact.
> (Olli Rehn)[1]

Introduction

On January 1, 2001, Greece became the twelfth member of the Eurozone, after being left out when the single European currency was launched at the beginning of 1999 for failing to meet any of the convergence criteria (Maastricht Criteria), but primarily those on inflation and the budget deficit.

Costas Simitis, at the time prime minister of Greece, very proudly said on December 31, 2000 that his country "is already experiencing euro conditions. We all know that our inclusion in EMU ensures greater stability for us and opens up new horizons" and that the Greek government hailed the achievement of becoming part of the Eurozone. However, the president of the European Central Bank (ECB) at that time, Wim Duisenberg, was already warning that the Greek government had to keep working hard to improve its economy and comply with the requirements of the Stability and Growth Pact designed for economic and financial stability. At the same time, some analysts cautioned that the euro could suffer from the inclusion of a weaker European nation, prompting the ECB to reiterate to East European member states which wanted to join the Eurozone that they had to strictly respect all Maastricht Criteria, but mainly the budget deficit rule of 3%, because the EU risked being accused of a double standard.

On November 15, 2004 Greece admitted that it had fudged the convergence criteria to qualify for the Eurozone. In particular, Greece acknowledged that it had joined the Eurozone in 2001 on the basis of figures that showed its budget deficit to be much lower than it really was. The Greek government explained that its deficit was never below the 3% required by the EU but that the deficit became unmanageable between 2000 and 2003 due to hosting the 2004 Summer Olympics.[2] No government was able to control the deficit or comply with the Stability and Growth Pact (SGP) requirements. Eurostat, the EU's statistics agency, sent a delegation to Athens to examine the country's budget figures. This was not the first time that Eurostat expressed concerns with the data provided by Greece. In March 2002, Eurostat had refused to validate data transmitted by the Greek government, and after further analysis the Hellenic Statistical Authority[3] had to revise the debt level by several percentage points. However, in September 2002 Eurostat once again refused to validate Greek government data, which after being reviewed turned what had been a surplus into a deficit.

In March of 2004, shortly before Greek elections, Eurostat again refused to validate Greek numbers. When the new government of the conservative party, New Democracy, was inaugurated, it promised an objective financial audit of all government accounts. Initially, all parties agreed to this decision, which was even applauded by George Papandreou, president of the Panhellenic Socialist Movement (Pasok), by then the main opposition party. But this promise did not materialize and neither outside auditing firms nor the central bank was ever asked to carry out any audit of government accounts. Instead, the New Democracy government investigated the years 1997–2003 and gave the data to Eurostat, which published it in a report.[4] Despite the evidence, the European Union never took any decision at all on possible disciplinary action against Greece for not respecting the SGP.

On March 29, 2005, however, the New Democracy party imposed an austerity budget in an attempt to slash Greece's deficit and get public finances back on track after the cost of hosting the 2004 Olympics. Some of the measures included a dramatic tax increase on alcohol and tobacco, and an increase in VAT from 18% to 19%, but the main goal was to cut public spending by 3.5 billion euros and reduce Greece's public sector deficit, which at 6.1% of GDP in 2004 was well above the permitted ceiling of 3%, to 3.5% of GDP in 2005. After a year of austerity measures, the Greek economy experienced strong economic growth in the spring of 2006, with GDP rising 4.1% in the first three months of 2006; Unfortunately, this was only a temporary improvement and in 2009 the Greek economy contracted by 0.3% and the national debt rose to 262 billion euros, compared to 168 billion euros in 2004. The situation forced the New Democracy government to call for new elections, asking the Greek people for a new mandate to tackle the looming financial crisis. On October 4, 2009, Papandreou's Pasok party took back power from the New Democracy party. And shortly after that, concerns about the debt began mounting as Papandreou admitted that the Greek economy was in a difficult position and European finance ministers expressed concern about the size of the country's debt. This fear materialized on December 8, 2009, when Fitch downgraded its credit rating of Greece's long-term debt to BBB+, from A- which combined the Greek crisis with the worldwide economic crisis.

This downgrade increased Athens' cost of borrowing and marked the beginning of a complicated sequence of events. On December 14, 2009 Papandreou announced a radical set of reforms designed to cut the deficit by four percentage points, as a proportion of GDP, between 2010 and 2011. In a televised address to the nation, he issued a clear warning:

> There are certain moments in the history of a nation when the choices made define the decades to come. Today is such a moment. It is time to address and resolve, once and for all, deep-rooted problems that are holding the nation back.
> (Smith 2009, 1)

But the austerity measures irritated society and on December 17, 2009 thousands of workers went on strike and took to the streets to protest the cutbacks, demanding, instead, more government spending to help counter the difficult economic situation.

Despite the measures, 2010 was a turning point for the country. By January 28, 2010 the spread between the interests charged on credit to Greece and the largest and strongest economy in the Eurozone, Germany, widened sharply to 4% as bond holders demanded a higher interest rate, amid concerns about the country's budget deficit as well as fears that it might eventually be forced out of the single currency zone.

The lack of international trust as to the state of the Greek economy forced Papandreou to announce another austerity package which included a severe freeze on public sector pay and higher taxes for low- and middle-income households. This announcement was followed by a strike and street protests by public sector workers, who clashed with riot police in Athens.

The economic and social situation forced European leaders to gather in Brussels on Thursday February 11, 2010, for an emergency summit amid growing speculation that they would rescue Greece in what would be the first bail-out program of a Eurozone country. In fact, it was Joaquín Almunia, the commissioner for monetary affairs at the time, who told the European Parliament that the summit should prepare an aid package to Athens "in exchange for clear commitments that they will meet their responsibilities" (Traynor 2010). German Chancellor Angela Merkel opposed a quick bail-out program for Greece at the meeting, arguing that the country needed to tackle its debt problems by itself. Not only had Greece for years reported dubious national accounts information to the Eurostat agency, but there was concern about the role played by Goldman Sachs. U.S. Financial regulators in fact scrutinized Goldman Sachs in 2010 for its role in helping the Greek government to structure a string of complex derivatives deals and borrow billions of dollars in exchange rate swaps, which did not officially count as debt under Eurozone rules (Clark, Stewart and Moya 2010).

When Eurozone member states failed to provide help to the deteriorating Greek economy, Papandreou launched a campaign to persuade world leaders on both sides of the Atlantic to support Greece as it struggled with debts of 300 billion euros, and a budget deficit that by 2010 had swelled to 12.7% of GDP. Thus, on March 9, 2010, Papandreou met with President Obama during an official visit to the United States and asked for help in cracking down on financial speculators such as "hedge funds and currency traders, who he blames for aggravating problems and making it harder for Greece to borrow money" (Warden 2010). After months of difficult negotiations in Athens involving the International Monetary Fund (IMF), the European Commission and the European Central Bank, the

Eurogroup on May 2, 2010 approved the first bail-out of a Eurozone member state by agreeing on a three-year package.

Since May of 2010, Greece has been receiving financial support from Eurozone member states and the IMF to cope with its financial difficulties and economic challenges through three "Economic Adjustment Programmes"[5]—with the last one being the most problematic of the three.

The First Economic Adjustment Programme was signed on May 2, 2010 when the Eurogroup agreed to provide Greece with bilateral loans pooled by the European Commission in what is called the "Greek Loan Facility" for a total of 80 billion euros.[6] The European Commission decided that this amount was to be disbursed from May 2010 through June 2013. However, due to the crisis in Portugal and Ireland and the fact that Slovakia decided not to participate in this program, the amount was later reduced by 2.7 billion euros. This financial assistance was part of a joint package, with the IMF committing an additional 30 billion euros under a stand-by arrangement (SBA).

The Second Economic Adjustment Programme[7] for Greece was agreed on March 14, 2012 by the Eurozone finance ministers. Member states and the IMF agreed to add to the first program an additional €130 billion for the years 2012–14. While the financing of the first program was based on bilateral loans, the second program was going to be financed by the European Financial Stability Facility (EFSF), which had been fully operational since August 2010.[8] However, the IMF was also part of this second program, contributing 19.8 billion euros. That meant that the second program provided financial assistance totaling about 164 billion euros until the end of 2014; it was further agreed that in this second aid package there should be private sector involvement (PSI) to improve the sustainability of Greek borrowing.[9]

The Second Economic Adjustment Programme expired on June 30, 2015 and was immediately followed by a request on July 8, 2015 for a third assistance program. On August 19, the European Commission agreed to the Third Economic Adjustment Programme[10] after signing a Memorandum of Understanding (MoU)[11] with Greece that paved the way for mobilizing up to 86 billion euros in financial assistance to Greece over three years (2015–2018). What's more, the Greek authorities signed a Financial Assistance Facility Agreement with the European Stability Mechanism (ESM) to specify the financial terms of the loan. However, this third program linked the disbursement of funds to effective progress in meeting the requirements included in the MoU. The requirements, which provoked much public debate, were designed to help Greece improve its public finances, enhance its competitiveness, cut employment and help Greece return to a sustainable growth path.

The bail-out program: rules are meant to be broken

The EU and the Eurozone were at a crossroads in 2010 when they had to deal with the Greek crisis and later with Ireland, Portugal and Spain. These economic problems arose because the Treaty of Lisbon did not provide the tools needed not only to solve any financial or economic problems that might arise but, more importantly, to prevent them from ever developing in the first place. The Stability and Growth Pact, which requires countries to maintain their public finances within a certain agreed level, was never properly supervised and no sanctions were ever imposed on countries that were not obeying the requirements.

The Treaty of Lisbon failed to correct these well-known deficiencies and made the legal framework even more confusing, retaining the so-called "no-bail-out rule" yet introducing a blurry "exit clause"—two moves that clearly were inadequate to deal with the problems at hand. That left the Eurozone and the EU in a gridlock that has been damaging its image and putting in jeopardy the survival of the project.

Nonetheless, the economic crises experienced by some Eurozone nations have made probable what was unthinkable when the Treaty of Lisbon was under consideration: the expulsion or withdrawal of a member state from the Eurozone. Expulsion from the Eurozone is considered less likely because it would definitely hurt the image of the EU and its members. But a growing number of scholars, economists and average members of society regard a country's voluntary withdrawal from the Eurozone, while it remains in the EU to sort out its finances, as the most beneficial option. In fact, the idea of a country voluntarily leaving the Eurozone while remaining in the EU is the most widely recommended solution to the current problems. However, there is the possibility of a negotiated withdrawal, which would be significantly different from a unilateral or voluntary withdrawal.

Neither of these alternatives are contemplated in the Treaty of Lisbon, however. The treaty only considers the complete exit of a country or group of countries from the EU. Article 50 of the Treaty of Lisbon says that "Any Member State may decide to withdraw from the Union in accordance with its own constitutional requirements."[12] But this article refers to leaving the EU altogether, with the possibility of rejoining the union following the procedures in Article 49. That article explains that, "Any European State which respects the values referred to in Article 2 and is committed to promoting them may apply to become a member of the Union."[13] Article 2 further states that:

> The Union is founded on the values of respect for human dignity, freedom, democracy, equality, the rule of law and respect for human rights, including the rights of persons belonging to minorities. These values are common to the Member States in a society in which pluralism, non-discrimination, tolerance, justice, solidarity and equality between women and men prevail.

In this case, the country would have to reintroduce its old currency or create a new one, restructure its central bank and give it full monetary powers. There would also be a legion of difficulties related to the rights and obligations of every natural or legal person inside or outside the country withdrawing from the Eurozone. Most importantly, reintroducing the old currency or a new one would likely lead to the continued use of the euro in the country, due to the uncertainty that would surround the new national currency.

The Maastricht Treaty included a so-called "no bail-out" clause that was retained in the Treaty of Lisbon, at Germany's insistence, to prevent a budgetary problem in one country from spilling over to the EU as a whole. However, the Lisbon Treaty's Article 122 states that any member state "seriously threatened with severe difficulties caused by natural disasters or exceptional occurrences beyond its control" can receive financial assistance from other member states. The question is if the debt crisis experienced in Greece could qualify as an "exceptional occurrence." The problem with Greece is that these exceptional occurrences are man-made, and yet are negatively affecting the EU and the Eurozone by undermining the strength of the Eurozone. In the Greek case, there was debate on whether the "no bail-out rule" should be applied, or whether Greece should be helped, and how. Germany's economic minister at the time, Rainer Brüderle, stated that he did not believe "that a bailout is the right way because German and French taxpayers can't pay for Greece. Maybe they will give certain help, but first it is for the Greeks to solve their problems" (Randow and Lacqua 2010).

The impossibility of a voluntary withdrawal from the Eurozone rests on the wording and spirit of Articles 4(2), 118 and 123(4) and Protocol 24 of the Treaty establishing the European Community which explicitly refer to the "irrevocable fixing" of the conversion rates as well as to the irreversibility of the process of adopting the euro. Since joining the Eurozone and adopting the euro is voluntary, participating in the EMU becomes a legal obligation because the agreement is irrevocable and the monetary union process is irreversible. Thus, leaving the EMU but remaining in the EU is impossible, and leaving the EMU can only happen if a country leaves the EU. However, it is understood that unilateral withdrawal is possible as a remedy or relief measure if member states constantly breach the treaties or have difficulties complying with their obligations.

Since members do not have the right to voluntarily withdraw, is there a mechanism by which member states can expel a fellow country? This situation was already contemplated when Irish voters rejected the Lisbon Treaty in June 2008. A procedure to legally expel a member states whose economic and financial behaviour might be endangering the survival of the Eurozone and the EU can only be possible if Article 48 of the Treaty is amended and if there is unanimous consent by all member states.

There are a number of reasons that can explain why neither an expulsion clause nor withdrawal possibilities were included in the treaties. First, the idea of the EU was to present this union as an organization where member states share a full commitment to the project. Second, allowing for the possibility of expulsion or withdrawal would increase adverse selection and moral hazard.

The Greek tragedy that erupted in 2010 was just the tip of the iceberg, because some other member states suffered similar situations. However, despite the rigidity of the legal framework, the depth of the crisis required flexibility to prevent the union from disappearing. This has shown that the phrase *pacta sunt servanda* rarely reflects reality and that "where there is a will, there is a way." In fact, the spirit and the letter of the very last paragraph of the joint statement issued by the Heads of State and Government, after agreeing to a blurry financial aid package for Greece, asked:

the President of the European Council to establish, (. . .) a task force (. . .) to present to the Council, before the end of this year, the measures needed to reach this aim, exploring all options to reinforce the legal framework.

(European Council 2010)[14]

Thus, it becomes paramount to amend the treaty in order to accommodate solutions that were unthinkable years ago but might nevertheless become the only way to save the union. It is now the best time for the EU project to change and improve its provisions, which would have never taken place in calmer times. The project is facing its biggest crisis and the EU should apply Albert Einstein's idea:

> The greatest inconvenience of people and nations is the laziness with which they attempt to find the solutions to their problems. . . . Let us stop, once and for all, the menacing crisis that represents the tragedy of not being willing to overcome it.

Greece after Syriza: the beginning of a new relationship

Indirect presidential elections were held in Greece for a successor to Karolos Papoulias. Prime Minister Antonis Samaras and Deputy Prime Minister Evangelos Venizelos asked the Speaker of the Parliament on December 9, 2014 move forward the elections.

Samaras announced the candidacy of New Democracy politician Stavros Dimas, jointly supported by the ruling New Democracy–Pasok coalition, for the presidency. But Dimas failed to secure the required majority of MPs, despite the fact that there were three rounds of voting in December: the first round was held on December 17, the second on December 23 and the third on December 29. As a consequence, Samaras asked incumbent president Papoulias on December 31 to issue the presidential decree required by the Constitution to formally dissolve parliament and call for new election—set for January 25 of 2015.

The Coalition of the Radical Left founded in 2004, Syriza, won the election, became the largest party in the Greek parliament and chose party chairman Alexis Tsipras to serve as prime minister. On January 26, 2015, Tsipras and Independent Greeks (Anel) leader Panos Kammenos formed a coalition government, with Tsipras becoming prime minister while Greek-Australian economist Yanis Varoufakis was appointed minister of finance (Inman 2015) and put in charge of negotiations with EU authorities. On February 5, 2015 the new parliament was inaugurated and immediately resumed the presidential election. On February 17, 2015, Tsipras nominated veteran New Democracy politician and former Interior Minister Prokopis Pavlopoulos, who was elected on February 18, 2015 as the new President of the Republic with 233 out of 300 votes.

Since 2010, Greece had been struggling to solve a debt crisis that continued despite the economic and financial help provided by the institutions. The fact that the ruling ND–Pasok coalition could not ensure the election of a president, that a snap election became a reality, and that the leftist anti-austerity Syriza was leading in opinion polls, caused widespread anxiety over Greece's economic and political future. On December 30, 2014, the Athens Stock Exchange fell by 9.5% and interest rates paid on 10-year loans issued by the Greek government rose to 9%. (BBC News 2014) Since that date, Greece and the EU have gone through some tough times. On July 2015 Yanis Varoufakis was replaced by Euclid Tsakalotos as minister of finance. Tsipras resigned as prime minister on 20 August 2015 and a snap election was set for September 20, 2015 (BBC News 2015) because at least 25 Syriza MPs were in disagreement with the terms of the bail-out signed by Tsipras and split to form a new party, called Popular Unity and led by Panagiotis Lafazanis.

During the six months between the January 25 election and Tsipras' resignation in August, many political and economic events put the relationship between Greece and the EU at severe risk.

First, on February 28, the second economic assistance program was set to expire. With the new election and the success of Syriza, the future of the project suffered from significant political uncertainty, especially after Varoufakis declared that the government had "no intention of co-operating with a three-member committee whose goal is to implement a programme whose logic we consider anti-European" (BBC News 2015c). After more harsh rhetoric and intense negotiations, the Greek government on February 18 requested an extension of the Master Financial Assistance Facility Agreement. The Eurogroup agreed to a four-month extension, based on the Greek government's commitment to a comprehensive list of reforms and their acceptance by parliament (Traynor 2015). The extension was finalized on February 27 and was to expire on June 30, 2015.

On that date, the country failed to pay the approximately 1,600 million euros owed to the International Monetary Fund, becoming the first developed country to default on payments to the institution (Robins-Early 2015). On April 9, 2015 Greece repaid a 450 million euro IMF loan installment (Associated Press 2015b), and on May 11, 2015 Greece, one day earlier than scheduled, tapped emergency reserves in its holding account at the International Monetary Fund to make a 750 million euro debt payment to the Fund (Maltezou and Papadimas 2015). However, Greece could not make any of the payments due to the IMF—on June 5 for about 300 million euros; June 12 for 345 million euros; June 16 for 576 million euros; June 19 for 345 million euros; and June 30 for about 1.5 billion euros (Associated Press 2015a).

The International Monetary Fund (IMF) communications director Gerry Rice confirmed that:

> The SDR 1.2 billion repayment [about EUR 1.5 billion] due by Greece to the IMF today has not been received. We have informed our Executive Board that Greece is now in arrears and can only receive IMF financing once the arrears are cleared. I can also confirm that the IMF received a request today from the Greek authorities for an extension of Greece's repayment obligation that fell due today, which will go to the IMF's Executive Board in due course, . . .
>
> (IMF Communication Department 2015)

June 30, 2015 was also an important date because the second economic program expired without any agreement on financial assistance to Greece despite four months of negotiations on the economic future of the country. During this time, it was clear that Greece needed financial help and that the country was facing a real threat of default, which forced both parties to try to agree on an extension of the second bail-out deal. However, on June 26, 2015 Greece unilaterally broke off negotiations with the Troika and called for a surprise referendum. On June 26, 2015 the Eurogroup issued the following statement:

> Since the 20 February 2015 agreement of the Eurogroup on the extension of the current financial assistance arrangement, intensive negotiations have taken place between the institutions and the Greek authorities (. . .) Regrettably, (. . .), this proposal has been rejected by the Greek authorities who broke off the programme negotiation.
> (European Council 2015)[15]

Further, the European Commission made public the latest proposal agreed by the European Commission, European Central Bank and International Monetary Fund, although:

> neither this latest version of the document, nor an outline of a comprehensive deal could be formally finalized and presented to the Eurogroup due to the unilateral decision of the Greek authorities to abandon the process on the evening of 26 June 2015.
> (European Commission 2015)[16]

However, only a few hours after abandoning the negotiations, Tsipras announced on television that a referendum was to be held on July 5, 2015.[17] It required citizens to approve or reject the offer proposed by the Troika on June 25, 2015 in order to obtain the last tranche of money of the second bail-out deal, which had been held back by the Troika since February 27, 2015. This proposal contained a list of 10 prior-action items offered by the commission, but withdrawn when negotiations were abandoned.[18]

On June 28 the referendum was approved by the Greek Parliament with the votes in favor of Syriza, Anel and Golden Dawn (La Vanguardia 2015), and the Greek government had to order strong capital controls that forced banks to remain closed and imposed limits on cash withdrawals at ATMs of 60 euros a day for person (Pérez and Sánchez-Vallejo 2015). The referendum was held on July 5 with a participation rate of 62.50%, and 61.31% choosing "NO,"[19] which showed an overwhelming rejection of the policies proposed by the European Union rescue (Maltezou and Papadimas 2015).

But Varufakis resigned as finance minister on July 6, 2015, the day after the referendum, and on July 8, 2015 Euclid Tsakalotos, his successor, made an official request for stability support—in the form of a loan facility—to the ESM to be used for meeting debt obligations and to ensure stability of its financial system. A separate request for financial assistance was sent to the International Monetary Fund (IMF) on 23 July 2015.[20]

On July 8, 2015, Tsakalotos also submitted to the head of the ESM a simple one-page request to the Eurozone's 500 billion euros bail-out fund, the European Stability Mechanism, for a new three-year program in the following terms:

> On behalf of the Hellenic Republic ("the Republic" or "Greece"), I hereby present a request for stability support within the meaning of Articles 12 and 16 of the ESM Treaty given the risk to the financial stability of Greece as a member state and of the euro area as a whole.
>
> (Reuters 2015)

The Greek Parliament approved the prime minister's request on July 10, 2015 and the completed package was forwarded to the euro group, which then scheduled a "crisis summit" on July 12 to consider the request, which then offered a dramatic turnaround of "pension cuts, tax increases and other austerity measures" (Steinhauser and Fairless 2015). At the Euro Area Summit which took place on July 12–13, the leaders of euro area countries reached an agreement with Greece on a set of prior actions that had to be implemented urgently in order to start negotiations on an overarching reform agenda, to be detailed in a MoU.

On July 13, the Syriza-led government accepted the conditions imposed by the Eurogroup, in exchange for a third bail-out package. Curiously, the conditions attached to the third assistance program contained even larger pension cuts and tax increases than the one rejected by Greek voters in the referendum. This new package was approved following a stormy debate in which dozens of lawmakers on the left rebelled against Tsipras. Nonetheless, the package passed with 222 votes in favor in the 300-seat chamber but with the opposition of 62 Syriza lawmakers—including former Finance Minister Varoufakis. On July 15 and 22 the Greek lawmakers approved several sets of legislation related to the conditions attached to the financial assistance package (Maurice 2015).

On July 16, 2015, two days after it had voted against it (Maurice 2015), the UK accepted the proposal to grant Greek a short-term loan. And on July 17, the German Parliament voted in favor of opening negotiations on the third bail-out. (Mahony 2015) Thus, on July 17, 2015, the Council approved:

> a decision granting up to 7.16 billion euros in short-term financial assistance to Greece under the European Financial Stabilization Mechanism (EFSM). The loan will have a maximum maturity of three months and will be disbursed in up to two installments. It will allow Greece to clear its arrears with the IMF and the Bank of Greece and to repay the ECB, until Greece would start receiving financing under a new program from the European Stability Mechanism (ESM).[21]

Also on July 17, the Eurogroup asked the institutions to start negotiations on a MoU to detail the conditions for a third financial assistance facility of up to 86 billion euro over three years which will cover the period 2015–2018 in accordance with Article 13 of the ESM Treaty.[22] On August 11, Greek authorities and the institutions reached a staff-level agreement on the MoU, and euro area finance ministers endorsed it three days later—after Greek authorities had passed another set of legislation, the so-called "prior actions"—stating that:[23]

> The Eurogroup welcomes the agreement that has been reached between Greece and the European Institutions, with input from the IMF, on the policy conditionality underlying the new ESM macroeconomic adjustment programme.

This new program therefore followed a July 8 request for financial assistance by the Greek government, after expiration of the country's second program on June 30, and allowed the European Commission to sign another MoU on August 19 with Greece following approval by the ESM Board of Governors for further stability support, accompanied by a Third Economic Adjustment Programme. The financial assistance is expected to allow the Greek government

> to cover financing needs, make overdue payments, and address financial sector needs in order to mitigate hindrances to economic activity, as well as repay a short-term bridge loan of EUR 7.16bn that was disbursed under the European Financial Stabilization Mechanism on 20 July.[24]

The first disbursement of funds of 13 billion euros contemplated under this third program was made on August 20, 2015 and an additional 10 billion euros was to be released immediately for bank recapitalization.

On August 20, 2015, the same day that Greece received the first 13 billion euros payout from the third bail-out package that enabled the government to repay 3.2 billion euros to the ECB and avoid default, Tsipras announced his resignation and snap elections for September 20 (Kitsantonis and Yardley 2015). This move was designed to allow him to capitalize on his popularity among voters and remain in power, in a stronger position and without the anti-bailout Syriza rebels to interfere when the time comes to implement the toughest parts of this third program.

Tsipras has remained in power after pledging to end austerity and restore Greek dignity amid a standoff with the euro region. He won the September 20, 2015 election—despite yielding to the demands of European leaders for more austerity in the crisis-hit country—and has secured a new mandate. Voting is mandatory in Greece, but the turnout was only 56%, the lowest participation level since at least the 1990s. Syriza received 35.5% of the votes, a level of support barely diminished from the emphatic victory that catapulted him into power in January 2015. His new left-wing government took office on September 23 as he renewed the governing coalition he forged on January 26, 2015, with Panagiotis Kammenos the founder of the right-wing anti-austerity party "Independent

Greeks." On the new cabinet, Kammenos was named minister of defense and Tsakalotos was reappointed as finance minister in charge of implementing the MOU signed on August 19 and tackling the painful economic reforms. Finally, the Syriza members who revolted against the bail-out agreement and split from the party formed a new party, Popular Unity. This party advocates not only a Greek withdrawal from the Eurozone but also the reinstatement of the drachma as the national currency (BBC News 2015a).

Final words

Since January 2015, Greece has been on the verge of collapse many times and close to leaving the EU, with the consequent economic and social chaos. After nearly eight months of political and economic paralysis, a new Greek Parliament and government cabinet were sworn in after approving a third financial assistance program.

Syriza came to power in January of 2015 promising to bring the country out of its deep crisis and abandon the unpopular austerity measures and reforms. However, after a dramatic standoff that caused the country to suffer weeks of banking paralysis, the government approved a third international bail-out program that requires compliance with economic and fiscal conditions that are much tougher than previous plans. Tsipras, despite a political discourse of communist-like utopia and anti-European populism, had to step over every single one of the red lines that he promised his constituents that he would never cross. The promises of the radical left that captivated voters in Greece turned out to aggravate the already strained situation, increasing the levels of poverty, economic chaos, political instability and social tensions.

Tsipras has a new mandate to help the country and his fellow countrymen, many of whom are complaining that Greece is paying debt with more debt, and that the money is not going to help the Greek people. Thus, the approval and adoption of the third bail-out does not guarantee that the country will avoid the worst-case scenario. In fact, it is too early to completely rule out that final outcome. However, the most difficult decisions have been made and the new political consensus in the country must ensure that the necessary measures and policies are implemented in order to turn around the country's economic outlook.

Notes

1 European Commission. "Remarks of European Commission Vice-President Rehn at the Eurogroup press conference of 14 May 2012." Press Release Database, May 14, 2012. http://europa.eu/rapid/press-release_MEMO-12-347_en.htm.
2 Between 2000 and 2003, as the cost of hosting the 2004 Summer Olympics reached 7 billion euros (£4.8 billion).
3 Hellenic Statistical Authority. http://www.statistics.gr/portal/page/portal/ESYE.
4 Eurostat. "Report by Eurostat on the revision of the Greek Government deficit and debt figures" (PDF). November 22, 2004.
5 European Commission. "Financial assistance to Greece." Economic and Financial Affairs. http://ec.europa.eu/economy_finance/assistance_eu_ms/greek_loan_facility/index_en.htm.

6 European Commission. "First Economic Adjustment Programme for Greece." Economic and Financial Affairs. http://ec.europa.eu/economy_finance/assistance_eu_ms/greek_loan_facility/index_en.htm.
7 European Commission. "Second Economic Adjustment Programme for Greece." Economic and Financial Affairs. http://ec.europa.eu/economy_finance/assistance_eu_ms/greek_loan_facility/index_en.htm.
8 European Financial Stability Facility. "About EFSF." http://www.efsf.europa.eu/about/index.htm.
9 European Commission. "Second Economic Adjustment Programme for Greece." Economic and Financial Affairs. http://ec.europa.eu/economy_finance/assistance_eu_ms/greek_loan_facility/index_en.htm.
10 European Commission. "Third Economic Adjustment Programme for Greece." Economic and Financial Affairs. http://ec.europa.eu/economy_finance/assistance_eu_ms/greek_loan_facility/index_en.htm.
11 European Commission. "Memorandum of Understanding between the European Commission acting on behalf of the European Stability Mechanism and the Hellenic Republic and the Bank of Greece." Economic and Financial Affairs. http://ec.europa.eu/economy_finance/assistance_eu_ms/greek_loan_facility/pdf/01_mou_20150811_en.pdf.
12 The Lisbon Treaty, Article 50. http://www.lisbon-treaty.org/wcm/the-lisbon-treaty/treaty-on-European-union-and-comments/title-6-final-provisions/137-article-50.html.
13 The Lisbon Treaty, Article 49. http://www.lisbon-treaty.org/wcm/the-lisbon-treaty/treaty-on-european-union-and-comments/title-6-final-provisions/136-article-49.html.
14 European Council (2010). "Statement by the Heads of State or Government of the Euro Area—25 March 2010." http://www.consilium.europa.eu/uedocs/cms_data/docs/pressdata/en/ec/113563.pdf.
15 European Council. "Eurogroup statement on Greece." Council of the European Union, June 27, 2015. http://www.consilium.europa.eu/en/press/press-releases/2015/06/27-eurogroup-statement-greece/.
16 European Commission. "Information from the European Commission on the latest draft proposals in the context of negotiations with Greece." June 28, 2015. http://europa.eu/rapid/press-release_IP-15-5270_en.htm.
17 Official Referendum Site: http://www.referendum2015gov.gr/en/.
18 European Commission. "List of prior actions—version of 26 June 20 00.pdf." Press Release Data Base. http://europa.eu/rapid/press-release_IP-15-5270_en.htm.
19 Referendum "NO" campaign site: http://oxi2015.gr/.
20 European Commission. "Financial assistance to Greece." Economic and Financial Affairs. http://ec.europa.eu/economy_finance/assistance_eu_ms/greek_loan_facility/index_en.htm.
21 European Council. "EFSM: Council approves €7bn bridge loan to Greece." July 17, 2015. http://www.consilium.europa.eu/en/press/press-releases/2015/07/17-efsm-bridge-loan-greece/.
22 European Commission. "Treaty establishing the European Stability Mechanism (ESM)." http://europa.eu/rapid/press-release_DOC-12-3_en.htm.
23 European Council. "Eurogroup statement on the ESM programme for Greece." Council of the European Union. August 14, 2015. http://www.consilium.europa.eu/en/press/press-releases/2015/08/14-eurogroup-statement/.
24 European Commission. "Financial assistance to Greece." Economic and Financial Affairs. http://ec.europa.eu/economy_finance/assistance_eu_ms/greek_loan_facility/index_en.htm.

9 The United Kingdom and Turkey

It's complicated

> Enlargement is about sharing a project based on
> common principles, policies and institutions.
> (European Commission 2011, 17)[1]

The UK and the EU: an interesting love–hate relationship

The United Kingdom, made up of Scotland, Wales, England and Northern Ireland, joined the European Economic Community (EEC) in 1973 through the efforts of Conservative Prime Minister Edward Heath. From that moment on, the relations between the UK and the European bloc have been turbulent because the various UK governments have expressed varying degrees of reservations whenever the European project has sought to take further steps towards integration.

The UK applied to be part of the EEC in 1963 and 1967, but French General Charles de Gaulle vetoed both initiatives. The reason for de Gaulle's attitude has been studied at length. However, the main hypothesis is that de Gaulle wanted to build a Europe without the influence of London or Washington. Nevertheless, relations between the UK and the European Union changed over time and in 1973 the UK joined the EU with almost 70% of the UK's population favoring it. But the arrival in 1979 of Conservative Prime Minister Margaret Thatcher reversed this trend. At that time, the country was facing a deep economic crisis, and so the Iron Lady tried to renegotiate her country's economic relations. She was criticized for being a Euroskeptic yet her policies benefited the coffers of the UK and helped to improve the lives of voters who re-elected her three times.

Thatcher was replaced in 1990 by the Conservative government of John Major, which also had troubled relations with Europe mainly because it was characterized as strongly Euroskeptical. Major was a tough negotiator on the UK's position within the EU, especially during the talks that led to the signing of the Treaty of Maastricht in 1992. This treaty was meant to advance the project toward the final stage of integration: the introduction of a common currency that would need greater political cooperation and could lead to political integration. Major negotiated an exemption clause in Maastricht, however, that gave the UK the option of not having to enter the third stage of Economic and Monetary Union (EMU), which would involve the adoption of the euro. This attitude toward a project that sought greater integration and, above all, toward the introduction of a common currency, was seen as an act of indifference towards the grand project.

In 1997, with the coming to power of Labour's Tony Blair, the UK government ended nearly 20 years of deep Euroskepticism. Blair began a period in which British officials were more inclined to favor an integrated EU, but without abandoning the pound sterling in favor of the euro. Under the later government of Gordon Brown, the UK ratified the Lisbon Treaty in 2008 despite high levels of public debate on the issue.

When Conservative David Cameron became prime minister in 2010 thanks to a coalition with the Liberal Democrats, relations with Europe again grew strained just as the Eurozone was experiencing a deep economic crisis. In fact, the UK appears to have focused at the time on renegotiating its relationship with the European Union and even recovered some of the powers it had transferred to Brussels. Cameron also announced that if re-elected in 2015, he would hold a referendum on whether the UK should stay in the European bloc. In fact, it has been repeatedly said that "it's time that the British decide" (Fresneda 2013). The proposal for a referendum sparked a great debate because some feared that the vote itself would have a negative effect on the UK's economic growth and job creation. Cameron noted that the referendum would not be carried out if the EU accepted a number of exceptions, especially in labor policy (Gallego 2013).

The United Kingdom and four reasons for its anti-EU attitude

The explanation for the difficult relationship between the United Kingdom and the EU is simple. On the one hand, the UK has been going through a major economic crisis since 2005 that required significant financial resources and a tough restructuring of its economic and political landscape. Second, the crisis in other European countries has required the EU to adopt measures related to compliance with the Stability and Growth Pact that are not in the best interests of the UK, even though the country has been extremely conscientious when it comes to managing its own deficits and debts. And third, the UK is at odds with the EU when it comes to a possible implementation of the so-called Tobin tax, arguing that would negatively impact the interests of the City of London as a financial hub. Finally, the "Social Charter" remains a point of debate, and the two sides do not appear to be close to an agreement.

The economic crisis touched the UK when Northern Rock collapsed in 2007, deepened in 2008, and in 2012 the country still suffered two quarters of negative growth. This situation complicated the country's outlook because although the UK needed measures to promote economic growth, it also needed to implement a program of fiscal consolidation in order to reduce the budget deficit, which stood at more than 10% of GDP in January 2010.

In March 2010, the UK's public finances were worrying the EU and the European Commission so much that a few weeks before the General Election the two institutions publicly urged Brown to reduce the fiscal deficit, which exceeded 10% of GDP. This EU action, in the middle of the political campaign, stimulated the political debate yet voters gave the victory to David Cameron even though he had to make an agreement with the Liberal Democrats to form a stable government.

Despite the change of government, the UK economy went on to suffer the worst recession since the 1970s. The Cameron government was forced to carry out profound austerity programs and a significant fiscal adjustment (Europa Press 2013). And while Merkel and Cameron disagree on many issues, it appears that the two leaders have created a new European axis based on defending the need for economic austerity measures, especially at a time when French President François Hollande was not defending these same values.

Although the UK also carried out major tax reforms, it has not ratified the so-called European Fiscal Pact, which was signed on March 2, 2012 and entered into force on January 1, 2013. The agreement seeks to boost fiscal discipline through stricter monitoring mechanisms, especially for countries in the Eurozone. After more than 10 hours of negotiations on a plan to strengthen fiscal discipline in the Eurozone, Cameron rejected the pact, saying that it was not favorable to UK national interests and that the negotiators had not agreed to certain special exceptions that would have favored the British financial system. Cameron added that he could not put the pact before the British parliament because he did not believe in it (CNN Expansión 2011).

Another point of great tension between the United Kingdom and the Continent is the so-called Tobin tax. In 2012, trying to find extra revenues, the then-president of France, Nicolas Sarkozy, proposed this new fee to the European Commission, estimating that it could raise 57 billion euros a year. This so-called Robin Hood tax (Walker 2011) would be applied to transactions of stocks, bonds and derivatives made by financial institutions in the European Union. The purchase of shares and bonds would be taxed at 0.1%, and the purchase of derivatives at 0.01%. But if this tax is to be implemented only at the EU level, many such transactions will simply be moved to other countries to avoid the increase in the cost of transactions.

Cameron strongly opposed this tax and argued that although additional income was needed and that banks should shoulder some of the burden, this Tobin tax would damage the City, London's financial district, further sharpen the UK recession and eliminate a large number of jobs throughout Europe. It was estimated that nearly 80% of the proceeds from the Tobin tax would come from the City, which is also the financial center of the European Union (Watt 2011).

The last major point of contention arose after the Second World War, when the vast majority of Western European countries adopted social welfare and employment policies that provided generous support to the less advantaged sectors of society. These policies, interpreted differently in each country, create what is broadly known as the "European social model." During the 1970s and 1980s, politicians seeking to boost their nations' economic growth began to revoke certain social benefits and labor rights, sparking a significant debate with those who wanted to maintain the European model.

This struggle was fought most directly by Thatcher, representing the pro-market position, and the president of the EU Commission, Jacques Delors.

Delors presented the "Charter of Fundamental Social Rights" as part of the Maastricht Treaty in 1992. Thatcher opposed it and John Major criticized it at length at the Maastricht Summit. EU member nations finally agreed to include the Social Charter as an optional clause in the final version of the Treaty of Maastricht. This allowed for the UK's final ratification of the treaty. Blair signed it in 1997 and later he did not oppose the inclusion of a chapter on employment in the later Treaty of Amsterdam and toned down the British opposition to EU provisions on social rights.

Turkey and the European Union: the Cyprus debate

The relationship between Turkey and the European Union is extremely interesting. Turkey's political system was established in 1923 after the fall of the Ottoman Empire and the end of the Second World War. Turkey claims to be a democratic, secular and constitutional republic with a strategic location: a European Turkey, representing about 3% of its territory, and an Asian Turkey with 97% of the land, separated by the Bosphorus, the Sea of Marmara and the Dardanelles. Although Turkey has belonged to NATO since 1952 and the G20 since 1999, the country has never been considered fully European because only some 3% of its territory lies in the European continent. In addition, Turkey has experienced a dramatic drop in its population's enthusiasm for joining the EU since 2004. At that time, a significant 73% of Turks believed that accession to the EU would be positive, but in 2010 only 38% wanted to be part of the union (Morelli 2010).

Turkey's relationship with the European Union began in 1963, when it signed on to the European Economic Community in the so-called Ankara Agreement. An additional protocol signed in 1970 set the objectives for the accession, among them cooperation in trade and economic matters and the establishment of a customs union in three phases. A 1995 decision by the Association Council on the third phase of the Customs Union provided an important momentum for adapting Turkish legislation to EU legislation. To ensure the smooth functioning of the Customs Union, Turkey had to adopt, before its entry to the European bloc, a good part of the *acquis communautaire*—the EU's accumulated legislation, legal acts and court decisions—specially in the areas of customs regulations, trade policy, competition and protection of intellectual, industrial and commercial property.[2]

Turkey and the delayed accession process: fifty years of history

The European Union has specified a number of requirements and procedures that all countries should comply with in order to join the group. When a country is named as a "candidate" country, that nation must begin negotiations and adjustments to qualify for the Copenhagen Treaty and adopt EU requirements— basically respect for the standards, rules, and institutions of the member countries and respect for the citizens of all countries, including those of the candidate country. The EU nevertheless reserves the right to decide which candidates can join and which need further to progress the accession process.

The European Commission supports the accession process financially through the so-called Instrument for Pre-Accession Assistance (IPA) which aims to help countries carry out the political and economic reforms necessary for EU accession. Each of the countries receiving aid has different needs, so the IPA is a flexible tool that adapts to those differing needs. In the case of Turkey, the Commission's allocation of funds between 2007 and 2013 exceeded one billion euros.[3]

European Commission documents note that the IPA is a system of financial assistance to candidates or potential candidates for EU membership that is channeled through five components: transition assistance and institution building; cross-border cooperation; regional development; human resource development; and rural development.[4] The Commission also says that there are two types of countries that can benefit from IPA funding.[5]

- EU candidate countries (Croatia, Turkey and the former Yugoslav Republic of Macedonia) are eligible under the five components of the IPA.
- Potential countries of the Western Balkans (Albania, Bosnia and Herzegovina, Montenegro, Serbia and Kosovo under Resolution 1244/99 of the Security Council of the UN) are eligible only for the first two components.

The overall accession process is governed, however, by rules adopted at the European Council in Copenhagen in 1993 and known as the Copenhagen Criteria. Further, the candidate country must also adopt and comply with all EU laws and regulations, the *acquis communautaire*. Finally, countries must follow a set of rules divided into 35 chapters,[6] which are not negotiable. Candidate countries may only decide when and how they will adopt and implement them.

The Commission monitors how candidate countries implement these EU laws and other requirements, thus assisting and expediting the process of accession, and reports on the progress through annual reports. Accession of a country to the EU occurs once negotiations have been concluded on each of the 35 chapters and following approval by each of the member countries of the EU. At this time an Accession Treaty is signed to detail the terms and conditions by which the country enters the EU membership on a specified date.

The conditions that Turkey and other candidate countries must meet for a smooth and gradual integration into the European Union were established at a European Council meeting in Madrid on December 15–16, 1995. In a statement issued nearly three years later, the Commission stated that Turkey had the capacity to develop and implement legislation compatible with the EU but faced a number of weaknesses.

The Commission granted Turkey the status of candidate country in 1999 but reiterated that negotiations for accession would be opened only when Turkey met the Copenhagen Criteria, which state that all member countries should have stable institutions guaranteeing democracy, the rule of law, respect for human rights and respect for and protection of minorities.[7]

1   Free movement of goods
2   Free movement of workers
3   Right of establishment and freedom to provide services
4   Free movement of capital
5   Public procurement
6   Company law
7   Intellectual property law
8   Competition policy
9   Financial services
10 Information society and media
11 Agriculture and rural development
12 Food safety, veterinary and phytosanitary policy
13 Fisheries
14 Transport policy
15 Energy
16 Taxation
17 Economic and monetary policy
18 Statistics
19 Social policy and employment
20 Enterprise and industrial policy
21 Trans-European networks
22 Regional policy and coordination of structural instruments
23 Judiciary and fundamental rights
24 Justice, freedom and security
25 Science and research
26 Education and culture
27 Environment
28 Consumer and health protection
29 Customs union
30 External relations
31 Foreign, security and defence policy
32 Financial control
33 Financial and budgetary provisions
34 Institutions
35 Other issues

Figure 9.1 The 35 Chapters of the *acquis communautaire*.

Source: European Commission.

Tensions in relations between Turkey and the EU hit a peak when the EU announced that it would accept 10 new countries from the Baltic and Central and Eastern Europe in 2004, then Bulgaria and Romania in 2006, while Turkey remained without a clear timetable for accession. The official explanation offered in the Progress Report presented by the European Commission in 2002 noted that Turkey did not meet the political and human rights criteria for accession set in Copenhagen in 1993. A Commission recommendation on October 6, 2004 said that Turkey had finally met sufficient parts of the Copenhagen political criteria and recommended that conditional accession negotiations be started. Based on the recommendation, negotiations for Turkey's accession began in October 2005.[8]

Accession continues to face two serious problems, however. On the one hand, the Commission has repeatedly said that Turkey has failed to comply with the Copenhagen Criteria in areas such as the fight against torture and ill-treatment and the implementation of provisions relating to freedom of expression and religion and the rights of women and minorities.[9] On the other hand, the start of negotiations required Turkey to sign an extension of the Ankara Protocol of 1963 for the 10 countries that had joined the EU in 2004—which included Cyprus, meaning that Ankara would have recognized Cyprus as a country.

Cyprus and Turkey have had no diplomatic relations since Turkey invaded northern Cyprus in 1974 and created the Turkish Republic of Northern Cyprus in 1983, which has not been recognized internationally and is where Turkey maintains a military presence.

Turkey signed the Ankara Protocol in 2005, which extends the customs agreement to the 10 new EU member states, but included a statement that it would not recognize Cyprus. Because of this political dispute, relations between Turkey and the EU have been strained and the accession process is moving even slower.

When Cyprus assumed a six-month presidency of the European Union in July 2012, Turkey froze relations with the EU. After Ireland assumed the following presidency, Turkish Minister for European Affairs Egemen Bağış declared that the previous six months had not been easy and even called it a pseudo-presidency, but added that Turkey had always worked hard to maintain its links to the EU (TRT 2013). In addition, the Turkish government announced that it wanted to relaunch the process of accession by opening new discussions on the 35 Chapters (TRT 2013).

Until Turkey accepts the full Ankara Protocol, with the recognition of the sovereignty of Cyprus, eight of the 35 chapters will remain closed to negotiations. German Chancellor Angela Merkel has said, however, that the EU is in favor of opening other new chapters in order to advance the negotiations (La Voz de Galicia 2013).

The question of Turkey's membership carries with it an implicit debate on political, economic and social-geographical issues. From a social-geographical aspect, it is important to understand that Turkey's location and religion signify that the "European identity" of Turkish citizens remains split in two. Turkey's accession also would push the eastern borders of the European Union to Iraq, Iran and Syria.

The truths behind the Turkish accession: the dilemma

The Turkish Empire reached its peak in the sixteenth century under Süleyman the Great and its end came in the early nineteenth century, when Turkey became "the sick man of Europe" after the Turkish War of Independence. The modern Republic of Turkey was established in 1923 by Kemal Atatürk, who fought for the union of the new republic through a common language and the secularization of the state even though 95% of the population was Muslim.

The Lausanne Peace Treaty of 1923 set the borders of the new Turkish Republic and required the government to protect the religious rights of non-Muslim minorities, but with severe restrictions. In addition, the central government's relationship with the Kurds, almost 25% of the population, was and still is quite troubled because the majority Turkish population sees the Kurds, who insist on using their own language, as a threat to the unity of the country. This internal problem has brought years of armed violence to a conflict now widely viewed as a civil war.

The Kurds demand that Turkey either grant independence to the region known as Kurdistan or allow them to enjoy greater autonomy. The Kurdish people supported the Allies during the Second World War and as a reward for their loyalty the Treaty of Sèvres (1920) recognized Kurdistan as an independence country. This treaty was never ratified, however, and the Treaty of Lausanne (1923) voided it and divided the Kurdish territory between Turkey, Iran, Iraq and Syria.

The war between the Turkish state and the Kurdish minority has been repeatedly condemned by the EU and, while the situation has eased somewhat, a European Commission report in 2002 noted that the continued Turkish oppression of the Kurdish minority is a justifiable obstacle to Turkey's accession.

The Kurdish and Cyprus roadblocks have not had much of a significant impact on Turkey's accession negotiations because the talks have been paralyzed for a while. To access the EU, Turkey must comply with all the 35 Chapters on rules. But as of July 2012, Turkey had completed talks on only one chapter, was negotiating 13 other chapters but with very little progress, and faced blocks on 17 other chapters (Martínez de Rituerto 2012). What's more, the implementation of the legal framework against terrorism and organized crime has been suffering recurrent violations in the areas of freedom and security, the right to a fair trial and freedom of expression, assembly and association. There are restrictions on the media, including numerous court cases against journalists and other authors, and censorship is widespread. Turkish Prime Minister Recep Tayyip Erdoğan has complained that the EU has been inventing obstacles to obstruct EU accession.

The European Commission issued an unusually harsh report on the progress of Turkey in its accession process in October 2012, but reiterated its desire to push the talks forward to ensure that the EU remains the reference point for reforms in the country. Although some progress had been made on the adoption of the new constitution, the Commission expressed great concern over the respect of fundamental rights. It also pointed to Turkey's decision to freeze relations with the Presidency of the EU when Cyprus held it in the second half of 2012. The European Council also expressed serious concerns with regard to Turkish statements and threats and called for full respect for the Council Presidency, a fundamental institution of the European Union. During the Cyprus presidency, Turkey also had issued an ultimatum to the EU and set a deadline of 2023 for a successful conclusion of the accession process, saying that unless the deadline was met the EU would lose an ally (Euroxpress 2012).

From the economic point of view, the accession of Turkey is also a complicated issue. The Customs Union agreement between Turkey and the EU was signed in 1995, and since then Turkey has made significant progress in reforming laws regarding financial services policy, telecommunications, agriculture and trade. However, this agreement is only one step toward the so-called Single Market for the free movement of services, capital and people. While this Customs Union has helped trade and other relations between Turkey and the EU, new conflicts have been arising because of the new wave of free trade agreements between the EU and other countries, such as Mexico, Chile, South Africa and Korea. Those agreements allow imports from those countries to enter the Turkish market without paying tariffs. However, Turkish goods exported to those countries must pay tariffs that depend on bilateral agreements. What's more, if the EU reaches a full agreement with the United States and ASEAN countries,[10] the economic impact for Turkey could be even higher. Turkish Economy Minister Zafer Çağlayan has already warned that if Turkey is to remain in the Custom Unions, the EU should include Turkish goods in any agreements with third countries. Otherwise, Turkey should abandon the Customs Union and simply sign a free trade agreement with the EU (Kirisci 2013). Furthermore, the accession of Turkey would have great implications for the EU budget since Turkey has the lowest income per capita and has the largest agricultural sector of the European bloc. This means that Turkey would have to receive significant financial support, which would cause great harm to other countries that still receive financial aid.

The EU budget system requires the richer member states to contribute more to the budget. However, the distribution system is far more complicated, so some rich countries contribute proportionately more than others while some poor countries receive disproportionately more than others. Turkey's accession therefore would have a very significant effect on the budget because those who contribute would have to contribute more and those who now receive assistance would suffer a significant reduction in benefits. The EU budget is included in a seven-year spending plan, known as the "financial framework," that allows the bloc to program expenditures more effectively. On February 8, 2013 the financial framework for 2014–2020 was negotiated at a slightly lower level than the 2007–2013 budget because of the economic austerity at the time.

Due to all of these socio-geographic, economic and political challenges, the idea of a full accession by Turkey has never had much support within the EU. It has always been said that behind the Turkish question there are a series of very complex, controversial and unofficial reasons: Turkey has very high poverty levels; Turkey's borders with Syria, Iraq and Iran would extend the EU deep into the Asian continent; and the majority of the Turkish population is Islamic, while Europe has long been part of the Christian tradition.

Final words

The UK and Turkey are the two extremes of Europe, with each having distinctive characteristics that differentiate them from other EU countries. The UK's legislative and judicial sectors follow the rule of law or customary law, while the Continent follows the Napoleonic code and laws. British citizens have accepted religious reforms that offer a more liberal approach than in the rest of Europe. Democracy remains unchallenged in the UK, while other European countries have been less stable. In addition, the Anglican reforms pushed British culture toward commercialism and a free market. Britain was the last empire on earth and still remains part of a commonwealth where the Queen is the head of an association of nations that share standards, principles and languages. Although the British Empire virtually disappeared after the Second World War, the United Kingdom still maintains important international links with former colonies via the Commonwealth. The mentality of the British people remains influenced by the idea of the Empire and a large majority of the citizens view a full union with what they call "the mainland" with suspicion. Moreover, the economic cycles of the UK traditionally have been more closely linked to the economic cycles of the United States than the European ups and downs. In addition, the British pound remains a universal icon of strong value and represents the economic independence of the UK and the City of London.

Sultan Mehmet II pushed Turkey's border into a tiny part of European territory in the 1400s mainly because Rome provided little support to the city of Constantinople, now Istanbul. Turkey is now a Muslim majority republic and Europe is a secular continent with deep Christian roots. Many different religions now enjoy freedom in Europe, despite a history of religious wars and reformations. Europe now has acquired a level of religious maturity where such problems no longer have priority status.

This freedom is lacking in Turkey, either because of its interpretation of religion or the absence of reformations. Religion, however, is not the biggest problem for Turkey's accession to the EU, as indicated by the fact that Bosnia and Herzegovina, with a Muslim population, is expected to soon join the EU.

The biggest problem is the geography. The part of Turkey located in Europe would make sense as an EU member, but the rest of the country is in Asia and would clearly undermine the idea of a European Europe. The solution to the Turkish issue may not be easy, although in the not too distant past an imaginative solution brought the People's Republic of China and Hong Kong together under the principle of one country and two systems.

Notes

1. European Commission. 2011. *Enlargement strategy and main challenges 2006–2007.* Communication from the Commission to the European Parliament and the Council. http://ec.europa.eu/enlargement/pdf/key_documents/2006/nov/com_649_strategy_paper_en.pdf Brussels, November 8. http://ec.europa.eu/enlargement/pdf/key_documents/2006/nov/com_649_strategy_paper_es.pdf.
2. Europa."Estrategiadepreadhesión deTurquía."http://europa.eu/legislation_summaries/enlargement/ongoing_enlargement/community_acquis_turkey/e40113_es.htm.
3. European Commission. "Instrument for Pre-Accession Assistance (IPA)." http://ec.europa.eu/regional_policy/thefunds/ipa/turkey_development_en.cfm.
4. European Commission. "Overview: Instrument for Pre-accession Assistance." http://ec.europa.eu/enlargement/instruments/overview/index_en.htm.
5. European Commission." Instrumento de Ayuda de Preadhesión (IAP)." http://ec.europa.eu/regional_policy/thefunds/ipa/index_es.cfm.
6. European Commission. "Enlargement." http://ec.europa.eu/enlargement/policy/conditions-membership/chapters-of-the-acquis/index_en.htm.
7. Europa. "Criterios de adhesión (criterios de Copenhague)." http://europa.eu/legislation_summaries/glossary/accession_criteria_copenhague_es.htm.

8 Europa. "Estrategia de preadhesión de Turquía." http://europa.eu/legislation_summaries/enlargement/ongoing_enlargement/community_acquis_turkey/e40113_es.htm.
9 Europa." Estrategia de preadhesión de Turquía." http://europa.eu/legislation_summaries/enlargement/ongoing_enlargement/community_acquis_turkey/e40113_es.htm.
10 European Commission. "International affairs, free trade agreements." http://ec.europa.eu/enterprise/policies/international/facilitating-trade/free-trade/#h2-1.

10 Trends in immigration into the EU

History and challenges

> The severest justice may not always be the best policy.
> (Abraham Lincoln)[1]

Introduction

The European Union is made up of 28 countries with a total population of about 450 million people. The free movement of labor, capital, goods and services for EU citizens was a priority included in the Single European Act signed in 1987. Since 1950, the EU has continued to receive migrants from all over the world because it understands that its economic prosperity and political stability have become a strong factor in attracting migrants. Since the summer of 2015, however, the EU has seen a massive arrival of irregular migrants mainly through Italy and Greece and aiming to settle in northern European countries such as Germany and Austria. Irregular migration, defined as migrants who entered the EU with forged or no documents via land, air or sea routes, has therefore become an extremely complicated question. The European Commission, through the Directorate-General for Migration and Home Affairs, is working to address the different needs of regular migration, irregular migration and the asylum system.

The main debate on how to handle this crisis is been conducted at the European Commission, which had to rush on May 2015 to put together a comprehensive European Agenda on Migration in order to face the challenges of the migrant flow. However, some countries and politicians in the EU have proposed making this situation a "Schengen Area issue." This would blur the concepts of the Schengen Agreement and the idea of an internal market for EU citizens recorded in the Single European Act.

Migration is influenced by a combination of economic, political and social factors which are known as push factors if they negatively affect the migrant's country of origin or pull factors if they attract migrants to the migrants' destination. Migration has an impact on the destination countries as it may be used to solve specific labor shortages. In the country of origin, migration also impacts the labor market, and often the average age of the population.

According to the Eurostat,[2] on January 1, 2014, the number of people living in the EU who were citizens of non-member countries stood at 19.6 million, while the number of people living in the EU who had been born outside the community was 33.5 million. On that day, Germany had the largest numbers of non-national residents with 7 million, followed by the United Kingdom with 5 million, Italy with 4.9 million, Spain with 4.7 million and France with 4.2 million.

In these five member states, the total number of non-nationals represented 76 % of the total number of non-nationals living in all EU member states, indicating that acquiring the citizenship of an EU member state is a priority because of its legal implications. Official statistics show that in 2013 a total of 984,800 people obtained the citizenship of an EU member state, the highest number since 2002 and an impressive 20% increase from 2012. Spain had the highest number of persons acquiring citizenship in 2013, at 225,800, followed by the United Kingdom with 207,500, Germany with 115,100, Italy with 100,700 and France with 97,300. A report on the naturalization rates, which measure the ratio between the total numbers of citizenships granted and the stock of non-national residents at the beginning of a year, shows that in 2013 Sweden had the highest rate with 7.6 citizenships granted per 100 non-national residents, followed by Hungary with 6.5 and Portugal with 5.9. Citizenship is important because citizens of EU member states have the freedom to travel, work and study anywhere within the EU's borders. For the past decade, migration policies within the EU in relation to citizens of non-member countries were mainly concerned with attracting a particular migrant profile in an attempt to alleviate specific labor shortages. Other concerns include preventing unauthorized migration and the illegal employment of migrants who are not permitted to work, and promoting the integration of migrants into society.

The refugee crisis: the Single European Act vs the Schengen Agreement

The early part of the twenty-first century has been a difficult one for the European Union. It has suffered a brutal economic crisis with devastating effects on some Eurozone member states such as Ireland, Portugal, Spain, Malta and especially Greece, which since 2010 has been experiencing an economic crisis with profound implications for the country and the unity of the EU.

The European project is now suffering a major refugee crisis for which the EU was not at all ready. Since the early summer of 2015, the EU has been receiving tens of thousands of migrants who put their lives at risk to cross the Mediterranean Sea and escape from wars, persecution and poverty. Over the years, the EU has been exposed to migration and there have been attempts at regional cooperation on the thorny issue. In July of 2008, the Union for the Mediterranean[3]—which now, in 2016, consists of the 28 EU member states, the European Commission and 15 Mediterranean countries—was established as a relaunch of the Euro-Mediterranean Partnership, the so-called Barcelona Process, with the goal of promoting stability and prosperity throughout the Mediterranean region in order to reduce the incentives for irregular migration. Unfortunately, this project has all but disappeared since the 2010 revolts in Arab countries.

As the economic, social and political conditions in most of those countries worsened, a massive migration flow toward the EU began. Once these migrants arrive at any Schengen member state (most are EU member states), they have the freedom to cross borders of member states with no checkpoints or passport controls. The current migrant crisis should be considered a Schengen Agreement crisis and Schengen member states—not just the EU member states that are part of the Schengen Agreement—must be responsible for solving the situation.

When the EU project was first envisioned, the free movement of persons was a core principle that was recorded in the original Treaty of Rome and was a fundamental idea for the development of the European Economic Community. The idea was that EU nationals could travel freely from one member state to another, although a structured system of identity controls was to exist at the border between most member states. However, disagreements on the elimination of border controls among member states delayed this arrangement. Nonetheless, in 1985 five of the then-10 member states— Belgium, France, Luxembourg, The Netherlands, and West Germany—signed an agreement, near the town of Schengen in Luxembourg, for the gradual elimination of internal border controls. The agreement remained only partially implemented up until 1995. The goal of the Schengen Area was to gradually abolish passport and border controls at common internal borders while maintaining border controls with non-Schengen states.

Twenty-two EU member states were participating in the Schengen Area as of 2015. While Ireland and the United Kingdom opted out of the arrangement, Bulgaria, Croatia, Cyprus and Romania have expressed their wish to join the Schengen Area. What's more, Monaco, San Marino and Vatican City are considered to be de facto members of the Schengen Area because they are also considered de facto members of the EU and the Eurozone, even though they have not signed any documents that make them part of the project. Finally, Iceland, Liechtenstein, Norway and Switzerland are not EU members but have signed the Schengen Agreement.

The spirit of the Schengen Agreement should not be confused, however, with the idea behind the Treaty of Rome (1947) and the Single European Act (1986) which established the goal of a single market by the end of 1992. A single market is a type of trade bloc in which there is freedom of movement of capital, labor, goods and services for citizens of member states. The EU single market is an area free of borders that nonetheless maintains many differences in the areas of national tax systems, certain services sectors, financial services, energy and transport and the recognition of professional qualifications. The Single European Act was signed by the foreign ministers of Belgium, the Federal Republic of Germany, France, Ireland, Luxembourg, The Netherlands, Portugal, Spain, and the United Kingdom to provide their citizens with a borderless area. Denmark and Italy raised certain concerns, however. In the case of Denmark, the parliament rejected the Single European Act, forcing the Danish government to hold a non-binding referendum in an attempt to overcome the parliamentary rejection. Danish voters approved the Single European Act in February of 1986.

At the EU level, the European Commission, via the commissioner for Migration and Home Affairs,[4] deals with (1) legal migration, (2) irregular migration and return policies, and (3) efforts to establish a common European asylum system. EU measures on legal migration cover the conditions of entry and residence for certain categories of migrants, such as highly qualified workers who come under the "EU Blue Card Directive," as well as students, researchers, family reunifications and long-term residents. In November 2011, the European Commission launched the EU Immigration Portal to (1) provide first-hand information for foreign nationals interested in moving to the EU, (2) help migrants who are already in the EU and want to move from one EU member state to another, and (3) offer information about procedures in all 28 EU states for each category of migrants.

The Commission has identified irregular migration as a problem for both migrants and the host country, as well as a lucrative business for smugglers and organized crime. Therefore in October of 2013, the Task Force Mediterranean set out concrete actions to address the migration crisis and prevent the loss of lives in the Mediterranean. They included agreeing to the EU Action Plan against Migrant Smuggling and setting common rules for punishing criminal networks of migrant smugglers. Finally, the EU set up a common European asylum system for people fleeing persecution or serious harm in their own country and therefore in need of international protection.

The massive wave of migrants who have been arriving at EU countries that are members of the Schengen Agreement are automatically allowed to both claim asylum and travel exempt from border and passport controls through the area. This reality is shaking the foundations of the Schengen Agreement because member states are building border controls for the flow of migrants claiming asylum and refugee status. This is the case of Austria, where Foreign Minister Sebastian Kurz has declared that the "surge of migrants into Europe has become too big, and EU member states have a responsibility to protect their borders."[5] Sweden already imposed border controls after more than 120,000 migrants arrived in the first 10 months of 2015 alone.[6] Sweden was also drawing up plans to establish new controls on the Øresund Bridge to Denmark in an attempt to stop the flow of asylum seekers.[7] Slovenia and some of the Balkan countries—Croatia, Serbia and Macedonia—have also built border controls to stop the arrival of what they define as economic migrants from neighboring countries. Hungary has built fences along its border with Croatia and Serbia.

This crisis is having a devastating impact not just on the Single European Act and the Schengen idea of free movement, but on member states themselves because some countries are blaming others for failing to properly control their borders and leaving the burden of controlling migrants to other nations. This is the case of Hungary, which blames economically troubled Greece for her inability to control its border, which in turn is forcing other neighbors to take measures such as building new fences.

While all Schengen member states should realize that irregular migration is a shared responsibility, and that all member states must contribute to tackling this unprecedented challenge, it is only EU member states that are addressing the new migration crisis.

Migration and Home Affairs in the European Union: the legal and political framework

The Directorate-General for Migration and Home Affairs is the branch of the European Commission responsible for the European migration policy.

In 2005, the European Commission relaunched the debate on the need for a common set of rules for the admission of economic migrants, with a Green Paper that focused on an EU approach to managing economic migration and led to the adoption at the end of the year of a "Policy plan on legal migration." This plan stated, in part, that:

> The Hague Programme, endorsed by the European Council on 4–5 November 2004, stressed the importance of having an open debate on economic immigration at EU level, which—together with the best practices in member states and their relevance for the implementation of the Lisbon strategy—should be the basis for "a policy plan on legal migration including admission procedures capable of responding promptly to fluctuating demands for migrant labour in the labour market."[8]

In July of 2006, the European Commission adopted a policy statement on the fight against illegal immigration of third-country nationals that aimed to strike a balance between security and an individual's basic rights during all stages of the illegal immigration process. It also noted that the term 'illegal immigration' is,

> used to describe a variety of phenomena. They include third-country nationals who enter the territory of a member state illegally by land, sea and air, including airport transit zones. This is often done by using false or forged documents, or with the help of organized criminal networks of smugglers and traffickers. In addition, there is a considerable number of persons who enter legally with a valid visa or under a visa-free regime, but 'overstay' or change the purpose of their stay without the approval of authorities. Lastly there are unsuccessful asylum seekers who do not leave after a final negative decision.[9]

In September of 2007, the European Commission presented its Third Annual Report on Migration and Integration, which stressed that "consolidating the legal framework on the conditions for entry and stay of third-country nationals is essential for the development of a coherent EU approach to integration."[10] This report was followed by an October 2008 statement emphasizing the need to increase coordination, coherence and synergies on migration issues as one aspect of external and development policy. It added that a global approach to migration,

> can be defined as the external dimension of the European Union's migration policy. It is based on genuine partnership with third countries, is fully integrated into the EU's other external policies, and addresses all migration and asylum issues in a comprehensive and balanced manner.[11]

The EU heads of state and government met on December 2009 and adopted "the Stockholm Programme"[12] which stablished a framework and series of principles for the ongoing development of European policies on justice and home affairs—including migration—for the period 2010 to 2014. To bring about the changes agreed upon, the European Commission then enacted an action plan that agreed to create an area of freedom, security and justice for Europe's citizens in 2010.

The Stockholm Programme notes that the European Council,

> considers that the priority for the coming years will be to focus on the interests and needs of citizens. The challenge will be to ensure respect for fundamental rights and freedoms and integrity of the person while guaranteeing security in Europe. It is of paramount importance that law enforcement measures, on the one hand, and measures to safeguard individual rights, the rule of law and international protection rules, on the other, go hand in hand in the same direction and are mutually reinforced.

In May of 2015, due to the refugee crisis in the Mediterranean, the European Commission's Directorate-General for Migration and Home Affairs and other EU agencies presented a European Agenda on Migration[13] outlining measures to be taken immediately to respond to the crisis, as well as steps to be taken in coming years to improve the management of migration. This document, made public May 27, 2015, is of extreme importance because it explains the measures that the European Commission agreed to implement in order to improve the management of migration.

This document covers five main points, with the first three put forward for immediate implementation. The first point sets out provisional emergency relocation measures. The second point presents a number of recommendations for the establishment of a European resettlement scheme. The third puts forward an Action Plan against Migrant Smuggling.

The proposal for provisional emergency relocation measures notes in general that the Commission agreed to assist Italy and Greece by activating an emergency response mechanism under Article 78.3 of the Treaty on the Functioning of the European Union. In particular, the European Commission noted that the assistance,

> will apply to Syrian and Eritrean nationals in need of international protection that arrived in either Italy or Greece after 15 April 2015 or that arrive after the mechanism is launched. A total of 40,000 persons should be relocated from Italy and Greece to other EU member states based on a distribution key . . . over the next 2 years—corresponding to approximately 40% of the total number of asylum seekers in clear need of international protection who entered these countries in 2014. The Commission is ready to do the same if other member states—such as Malta—also face a sudden influx of migrants. Member states will receive €6,000 for each person relocated on their territory.[14]

This statement directly recognized the exposure of Greece and Italy, saying that in 2014 Italy,

> saw 277% more irregular border crossings than in 2013, representing 60% of the total number of irregular border crossings in the EU. A steady increase also occurred in Greece, with an increase of 153% of the number of irregular border crossings in 2014 compared to those in 2013, representing 19% of the total number of irregular border crossings in the EU overall. In both cases, this trend looks set to continue, with unprecedented flows of migrants continuing to reach their shores.[15]

The European Agenda on Migration recognizes Malta as well as the Western Balkan route as critical migration routes. With respect to the emergency reallocation scheme, the proposal includes all member states except for Italy and Greece, which are the beneficiary states, and emphasizes that the United Kingdom and Ireland have "opt-in" rights, meaning that these two countries will not participate in the distribution key. The reallocation scheme for Greece and Italy only applies to those applicants who appear to be in clear need of international protection, and Italian and Greek authorities will receive help from the European Asylum Support Office (EASO) and other relevant agencies in order to identify those persons.

The relocation criteria are subject to the existing Dublin Regulation, which contemplates relocation of family members in the same member state and on the basis of the best interests of the child if present. However, secondary movement of relocated persons from one member state to another is not allowed, and migrants must be returned to the member state of relocation. The Dublin Regulation[16] also aims to "determine rapidly the member state responsible for an asylum claim" and provides for the transfer of an asylum seeker to that country. Usually, the responsible country will be the one where the asylum seeker first entered the EU. Finally, the EU is to provide an extra 250 million euros to fund the transfer of the relocated persons for 24 months.

The European Agenda on Migration also sets out recommendations for the establishment of a European Resettlement scheme, with resettlement defined as:

> the process upon [an] assessment and request by the United Nations High Commissioner for Refugees ('UNHCR'), non-EU displaced persons in clear need of international protection are transferred from a non-EU country and established in an EU member state with the objective of admitting them and granting them a form of international protection. Currently, resettlement of refugees is voluntary, with EU efforts being a sum of all national actions. Currently, only 15 EU member states have resettlement schemes, with three other member states resettling on ad hoc basis. The remaining member states do not participate in resettlement.[17]

The key idea was to try to prevent displaced persons from having to resort to criminal networks, and to bring refugees safely and legally to the EU. The EU budget was to dedicate an extra 50 million euros in the next two years for this purpose.

Finally, the Action Plan against Migrant Smuggling for the years 2015 through 2020 sets out concrete actions to counter and prevent migrant smuggling while ensuring the full respect and protection of the human rights of migrants. This part of the plan focused on four main points:

1   Enhanced police and judicial response.
2   Improved gathering and sharing of information.
3   Enhanced prevention of smuggling and assistance to vulnerable migrants.
4   Stronger cooperation with third countries.

Following the publication of the European Agenda on Migration in May of 2015, many other documents shed light on the crisis at hand. Especially important was the "EU–Turkey Joint Action Plan"[18] of October 16, 2015, which set out,

> the understanding between the European Union (EU) and the Republic of Turkey to step up their cooperation on support of Syrians under temporary protection and migration management in a coordinated effort to address the crisis created by the situation in Syria. It follows from the EU–Turkey working dinner on 17 May and the informal meeting of the EU Heads of State or Government on 23 September 2015 where EU leaders called for a reinforced dialogue with Turkey at all levels. The action plan identifies a series of collaborative actions to be implemented as a matter of urgency by the European Union (EU) and the Republic of Turkey with the objective to supplement Turkey's efforts in managing the situation of massive influx of persons in need of temporary protection.

The second important document is the "Western Balkan Action Plan"[19] of October 25, 2015, which noted that,

> officials representing Albania, Austria, Bulgaria, Croatia, the Former Yugoslav Republic of Macedonia, Germany, Greece, Hungary, Romania, Serbia and Slovenia had agreed to improve cooperation and step up consultation between the countries along the [migration route] and decided on pragmatic operational measures that can be implemented as of tomorrow to tackle the refugee crisis in the region.

Countries in the refugee crisis: the UK, Denmark, Switzerland, the Balkan countries and Turkey

The EU is experiencing a migrant flow so large that it is testing the pillars of its foundation as member states reintroduce border controls and build border fences.

There is an important distinction between voluntary migrants[20] and forcibly displaced people,[21] which is indeed the challenge of the twenty-first century. The Office for the Coordination of Humanitarian Affairs has noted that:

As of the end of 2014, an estimated 60 million people were forcibly displaced due to conflict and violence worldwide. These are figures not seen since World War II and Africa is one of the regions most affected. Conflicts in the CAR and South Sudan, as well as the Boko-Haram related violence have recently triggered heightened levels of displacement. Close to a million Central Africans, i.e. a quarter of the population, and an estimated 2.3 million South Sudanese and 2.3 million Nigerians have been forcibly displaced in their countries or to the neighboring countries. Forced displacement is growing worldwide and patterns of displacement are changing. We must adapt and change the way work to address the new challenges.[22]

This number is expected to increase in 2015 as the refugee crisis intensifies, with people leaving Syria, Afghanistan, Libya, Egypt, etc., all hoping to arrive at the EU borders.

The same report explains that these conflicts not only are lasting longer but remain unresolved, leading to increasing numbers of people displaced and in need of humanitarian help. While donors have been providing assistance, fast-rising needs are outpacing resources and increasing the funding gap. Despite the current crisis, every EU member except for the Netherlands slashed contributions to the World Food Program in 2015. This meant that during 2015 the UN agency has been unable to hand out food vouchers to refugees in Jordan, Lebanon, Iraq, Egypt and Turkey. Austria, Estonia, Greece, Portugal and Slovakia cut all of their funds to the program, while Sweden's contribution dropped by 95%, followed by Lithuania by 69%, and Belgium by 54%. The UK decreased its assistance by 30% and Croatia, Latvia, Poland and Romania gave nothing at all in the past two years. In total, the EU contribution went from 895 million euros in 2014 to 675 million euros in 2015, even as the needs of the World Food Program were estimated at a minimum of 1 billion euros.[23]

While most EU member states have been impacted by the arrival of thousands of refugees, the UK has taken the opportunity to once again raise its concerns with respect to the free movement of people. On November 10, 2015, Prime Minister David Cameron sent a six-page letter to EU Council chief Donald Tusk setting out four proposals for reforms in areas of British concern about the EU. One of those proposals was related to immigration.

The UK opted out of the Schengen Agreement and has maintained its own controls on arriving foreigners. Yet immigration from outside and inside the EU remains an issue of concern for London. Thus, Cameron explained in his proposal that the UK has an open economy but that the free movement has put great pressures on the kingdom's school, hospital and public service systems. He added:

> We do want to find arrangements to allow a member state like the UK to restore sense of fairness to our immigration system and to reduce the current very high level of population flow from within the EU to the UK.[24]

He also referred to those EU member states that very easily grant citizenship to third-country migrants, allowing then to move freely within the community.

He further stated the EU should "go much further to fulfil its commitment to the free flow of capital, goods, and services"—significantly leaving out the free movement of labor and people. This letter had a significant impact because EU leaders were expected to use a summit scheduled for December 17, 2015 to set the guidelines for an agreement on British demands for EU reforms to be decided at another gathering in February of 2016.[25]

Denmark is already one step ahead of the United Kingdom because Danish voters clearly rejected joining the EU justice and home affairs policies during a referendum on December 3, 2015. Demark therefore once again refused a deeper integration with the EU, because it had already opted out of this part of EU policy when it ratified the Maastricht Treaty. The Danish vote has not been given the level of attention it merited, because its results set a precedent for the so-called Brexit referendum and opened a new agenda of less EU rather than more. It also opened a debate for nations that may want to return to national sovereignty. It must be understood, however, that the Danish vote on the referendum was about deeper integration on a very specific political area, while the UK referendum is about leaving the EU altogether if British requests are not accepted.

Switzerland is an interesting case because since March 2009 it has been part of the Schengen Agreement. The Swiss voted against mass immigration, however, in a 2014 referendum that noted, "The initiative introduces a quota system, limiting the number of residence permits granted to foreigners and asylum seekers."[26] Supporters of quotas believe free movement has put pressure on housing, health, education and transport services and that foreign workers have driven down salaries. On the other hand, many business leaders believe that free movement is key to Switzerland's economic success, because it would allow employers to hire skilled staff from across Europe. Ever since the referendum, the Swiss Federal Council and Swiss Federal Assembly have worked to turn the result into legislation—figuring out a way to implement immigration quotas for both foreigners and asylum seekers without affecting the Swiss–EU Bilateral Agreement on the Free Movement of Persons, which went into effect in 2004.[27]

If the two bodies create and implement a quota system which would include a cap on immigration from EU countries, that would be a direct violation of the agreement. Given the EU's uncompromising stance on the principle of free movement of persons, it seems likely that the EU will seek to terminate the treaty as soon as the Swiss adopt legislation that goes against it. Without these agreements, Switzerland is bound to lose substantial access to European institutions and markets alike. Since the 2014 referendum, EU–Swiss relations have been strained because the decision to open the country's borders 12 years ago was negotiated as part of a package of agreements that allowed Swiss companies to have access to the common market.

On December 4, 2015, and in the middle of the refugee crises, the Swiss government announced it will honor the result of the 2014 referendum and will impose a unilateral quota by March 2016 if it is unable to strike a deal with the EU. That a significant change, considering that in May of 2015, Switzerland agreed with the EU plans to take in 20,000 refugees over the next two years and distribute them across the continent according to a quota system.[28] The referendum's result was expected because a Basel University survey published in August of 2015 showed that a significant majority of those questioned, 83.1%, wanted Switzerland to provide generous assistance in those countries where the refugee crisis was taking place, rather than to accept more refugees into Switzerland. The survey also showed that two-thirds of the people polled feared that allowing too many refugees into Switzerland would hurt the country's prosperity, and 44.6% said Swiss borders should be closed temporarily.[29]

During the refugee crisis, the European Commission launched 40 inquiries against 19 member states to force them to follow asylum rules. This decision was decisive because the Czech Republic, Hungary, Romania and Slovakia refused to accept the refugee-sharing scheme. Those four countries along the migratory route closed their borders on November 19 to those not coming from war-torn countries such as Syria, Afghanistan or Iraq, leaving thousands desperately seeking a better life stranded at Balkan border crossings. Many of those stranded could not provide documentation that they came from war-shattered nations, even if they did. The closure of the borders triggered pile-ups along the Balkan corridor of people who wanted to reach wealthy EU states, mostly Germany and Austria. Although Syrians are the biggest group among the asylum seekers, Pakistanis, Bangladeshis or Sri Lankans who were fleeing poverty also joined the surge of refugees.

The restrictions also drew criticism from the UN High Commission for Refugees, which alleged that the countries were selecting migrants on the basis of their nationality, which violated international rules on refugee status that say that every person has the right to ask for asylum. This action was taken despite the fact that on October 25 leaders from the Western Balkan migration route agreed on a 17-point plan to create 100,000 places for migrants, refrain to pushing them towards neighboring countries, work towards strengthening border controls and registration, and create a permanent migrant information system. This plan also included an agreement to increase provision of temporary shelter, rest, food, health, water and sanitation services to all in need.[30]

One country critical to the migrant crisis is Turkey. On September 23, EU leaders met in Brussels to agree on how to help Turkey maintain Syrian refugees within its borders, fight smuggling networks, strengthen its external borders and aid other countries in the Middle East and Africa. Turkey indeed has become "the key" to the migration crisis because it hosts more than 2 million refugees four years after the civil war broke out in neighboring Syria. Russia and Turkey had been negotiating an agreement to build a $12 billion "Turkish Stream" pipeline to carry Russian gas to Turkey and to other European countries. The pipeline proposal replaced the South Stream project, which was going to transport natural gas from Russia through the Black Sea to Bulgaria and through Serbia, Hungary and Slovenia to Austria, but was canceled because of problems with the European Union's competition and energy legislation. Negotiations on the Turkish Stream project were called off on December 3, 2015 after Turkey shot down a Russian warplane near the Turkish–Syrian border. Turkey had all but given up on EU membership, tired of the warnings from Brussels on civil rights and the Kurdistan issue, and so it had turned to Moscow, particularly when the negotiations over the Russian pipelines began. The confrontation over the downed Russian fighter, however, appears to have forced Turkey to look to Europe again.

Turkey needs help from the EU with the Syrian refugee crisis, and the EU needs Turkey to control the constant flow of migrants arriving. And now Turkey is using the crisis to ask EU leaders to lift EU visa restrictions for Turkish citizens, and to move ahead faster on Turkey's 50 years of trying to join the EU, a process that has been frozen for years. This issue was addressed during the summit that took place October 15, 2015 in Brussels, with the presentation to an "EU–Turkey joint action plan" that noted that both the EU and Turkey are facing common challenges that require coordinated responses. Accordingly,

> the Action Plan tries to address the current crisis situation in three ways: (a) by addressing the root causes leading to the massive influx of Syrians, (b) by supporting Syrians under temporary protection and their host communities in Turkey (Part I) and (c) by strengthening cooperation to prevent irregular migration flows to the EU (Part II). The EU and Turkey will address this crisis together in a spirit of burden sharing. The plan builds on and is consistent with commitments taken by Turkey and the EU in other contexts notably the Visa Liberalisation Dialogue. In both parts it identifies the actions that are to be implemented simultaneously by Turkey and the EU.[31]

Despite the need for cooperation, the EU criticized Turkey for its deteriorating media freedom and backsliding on the independence of the judiciary, and urged Ankara to resume peace talks with Kurdish rebels in a November 10, 2015 report on Turkey's progress on its accession application.[32] Release of the report was delayed until after Turkey's November 1, 2015 elections because the EU was concerned that the criticism of Ankara's performance could complicate negotiations with Turkey on the flow of migrants into the continent.[33]

Despite the unfavorable report, which kept the accession of Turkey on hold, Turkish and EU leaders met in Brussels on November 29, 2015 to finalize an agreement on slowing down the flow of refugees coming from Turkey that covered financial and political concessions, with the bloc offering 3 billion euros to help Turkey run refugee facilities in its territory, accelerating talks on the visa issue, restarting the EU accession talks and upgrading diplomatic relations. The summit therefore confirmed that after years of difficult relations, the EU and Turkey have suddenly improved their relationship amid the outbreak of the refugee crisis. On November 30, 2015—just one day after the EU–Turkey summit in Brussels—Turkish authorities arrested a large group of migrants and smugglers. Turkey also started to guard the Greek island of Lesbos, the main point of EU entry for migrants arriving through Turkey. The UN High Commissioner for Refugees (UNHCR) has announced that between January and November 26, 2015 about 431,000 people reached Lesbos. Greece, which has tried to avoid cooperation with EU demands on migrants and refugees as it faced its own economic and political problems, had to accept EU border regulations after it saw more than 700,000 people arrive on its shores since the beginning of the year.

Final words

The European Union is living one of the most important moments of its history. The economic crisis in Greece is having a devastating effect on the bloc's finances, and the refugee crisis is having a devastating effect on integration, nation states' relations, and politics.

On the economic side, most of the EU members are just recovering from a deep recession, with the governments buried in debts and deficits after they exhausted their financial reserves helping society with high levels of unemployment and implementing many social policies oriented towards lowering the impact of the economic crisis.

On the political side, the EU is experiencing a massive human exodus due to a mixture of political, economic and environmental issues. The Office for the Coordination of Humanitarian Affairs said in November 2015 that:

> Alongside conflicts and violence, climate change has also become a major trigger of displacement. More severe droughts and more frequent natural disasters increasingly drive people from their homes. Last year alone, at least 800,000 people were displaced due to disasters on the African continent.[34]

The difficult economic situation in the EU's southern members is flooding northern EU states like Germany, Austria and the UK with EU nationals looking for a better job opportunity and living standards. Furthermore, the EU is witnessing a massive arrival of refugees from Middle Eastern and African countries that is putting pressure on economic, political and even social relations among EU member states. National borders taken down after the Second World War as a sign of neighborly friendship and trust are being raised again, and a long-forgotten fear of the "other" is once again gaining political ground in the heart of Europe. This wave of refugees is allowing political parties with all-but moribund ideas to experience a comeback across Europe at the national and even European levels. The EU should prevent those radical political views and economic difficulties from pushing currently non-integrated migrants and new waves of migrants into ghettos. Governments also must be vigilant to prevent any already existing ghettos from being turned into anything similar to the infamous ghettos of Nazi-occupied Europe or Japanese-occupied Shanghai. Thus, the EU should not forget that securing external borders and securing the well-being of citizens are fundamental to the survival of the project, or the EU will fall like the Roman Empire.

In the middle of this crisis is Turkey. Geographically, the largest part of the country is located in Western Asia and just a small portion is located in Southeast Europe, which is why Turkey wants to be part of the EU. But Turkey has a poor human rights record and its economy was only the 70th freest according to a report on 186 countries.[35] One democracy index ranked it in 88th place out of 1216 countries, between Ecuador and Sri Lanka.[36]

Turkey has asked for a political and economic payment to help the EU contain the massive inflow of refugees. The political price has been the reopening of the EU accession talks and the economic price was the generous packet of financial assistance of about 3 billion euros. The EU should not be proud of having to pay Turkey to assist in the conflict. And EU institutions and politicians should be held accountable for their negligence. After decades of meetings, councils, regulations and press releases, the EU has been unable to secured its border and provide the necessary resources to deal with a massive inflow of refugees. During all these years, EU experts, politicians and technocrats could have asked many democratic and developed countries for advice on how to deal with massive and sudden migrations flows. For instance, the United States experienced refugee crises during both world wars during its lengthy hostile relations with Cuba. Since the Cuban Revolution in 1959, more than one million Cubans of all social classes have left the island to seek asylum in the United States; in fact, the U.S. Census of 2000 showed that 1,241,685 Americans claimed Cuban descent. They are considered to be the most successful Hispanic immigrant group, with educational and economic profiles near those of the U.S. population as a whole.

Notes

1 Your Dictionary. http://quotes.yourdictionary.com/author/abraham-lincoln/172508#vsy pRGcKOZzt3iCM.99.
2 Eurostat. "Migration and migrant population statistics." http://ec.europa.eu/eurostat/statistics-explained/index.php/Migration_and_migrant_population_statistics#Migrant_population (accessed November 11, 2015).
3 European Union External Action. "Euro–Mediterranean Partnership (EUROMED)." http://www.eeas.europa.eu/euromed/index_en.htm (accessed November 20, 2015).
4 European Commission. "Migration and Home Affairs." http://ec.europa.eu/dgs/home-affairs/what-we-do/policies/european-agenda-migration/index_en.htm (accessed November 21, 2015).
5 Euobserver. 2015. "Austria's foreign minister says border fences work." https://euobserver.com/tickers/130812 (accessed November 2, 2015).
6 Euobserver. 2015. "Sweden reintroduces border controls." https://euobserver.com/migration/131078 (accessed November 11, 2015).
7 Euobserver. 2015. "Greece accepts EU border help under Schengen threat." http://euobserver.com/migration/131387 (accessed December 1, 2015).
8 European Commission. "A policy plan on legal migration." http://europa.eu/rapid/press-release_MEMO-05-494_en.htm (accessed November 2, 2015).
9 European Commission. "A policy plan to fight illegal migration." http://europa.eu/rapid/press-release_MEMO-06-296_en.htm (accessed November 13, 2015).
10 European Commission. "Third Annual Report on Migration and Integration: an overview of policy developments on integration of third-country nationals at EU and national level." http://europa.eu/rapid/press-release_MEMO-07-351_en.htm (accessed November 13, 2015).
11 European Commission. "Strengthening the global approach to migration." http://europa.eu/rapid/press-release_MEMO-08-613_en.htm (accessed November 21, 2015).

12 European Commission. "The Stockholm Programme—An open and secure Europe serving and protecting citizens." http://eurojust.europa.eu/doclibrary/EU-framework/EUframeworkgeneral/The%20Stockholm%20Programme%202010/Stockholm-Programme-2010-EN.pdf (accessed November 2, 2015).
13 European Commission. "A European Agenda on Migration." http://ec.europa.eu/dgs/home-affairs/what-we-do/policies/european-agenda-migration/background-information/docs/communication_on_the_european_agenda_on_migration_en.pdf (accessed November 15, 2015).
14 European Commission. 2015. "European Commission makes progress on Agenda on Migration." http://europa.eu/rapid/press-release_IP-15-5039_en.htm (accessed November 2, 2015).
15 European Commission. 2015. "First measures under the European Agenda on Migration: questions and answers." http://europa.eu/rapid/press-release_MEMO-15-5038_en.htm (accessed November 16, 2015).
16 European Commission. 2003. Dublin II Regulation. http://eur-lex.europa.eu/legal-content/EN/TXT/HTML/?uri=URISERV:l33153&from=EN (accessed November 2, 2015).
17 European Commission. 2015. "First measures under the European Agenda on Migration: questions and answers." http://europa.eu/rapid/press-release_MEMO-15-5038_en.htm (accessed November 16, 2015).
18 European Commission. 2015. "EU–Turkey Joint Action Plan." http://europa.eu/rapid/press-release_MEMO-15-5860_en.htm (accessed November 12, 2015).
19 European Commission. "Meeting on the Western Balkans migration route: leaders agree on 17-point plan of action." http://europa.eu/rapid/press-release_IP-15-5904_en.htm (accessed November 9, 2015).
20 People who voluntarily move to other countries in search of better economic opportunities or to reunite with their families.
21 People who are left with no choice but to flee, those who seek protection from conflict, violence or persecution.
22 United Nation. 2015. "Remarks to the specialized technical committee of the African Union on migration, refugees and displaced persons." https://docs.unocha.org/sites/dms/Documents/23%20Nov%2015%20ASG%20Technical%20Committee%20AU.pdf (accessed November 23, 2015).
23 Nielsen, Nikola J. 2015. "Six EU states slash food aid for Syria refugees." *Euobserver*. http://euobserver.com/migration/130400 (accessed September 23, 2015).
24 David, Cameron. 2015. "A new settlement for the United Kingdom in a reformed European Union." https://s3.eu-central-1.amazonaws.com/euobs-media/9b90d4765b6d2a021f299bae5b5ab433.pdf (accessed November 10, 2015).
25 Maurice, Eric. 20150. "EU aims for UK deal in February." *Euobserver*. http://euobserver.com/political/131388 (accessed December 3, 2015).
26 Valentin Jeutner. 2015. "Swiss accept initiative to 'Stop Mass Immigration': legal implications (Part I)." *Cambridge Journal of International and Comparative Law*. http://cjicl.org.uk/2014/02/26/swiss-accept-initiative-stop-mass-immigration-legal-implications-part/ (accessed November 25, 2015).
27 Schweizerische Eidgenossenschaft. 1999. "Swiss–EU Bilateral Agreement on the Free Movement of Persons." http://www.sbfi.admin.ch/diploma/01793/01794/index.html?lang=en (accessed November 2, 2015).
28 Swissinfo. 2015. "Swiss praise EU refugee proposals." http://www.swissinfo.ch/eng/politics/quota-system_swiss-praise-eu-refugee-proposals-/41428716 (accessed November 25, 2015).
29 EUbusiness. 2015. "Swiss say will help Balkans deal with refugee crisis." http://www.eubusiness.com/news-eu/europe-migrants.1433/ (accessed.November 28, 2015).
30 European Commission. 2015. "Leaders' meeting on refugee flows along the Western Balkans Route." http://europa.eu/rapid/press-release_IP-15-5904_en (accessed October 28, 2015).

31 European Commission. 2015. "EU–Turkey Joint Action Plan." http://europa.eu/rapid/press-release_MEMO-15-5860_en.htm (accessed November 12, 2015).
32 European Commission. 2015. *Turkey 2015 report.* http://ec.europa.eu/enlargement/pdf/key_documents/2015/20151110_report_turkey.pdf (accessed November 13, 2015).
33 At the time of writing, the Turks were going to the polls on November 1, 2015 to elect a new parliament for the second time, since the result of the previous election held in June 2015 had resulted in no party being able to form a unilateral government.
34 United Nation. 2015. *Remarks to the specialized technical committee of the African Union on migration, refugees and displaced persons.* https://docs.unocha.org/sites/dms/Documents/23%20Nov%2015%20ASG%20Technical%20Committee%20AU.pdf (accessed November 30, 2015).
35 The Heritage Foundation. "2015 Index of Economic Freedom." http://www.heritage.org/index/about (accessed November 30, 2015).
36 The Economist. 2012. "Democracy Index." http://pages.eiu.com/rs/eiu2/images/Democracy-Index-2012.pdf (accessed December 8, 2015).

Part IV
The European Union and the challenges beneath the surface

Part IV

11 The future of the European Union

The Union must go

> Blood, toil, tears and sweat.
> (Winston Churchill)[1]

Introduction

The European Union is facing the worst crisis since its founding in the wake of the Second World War. The project is at a crossroads and any solutions will require blood, toil, tears and sweat.

At present, the debate on solutions focuses on the choice between two options: cutting costs or increasing them. But this seeming paradox is only the most visible part of a profoundly complex process. Answers to the problems of European identity, democratic deficit, the welfare state and the standardization and implementation of economic policies remain the major outstanding chapters in EU history.

The EU has lived sweet moments. It was born of the desire to leave behind the struggle and devastation of two world wars that ravaged the European continent and the need to become a solid bloc in order to successfully face worldwide economic competition. But the initial success of the euro tended to hide the systemic weaknesses and risks of the project.

There are EU countries enjoying positive trade balances and countries with budget deficits financed by credits that have not been used to increase competitiveness, but rather to finance unproductive spending and housing bubbles.

Unfortunately, it can be factually said that the EU now consists of creditor countries and debtor countries, where debtor countries often times accuse creditor countries of being unsupportive and demand the easing of the conditions of their debts. Debtor countries do not want to understand that becoming debtors brings along a change of governance because the need for financial assistance—required by their own political mismanagement of economic resources—brings with it the transfer of national sovereignty. This *quid pro quo* makes the situation difficult and subtle because excessive pressure from creditor countries is increasing poverty and worsening living standards in the debtor countries. Moreover, creditor countries are under pressure from their taxpayers because the financial help they provide amounts to a transfer of economic resources provided by taxpayers.

Unfortunately, the experience so far has shown that this transfer of resources takes place from north to south. Countries like Italy, Spain and even France would have carried out two to three competitive devaluations, relative to the northern countries, since adopting the euro. Instead, they have accumulated tensions in the domestic production of goods and services that have been slowing productivity and increasing deficits and public debt. At the same time, the creditor countries like those in Northern Europe have benefited from extending their markets to reach the countries of the former Soviet Union, China and Latin America.

In the absence of the EU and the euro, the debtor countries would have had the option to continue with their policy of devaluations to gain market share but impose a loss in the export cycle of other countries—a loss that the other countries somehow might be able to counteract by exporting to other countries. Nonetheless, devaluation policies are always specially damaging. Despite the recent opening of new markets, the cost of EU disintegration or the exit of a debtor country would ultimately be a bad solution for the world economy.

Today's globalized world needs strong economic groups, and a united Europe is more efficient than a divided Europe or a two-speed Europe. Therefore, the balance must be very subtle and southern countries, which have a different vision of economic balance, need to undergo a reformation. But the northern countries cannot leave the south to its own devices as that would mean the end of the project. How to accomplish this is the most serious challenge facing the EU today.

The European identity

It has been said that comparisons are hateful. However, in times of crisis it is necessary to look for reference points that help to define the target. The United States is a good example of how a common identity provides a strong unity and cohesion. The identity for the United States comes from the language, the dollar, the anthem, the flag and paying taxes. It is true that the U.S. is a federation, which the founding fathers of the EU never wanted. However, the EU now needs to develop a strong European identity in order to survive.

European identity can be achieved despite the existence of national languages but the facts indicate the predominance of some languages over others. Today, English is practically accepted as the common language in the EU, without a negative impact on the other national languages. The countries that use English as their mother tongue or those countries that use English as a second language tend to be more integrated and have greater economic success and a greater ability to seize the opportunities of globalization. Specifically, the study by the European Commission[2] on the use of different languages showed that 56% of EU citizens can hold a conversation in a language other than their native tongue. In fact, the study showed that English is the most used language among EU countries where Germany and several Northern European countries use English as a second language. Interestingly, native English-speaking citizens tend not to speak any other language. In fact, 66% of Irish and 62% of Britons do not speak a second language. But they are not alone, since 59% of Italians, 58% of Portuguese and 56% of

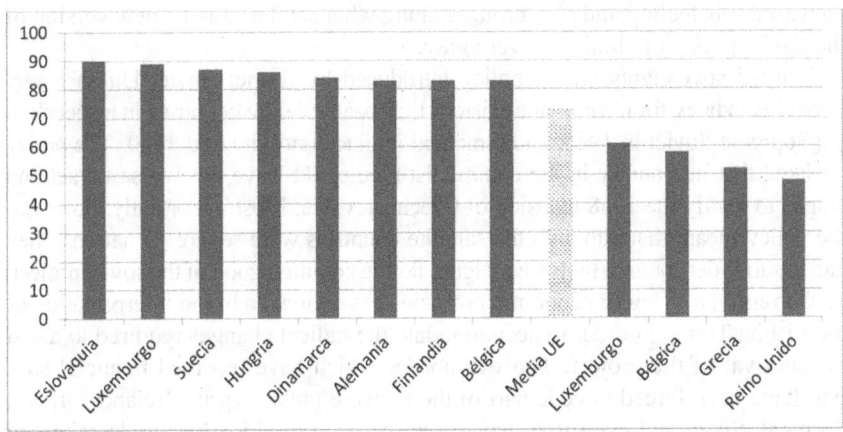

Figure 11.1 Proportion of residents expressing European identity, Summer 2009 (%).
Source: European Commission.

Spaniards also say they do not speak a second language.[3] Further, those countries where this type of bilingualism does not exist tend to be less integrated with the rest of Europe.

Therefore, if a solid economic bloc is characterized by a common language and currency, symbols like the flag and the anthem and the payment of taxes, the EU falls far short: it has no common language acceptable to all members; the euro is used only in some countries; there are taxes, but each country decides its own rates; and citizens are very much indifferent to the EU flag and the anthem, which are only formally present in the events of the EU bureaucracy.

European youth may be the future of the project, however. The Eurobarometer 71 survey showed that 83% of highly educated young people feel European, compared with 78% of those with less education.[4] These numbers make sense because 30% of the EU's youth are unemployed, which understandably makes them unsupportive of the project. Furthermore, the existence of academic programs for student mobility designed to assist the integration of European youth have not proven effective and only benefited some elites. It is, on the contrary, a paradox that the economic crisis has reduced these scholarships and exchange programs due to austerity policies, even as European youth are compelled to migrate to other European countries because of necessity.

The economic deficit: limited sovereignty

Since the EU was created, citizens have been denouncing a political system which they believe suffers from has been called a "democratic deficit." Some citizens believe that the union and its agencies lack democratic legitimacy because they are inaccessible to citizens by the complexity of their structure and operations.

The economic crisis and the need to provide some countries with financial aid has increased this feeling and also brought along what can be called a new version of the Soviet policy of "limited sovereignty."

Limited sovereignty was a policy introduced by former Soviet Union leader Leonid Brezhnev for Central and Eastern European satellite countries in a speech to the Supreme Soviet in 1968, and remained in place until the mid-1980. The policy declared that no country in the communist bloc could leave the Warsaw Pact and helped to justify the 1968 invasion of Czechoslovakia. Most importantly, however, the policy meant that although the satellite countries were sovereign nations, they had to surrender some of their sovereignty for the common good of the soviet project.

Currently, a string of economic problems have forced a broad interpretation of the Lisbon Treaty in order to accommodate the radical changes required to assist the survival of the project. Those countries which have received financial support have been forced to cede part of their sovereignty. Cyprus, Ireland, Greece, Portugal, Spain and even Italy have seen the need to abide by the decisions of Europe and have experienced "limited sovereignty"—luckily, with a far less nefarious meaning than in the Soviet Union. But this limitation of sovereignty has proven crucial for meeting the financial and economic obligations imposed to join the path of economic orthodoxy for the welfare of the union.

The economic orthodoxy promoted from decision centers such as Brussels and the International Monetary Fund (IMF) has been violently contested by leftists and nationalists. The economic crisis has revealed a strong antagonism between the two fundamentally ideological approaches that emerged from the very foundations of the EU: on the one hand, those left, green, radical and nationalist ideologies which defend the idea of the nation state and on the other, the socialist and conservative parties which prefer a "Europe of nations."

A European Union based on distinct nation states risks becoming an ultra-federal or cantonal Europe with difficult governance. The Europe of nations is the mostly widely accepted view, endorsing an EU of institutions, the pragmatism of decisions based on hierarchy, and the greater weight in the EU's decision-making of countries with a successful track record of managing their economies.

The problem facing the European Union today is that traditional national institutions remain operative while the European institutions are still maturing. Companies that need to renovate their operations must sometimes first eliminate a number of subsidiaries and departments, directors and associates, and update rules and regulations, and then they can move forward with a new structure, management and even a new business plan. The EU should follow a similar path, first by reorganizing national institutions, parliaments, official bulletins, and regional and departmental laws, and later by moving forward toward an integrated and renewed EU. Unfortunately, the first phase has never been an option and the second phase is still at the planning stage. As a consequence, European citizens still believe in their nation state and show very little interest in the elections to the European Parliament, an attitude that has been exacerbated by the economic crisis. The low turnout for both elections showed that Europeans were uninterested in the balloting. A historical analysis shows that from the first elections in 1972 to

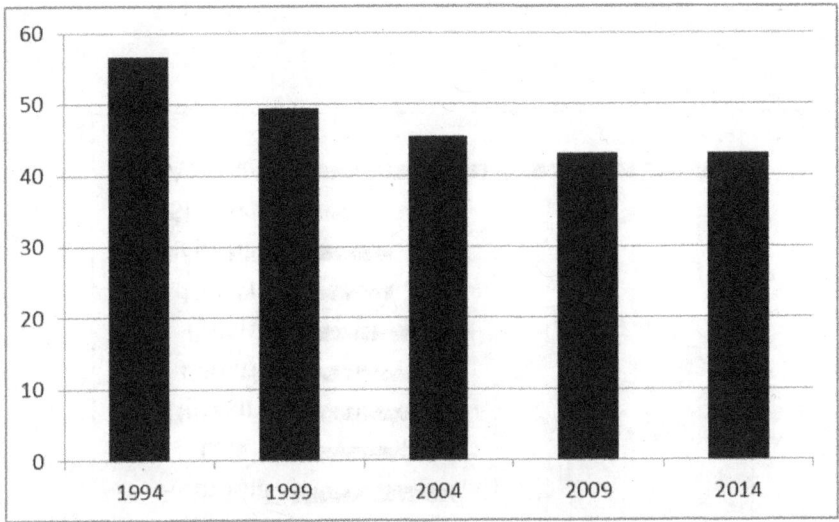

Figure 11.2 Voter turnout in European elections, 1994–2014 (%).
Source: European Parliament.

the latest in 2014, the rate of participation has been declining. In 1972 the turnout was 62%, in 1994 it was 57%, in 2009 was 43% and in 2014 it stayed at 43.09%.

Another concern in the last two elections was that the participation was extremely low in those Eastern European nations that had most recently joined the EU. Slovakia, for example, had the lowest participation rate in 2009, with only 19.64% of the eligible voters taking part and less than 15% in 2014. In the other Eastern European countries, the participation rate did not even reach 30%. Fortunately, there are countries with a longer history in the EU where the participation rate has been higher. For example in Belgium and Luxembourg participation in elections is compulsory so the turnout is usually close to 90% of the voters.[5]

There are two explanations for the low voter turnout. First, in the European Parliament elections, representatives are elected by citizens whose only options are candidates nominated by political parties in closed lists in each EU member state. There is no possibility for citizens to vote for politicians of another country who could better represent their interests or political and economic beliefs. Second, in many countries candidates for the European Parliament are politicians who are past their prime political years in their own countries and are relegated to Europe as a way to complete their political life at an international level. Therefore, often times, national political parties do not send to Europe the best candidates who can help build the project. Finally, the extremely high number of parliament members—751—often raises questions as to the optimum size of a modern legislature, especially one where attendance is not mandatory and the floor frequently looks like an empty soccer stadium.

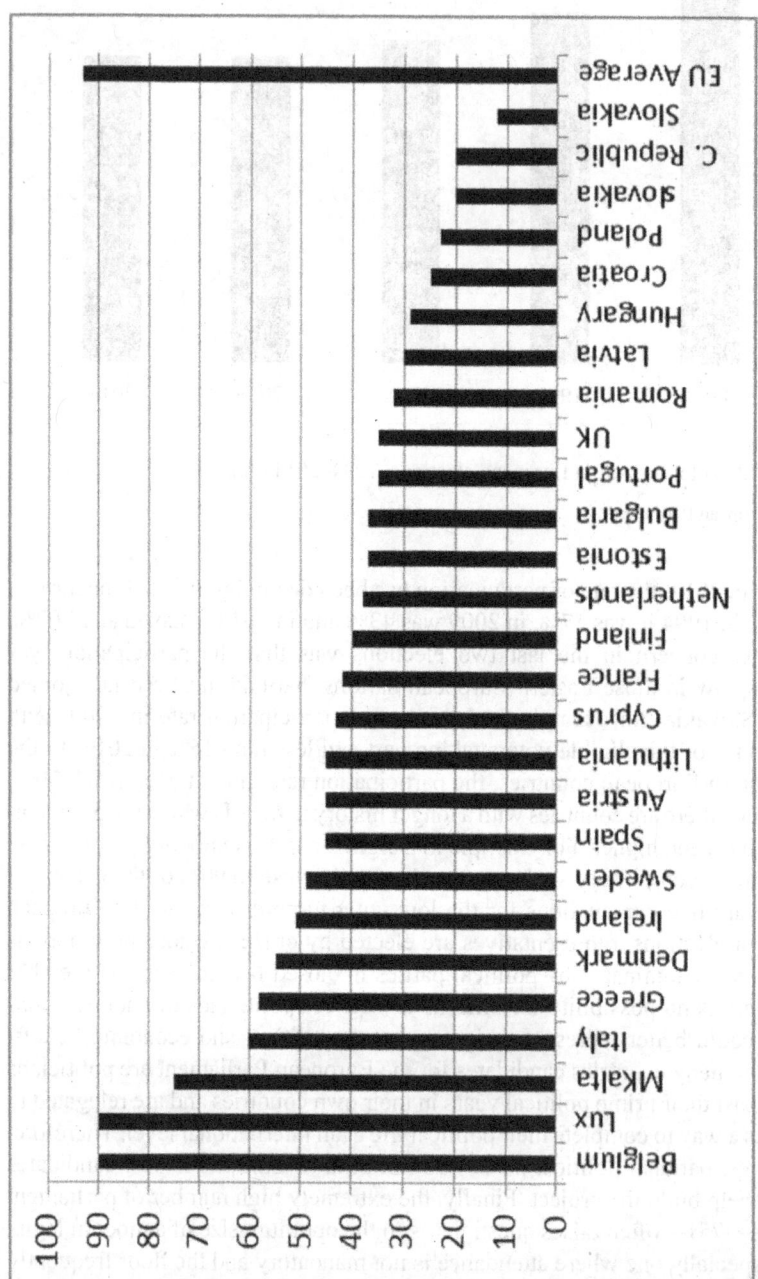

Figure 11.3 Voter turnout by state, 2014 (%).
Source: European Parliament.

Table 11.1 European Parliamentary election results: 2009 and 2014 compared

	2014	2009	% change
European United Left	52	35	+48%
Group of the Progressive Alliance of Socialists and Democrats	191	196	−2.55%
The Greens	50	57	−12%
Alliance of Liberals and Democrats for Europe	67	83	−19%
European People's Party	221	274	−19%
European Conservatives and Reformist	70	57	+22%
Europe of Freedom and Direct Democracy	48	31	+54%
Non-Attached Members	52	33	+36%

Source: European Parliament.

Despite the low voter turnouts, José Manuel Barroso who was the President of the European Commission in 2004-2014, has praised the elections as victories for the European project.[6] Critics have argued, however, that they show that EU leaders are out of touch with the European electorate. Not only is the low participation rate important, however, but there's been an increase in nationalist and extremist parties that are unwilling to work towards European unity and often act to the detriment of the cohesion of the project. For instance, the European United Left and the Europe of Freedom and Direct Democracy parties have seen significant increases in the number of their elected members.

The welfare state: a Ponzi scheme impossible to maintain

The *Encyclopedia Britannica* defines the welfare state as a system of government in which the state plays a key role in the protection and promotion of the economic and social welfare of its citizens. It is based on the principles of equal opportunity, equitable distribution of wealth and public support for those who do not enjoy the minimum living standards. It is a general term that can encompass a variety of forms of economic and social organization.[7]

The welfare state is not a concept invented in recent years. The idea of social protection has evolved from what might be called the state of love and charity in the Middle Ages to the welfare state of the twentieth century. In the Middle Ages, the protection for people in need revolved around the idea of charity, which was based on the alms of the citizens, municipal hostels and hospitals of religious organizations, houses of mercy and orphanages.

During the Renaissance helping people in need was no longer an act of charity for religious orders but part of the effort to increase social and economic well-being. The states began to develop a public welfare system, and the municipality, rather than the church, was the main institution responsible for social protection. Charitable social action relies on public altruism, which is always subject to discretion. In the modern era, the French Revolution promoted the concepts of equality, fraternity and liberty, and the state was obliged to care for the needy through social assistance. With the Industrial Revolution in the early nineteenth century and the creation of large masses of displaced people around the industrial belts, many governments were forced to adopt schemes for social insurance.[8]

The welfare state is based on public social assistance, which curiously was promoted mainly by conservative governments and opposed by socialist parties and trade unions which believed that its benefits would weaken their hold on voters. Generally, the welfare state is characterized by governments trying to maintain low levels of unemployment; offering health and accident insurance and unemployment and social assistance; providing free access to public education; and implementing social policies that seek to redistribute wealth in order to maintain social stability.

The welfare state in Europe began in the 1880s when Chancellor Bismarck was impressed by the Manifesto of Eisenach which promulgated Germany's first social laws. (BBC History) In the UK, the first social laws came when the Liberal party of Prime Minister David Lloyd-George in 1910 modernized the Old Poor Law dating from the early 1600s although it was the Beveridge Report of 1942 which really became the theoretical foundation for the current British welfare state. In France, the modern welfare state began during the Vichy regime in 1940. Finally, all dictatorships of the twentieth century could be categorized as welfare states. Modern welfare programs, unlike previous programs, offer a relative, not full, universal coverage. Modern examples of welfare states in the world are Germany, the Nordic countries, The Netherlands, and the UK.

Modern history has seen a series of events that helped the development of the welfare system. First, the Bolshevik Revolution of 1917 led the Russian government to improve the benefits of the welfare state, including social and medical assistance not as an act of charity but as a human right. Second, the welfare state increased its coverage in response to the Great Depression in certain countries where now the welfare state is a "cradle to grave" system—which often stymies citizen initiatives, weakens the economy and society and increases corruption. This type of welfare state during the Great Depression was seen as an intermediate system between communism and capitalism. Finally, after the Second World War many European countries began to offer a relatively wide coverage of social services in order to help the population. The welfare state, therefore, has not been a conquest of the workers but rather a government gift to help the welfare of its citizens.

The communist threat in Eastern Europe was a major reason for government decisions to implement the welfare state. But the maximum protection advocated by socialism has now collapsed and the citizens of Eastern Europe, who were once assured that the state would provide for them, have experienced a very different reality in the late twentieth century. What's more, social welfare coverage in communist countries was offset by the loss of private property and the freedom of association, free speech and other rights. The welfare state once provided by the People's Republic of China has completely disappeared and the country has replaced communism with capitalism in a rapid, convulsive about-turn.

Today, the services provided by the welfare states are based generally on benefits such as payments for pensions or unemployment, social services and in-kind assistance such as health services. Angela Merkel has said that, because of this wide coverage, Europe accounts for 7% of the world's population, produces 25% of global GDP but must finance 50% of the total social spending. It is obvious that Europeans must work hard to maintain their way of life.

After two world wars on the continent, Europe has lost its bellicose mood and defense budgets have been shrinking. What is more, since the 1950s Europe has not had to spend money on maintaining any empires. On the other hand, Europe is now under the U.S. defense umbrella, and can reallocate funds from its defense budget to social spending. This means that the U.S. must maintain an extremely high level of military spending for worldwide defense, and therefore it cannot spend more on a social welfare system that would provide more assistance to American citizens.

Europe has a birth rate that is zero or even negative and its adult population is growing exponentially. In short, the population pyramid has reversed with a narrow base and broad peak. European countries have always, for political and idiosyncratic reasons, demanded a welfare state and during the recent economic crisis the level of poverty rose in some countries. The lack of citizen initiative and the tendency to live off the state have made the welfare state even more necessary.

The welfare state is an obligatory social pact based on citizens' solidarity. An imposed solidarity that can only be maintained by increasing the state debt would not be much of an act of solidarity with future generations. One problem with the European welfare states is the existence of a "single box." The system is based precisely on the fact that there's no distinction among individuals, and the distribution criteria is random and often times discriminatory. Furthermore, the welfare states do not meet any capitalization criteria, which makes it a huge Ponzi scheme that mostly helps politicians to achieve power. The welfare state in Europe is doomed because it cannot be maintained and has been practically bankrupt for decades. The prospects for the welfare state, if maintained as a Ponzi scheme, are that it will collapse within a few years.

At present, there are some trends for timid reforms of the welfare state system. For example, changes in the model of public medical services are being considered in certain countries because they cannot continue offering universal health care. The differing state medical services in Europe also have helped to create a system of "health tourism" across European borders.

Some Western countries have private state entities that provide sensitive services to communities. However, it is not politically likely that a social security system would be privatized in the near future to make it more efficient and economical. Politicians simply do not want to lose control of revenues from social security fees paid by citizens because they can, through financial engineering, transfer funds from one activity to another that might prove more politically advantageous to them—the greater game of some governments in the European Union.

Notes

1 Winston Churchill. http://www.historyplace.com/speeches/churchill.htm.
2 European Commission. "Europeans and their languages." Special Eurobarometer 243, February 2006. http://ec.europa.eu/public_opinion/archives/ebs/ebs_243_en.pdf.
3 European Commission. "Europeans and their languages." Special Eurobarometer 243, February 2006. http://ec.europa.eu/public_opinion/archives/ebs/ebs_243_en.pdf.
4 European Commission. "Future of Europe." Eurobarometer 71, January 2010. http://ec.europa.eu/public_opinion/archives/eb/eb71/eb713_future_europe.pdf.
5 Parlamento Europeo. "Participación en las elecciones europeas." http://www.europarl.europa.eu/aboutparliament/es/000cdcd9d4/Turnout-(1979-2009).html.
6 Clive Leviev-Sawyer. 2009. "European Parliament elections 'victory for European project'—Barroso." *The Sofia Echo*, June 8. http://www.sofiaecho.com/2009/06/08/732475_european-parliament-elections-victory-for-european-project-barroso.
7 Encyclopædia Britannica. http://www.britannica.com/EBchecked/topic/639266/welfare-state.
8 Cristino Barroso Ribal. "Caridad, beneficencia, seguro social, asistencia social, y estado de bienestar." http://ctinobar.webs.ull.es/1docencia/Poltsociale/HISTORIA.pdf.

Bibliography

Agencias. 2011. "La Comisión Europea: el plan de rescate a Portugal no es fácil." *Expansión*, May 5. http://www.expansion.com/2011/05/05/economia/1304588655.html (accessed April 21, 2015).

Almunia, Joaquín. 2009. "EU interim forecast: coming out of the recession but uncertainty remains." *Europa*, Brussels, September 14. http://europa.eu/rapid/pressRelea-sesAction.do?reference=IP/09/1309&format=HTML&aged=0&language=EN&guiLanguage=en (accessed February 26, 2013).

APF. 2012. "Italia introduce 'regla de oro' en su Constitución." *El Economista*, April 17. http://eleconomista.com.mx/node/379486 (accessed December 9, 2012).

Arancibia, Salvador. 1982. "El partido socialista había meditado la devaluación de la peseta para cortar movimientos especulativos." *El País*, December 22. http://www.elpais.com/articulo/espana/PeREZ_ROYO/_JAVIER/MATUTES/_ABEL/GASOLIBA/_CARLES_A/SOLCHAGA/_CARLOS/BOYER/_MIGUEL/ESPAnA/MINISTERIO_DE_ECONOMiA_Y_HACIENDA/elpepiesp/19821222elpepinac_9/Tes/ (accessed September 11, 2008).

Associated Press. 2015a. "Greece misses debt payment to IMF as bailout expires." *MSNBC*, June 30. http://www.msnbc.com/msnbc/greece-misses-debt-payment-imf-bailout-expires (accessed June 30, 2015).

———. 2015b. "Greece repays IMF loan instalment despite cash crunch." *US Today*, April 9. <http://www.usatoday.com/story/money/2015/04/09/greece-repays-loan-instalment/ 25504405/ (accessed April 9, 2015).

Atkins, Ralph. 2006. "A coming of age for the European currency." *Financial Times*, December 28. Atkins, Ralph, and Quentin Peel. 2010. "Germans oppose Greek aid, poll shows." *Financial Times*, March 21. http://www.ft.com/intl/cms/s/0/ee055e82-3529-11df-9cfb-00144feabdc0.html#axzz2SGVWDjNP (accessed April 22, 2014).

Atlántico. 2013. "L'euro s'envole à 1, 35 dollar, Arnaud Montebourg s'inquiète." January 13. http://www.atlantico.fr/pepites/euro-envole-135-dollar-arnaud-montebourg-inquiete-623930.html#1rA31ZSPy7GoqEq6.99 (accessed January 25, 2014).

Aunión, J. A. 2007. "La educación Española retrocede." *El País*, December 5. http://www.elpais.com/articulo/sociedad/educacion/espanola/retrocede/elpepusoc/20071205elpepisoc_1/Tes (accessed September 10, 2009).

Baily, Martin N. and Jacob F. Kirkegaard. 2004. *A transformation of the European economy*. Washington: Peter G. Peterson Institute for International Economics.

Baker, Luke, and Michael Stott. 2013. "EU's Barroso urges leaders to stick to austerity goals." *Reuters*, February 26. http://www.reuters.com/article/2013/02/26/us-euro-summit-barroso-idUSBRE91P0ML20130226 (accessed March 20, 2014).

Bartel, Robert J. 1974. "International monetary unions: the XIXth century experience." *Journal of European Economic History*, 3, 3: 689–704.

BBC History. "Otto von Bismarck (1815–1898)." http://www.bbc.co.uk/history/historic_figures/bismarck_otto_von.shtml (accessed October 28, 2008).

BBC News. 2015a. "Greece crisis: Syriza rebels form new party." August 21. http://www.bbc.com/news/world-europe-34014083 (accessed August 21, 2015).

——. 2015b."Greece crisis: PM Alexis Tsipras quits and calls early polls." August 20. http://www.bbc.com/news/world-europe-34007859 (accessed August 20, 2015).

——. 2015c. "Greece's Varoufakis: 'No debt talks with EU-IMF troika." January 30. http://www.bbc.com/news/world-europe-31055069 (accessed January 30, 2015).

——. 2014. "Greek shares fall for third day on election fears." December 11. http://www.bbc.com/news/world-europe-30435311 (accessed May 2, 2015).

Bernanke, Ben S. 2010. "Economic policy—lessons from history." Speech at the 43rd Annual Alexander Hamilton Awards Dinner, Center for the Study of the Presidency and Congress, Washington DC, April 8. http://www.federalreserve.gov/newsevents/speech/bernanke20100408a.htm (accessed April 10, 2010).

Bild. 2011. "Jeder zweite Deutsche wünscht sich die D-Mark zurück." March 23. http://www.bild.de/BILD/politik/wirtschaft/2010/12/26/euro-umfrage-bild-exklusiv/deutsche-wollen-d-mark-wieder-haben.html (accessed June 23, 2013).

Blair, Tony. 2005. "Programme of the British Presidency." Statement to the European Parliament, Brussels, June 23. http://www.europarl.europa.eu/sides/getDoc.do;jsessionid=EEC841C80F8E54A229F29B24338B201E.node2?language=EN&pubRef=-//EP//TEXT+CRE+20050623+ITEM-004+DOC+XML+V0//EN (accessed June 28, 2008).

Caruana, Jaime. 2004a. "Foreword." International conference Dollars, debt, and deficits—60 years after Bretton Woods, co-organized by the Banco de España and the International Monetary Fund. Madrid, Spain, June 14–15, 2004. http://www.imf.org/external/np/res/seminars/2004/60/index.htm (accessed November 2, 2014).

——. 2004b. "60 years after Bretton Woods—a central banker's view." Opening remarks at the conference Dollars, debt and deficits—60 years after Bretton Woods, held at the Bank of Spain, Madrid, June 10. http://www.bis.org/review/r040618e.pdf (accessed on September 14, 2009).

Churchill, Winston. 1940. "Winston Churchill speech—'blood, toil, tears and sweat'." *Presentation Magazine*. http://www.presentationmagazine.com/winston_churchill_speech_blood_sweat_tears.htm (accessed April 18, 2010).

Clark, Andrew, Heather Steward, and Elena Moya. 2010. "Goldman Sachs faces Fed inquiry over Greek crisis." *The Guardian*, February 25. http://www.theguardian.com/business/2010/feb/25/markets-pressure-greece-cut-spending.

CNN Money. 2009. "Global 500." *Fortune 500*, July 20. http://money.cnn.com/magazines/fortune/global500/2009/countries/Ireland.html (accessed April 2, 2010).

Cohen, Benjamin J. 2003. "Global currency rivalry: can the euro ever challenge the dollar?" *Journal of Common Market Studies*, May: 1–23. http://repositories.cdlib.org/gis/8 (accessed February 16, 2008).

Cooke, Kieran. 2015. "Plummeting oil price casts shadow over fracking's future". *The Guardian*, 6 January, accessed at: http://www.theguardian.com/environment/2015/jan/06/oil-price-casts-shadow-over-frackings-future.

Council of the European Union. 2005. Council Decision of 12 July 2005 on Guidelines for the Employment Policies of the Member States. *Official Journal of the European Union*, 2005/600/EC. July 12. http://eurlex.europa.eu/LexUriServ/site/en/oj/2005/l_205/l_20520050806en00210027.pdf (accessed September 24, 2008).

———. n. d. "Ecofin Council." http://www.consilium.europa.eu/showPage.aspx?id=250&lang=EN (accessed February 1, 2010).

Coyle, Diane. 2005. Eurosclerosis revisited. *Strategy and Business*, 39. http://www.strategy-business.com/media/file/sb39_05210.pdf (accessed February 14, 2008).

Delors, Jacques. 1989. "Report on economic and monetary union in the European Community." Committee for the Study of Economic and Monetary Union. April 17. http://aei.pitt.edu/1007/1/monetary_delors.pdf (accessed November 23, 2013).

Deppler, Michael. 2007. "Economic and monetary integration in Europe as seen from outside." Directorate General for Economic and Financial Affairs. *European Economic News*, issue 6 (April). http://ec.europa.eu/economy_finance/een/006/article_5207_en.htm (accessed February 10, 2008).

Deschamps, Etienne. n. d. Le Projet d'Association économique atlantique de Jean Monnet.

Devries, P., J. Guajardo, D. Leigh, and A. Pescatori. 2011. "A new action-based dataset of fiscal consolidation." International Monetary Fund. Working Paper No. 11/128. http://www.imf.org/external/pubs/ft/wp/2011/wp11128.pdf (accessed January 27, 2014).

Economagic. http://www.economagic.com.

Economist, The. 2013. "Shale of the century." 2 June. http://www.economist.com/node/21556242 (accessed December 23, 2013).

EFE. 2013. "Fiscalía pide juzgar ex presidente Instituto Estadístico por falsear déficit." *El Diario*, January 22. http://www.eldiario.es/economia/Fiscalia-expresidente-Instituto-Estadistico-deficit_0_93091166.html (accessed April 24, 2013).

———. 2011. "Los conservadores irlandeses ganan las elecciones sin mayoría absoluta." *La Razón*, February 26. http://www.larazon.es/detalle_hemeroteca/noticias/LA_RAZON_360942/3192-el-conservador-fine-gael-gana-las-elecciones-irlandesas-segun-los-sondeos#.UXHFbsqkOeY (accessed May 2, 2014).

———. 2010a. "El Parlamento irlandés aprubó el plan de rescate." *Cinco Días*, December 15. http://www.cincodias.com/articulo/economia/parlamento-irlandes-aprueba-plan-rescate/20101215cdscdseco_23/ (accessed April 20, 2012).

———. 2010b. "Goldman Sachs ayudó a Grecia a ocultar su déficit público a Bruselas." *Libertad Digital*, February 15. http://www.libertaddigital.com/economia/goldman-sachs-ayudo-a-grecia-a-ocultar-su-deficit-publico-a-bruselas-1276384609/ (accessed April 22, 2014).

———. 1995. "La peseta se ha devaluado en seis ocasiones desde 1959." *El País*, September 18. http://www.elpais.com/articulo/economia/ESPANA/peseta/ha/sido/devaluada/ocasiones/1959/elpepieco/19920918elpepieco_18/Tes?print=1 (accessed September 12, 2009).

EFE Economía. 2013. "Turquía dejará la unión aduanera si la UE no le incluye en los tratados comerciales." *El País*, March 28. http://economia.elpais.com/economia/2013/03/28/agencias/1364475868_191458.html (accessed June 4, 2015).

Einstein, Albert. http://thinkexist.com/quotation/not_everything_that_counts_can_be_counted-and_not/15536.html (accessed September 10, 2009).

El-Agraa, Ali M. 1989. *The theory and measurement of international economic integration.* New York: St. Martin's Press.

El Mundo. 2005. "España es el país de la Unión Europea con mayor 'fuga de cerebros.'" February 18. http://www.elmundo.es/universidad/2005/02/11/actualidad/1108144411.html (accessed June 23, 2019).

Eurobarometer. 2012. Public opinion on the European Union. European Commission, Spring 2012. http://ec.europa.eu/public_opinion/archives/eb/eb77/eb77_first_en.pdf (accessed July 21, 2015).

Eurobarometer. 2005. Eurobarometer 64. European Commission, December 2005. http://ec.europa.eu/public_opinion/archives/eb/eb64/eb64_first_en.pdf.

EuroEFE. 2012. "Francia no deberá cambiar su Constitución para adoptar la 'regla de oro.'" August 9. http://www.euroefe.efe.com/1311_noticias/1700853_francia-no-debera-cambiar-su-constitucion-para-adoptar-la-regla-de-oro.html (accessed December 20, 2012).

Europa Press. 2013. "Cameron continuará con los ajustes para evitar que Reino Unido vuelva al abismo." March 7. http://www.europapress.es/economia/noticia-cameron-continuara-ajustes-evitar-reino-unido-vuelva-abismo-20130307195321.html (accessed January 14, 2015).

———. 2010. "Dificultades de los jóvenes científicos para regresar a España." *El País*, December 26. http://www.elpais.com/articulo/sociedad/Dificultades/jovenes/cientificos/regresar/Espana/elpepusoc/20101226elpepusoc_1/Tes (accessed January 13, 2014).

European Central Bank. 2008. "1998–2008: 10th anniversary of the EC." *Monthly Bulletin*, June: 1–156. Frankfurt am Main: European Central Bank. http://www.ecb.eu/pub/pdf/other/10thanniversaryoftheecbmb200806en.pdf (accessed August 28, 2008).

European Commission. 2011. *Enlargement strategy and main challenges 2006–2007*. Communication from the Commission to the European Parliament and the Council. http://ec.europa.eu/enlargement/pdf/key_documents/2006/nov/com_649_strategy_paper_en.pdf.

———. 2010a. "Report on Greek Government deficits and debts statistics." January 2010. http://ec.europa.eu/eurostat/documents/4187653/6404656/COM_2010_report_greek/c8523cfa-d3c1-4954-8ea1-64bb11e59b3a (accessed February 11, 2013).

———. 2010b. "Europe 2020." http://ec.europa.eu/europe2020/index_en.htmn (accessed March 29, 2010).

———. 2007. *Integrated guidelines for growth and jobs (2008–2010)*. Communication from the Commission to the Spring European Council. December 11. http://ec.europa.eu/growthandjobs/pdf/european-dimension-200712-annual-progress-report/200712-annual-report-integrated-guidelines_en.pdf (accessed November 6, 2008).

———. 2004. "Survey on the use of euro cash outside the EU." Directorate General for Economic and Financial Affairs, *Economy of the euro zone and the Union*, 195 (April). http://ec.europa.eu/economy_finance/publications/publication6321_en.pdf (accessed May 26, 2015).

———.1999. "Quarterly note on the euro-denominated bond markets." Directorate General for Economic and Financial Affairs, *European Economy*, 2 (April): 1–6. http://ec.europa.eu/economy_finance/publications/publication2645_en.pdf. (accessed October 2, 2008).

———. 1990. "One market, one money: an evaluation of the potential benefits and costs of forming an economic and monetary union." Directorate General for Economic and Financial Affairs, *European Economy*, no. 44 (October). http://ec.europa.eu/economy_finance/publications/publication7454_en.pdf (accessed March 8, 2008).

———. n. d. "EMU: A historical documentation." Directorate General for Economic and Financial Affairs. http://ec.europa.eu/economy_finance/emu_history/history/part_a_2.htm (accessed October 20, 2007).

———. n. d. "The White Paper and the Essen Strategy." Directorate General for Employment and Social Affairs. http://ec.europa.eu/employment_social/employment_strategy/origins_en.htm#2 (accessed November 12, 2007).

Euroxpress. 2012."Ultimátum de Turquía para su adhesión a la UE." October 31. http://www.euroxpress.es/index.php/Printer/noticias/2012/10/31/ultimatum-de-turquia-para-su-adhesion-a-la-ue/ (accessed July 4, 2014).

Federal Reserve. 2009. "Industrial production and capacity utilization." Federal Reserve Statistics Release, October 16, 2009. http://www.federalreserve.gov/releases/g17/Current/default.htm (accessed November 17, 2009).

Fresneda, Carlos. 2013. "Cameron preguntará a los británicos en 2017 si quieren seguir en la UE." *El Mundo*, January 23. http://www.elmundo.es/elmundo/2013/01/23/internacional/1358929895.html (accessed May 2, 2015).

Gallego, Javier. 2013. "La UE responde a Cameron que Reino Unido no es un socio privilegiado del club." *El Mundo*, January 23. http://www.elmundo.es/elmundo/2013/01/23/internacional/1358965600.html (accessed May 9, 2015).

García Delgado, José Luis, and José María Serrano Sanz. 2000. "From real to euro: the history of the peseta." *La Caixa*, Economic Studies Series No. 21. http://www.lacaixa.comunicacions.com/se/pbei.php?idioma=eng&llibre=21&resum=si (accessed October 12, 2012).

Girgis, Nancy. 2008. "EU Commission proposes €200 billion stimulus package." *CEP News*, November 26. http://www.economicnews.ca/cepnews/wire/article/173209 (accessed November 26, 2008).

Goldirova, Renata. 2007. "Stop blaming ECB and euro, Almunia tells France." *EUobserver*, September 28. http://euobserver.com/9/24866/?rk=1 (accessed March 26, 2013).

González, Miguel. 2012. "Rajoy anuncia que espera cerrar el déficit de 2012 en el 5,8% y no en el 4,4%." *El País*, March 2. http://politica.elpais.com/politica/2012/03/02/actualidad/1330689487_742509.html (accessed April 29, 2014).

Gros, Daniel. 2007. "Restoring popular support for integration in the EU." *Eurointelligence*, March 4. http://www.eurointelligence.com/article.581+M588aa09b633.0.htm (accessed January 20, 2008).

———, and Thomas Mayer. 2010. "How to deal with sovereign default in Europe: towards a Euro(pean) Monetary Fund." *Vox*, March 15. http://www.voxeu.org/index.php?q=node/4754 (accessed March 21, 2010).

Hirst, Tomas. 2014. "OPEC votes not to cut production, oil prices plummet." *Business Insider*, December 21, accessed at: http://www.businessinsider.com/opec-votes-not-to-cut-production-oil-prices-plummet-2014-11#ixzz3QnQou5c0.

Hymans, Jacques E. C. n. d. "Money for Mars? The euro banknotes and European identity." Draft chapter prepared for Robert Fishman and Anthony Messina, eds, *The year of the euro*. http://www-bcf.usc.edu/~hymans/Hymansfishmess.pdf.

Inman, Phillip. 2015. "Profile: Greece's new finance minister Yanis Varoufakis." *The Guardian*, 4 June.

Intereconomía. 2009. "La deuda que quiere reestructurar Dubai World alcanza los 26.000 millones de dólares." December 1. http://www.intereconomia.com/noticias-negocios/mercados-y-valores/claves/deuda-que-quiere-reestructurar-dubai-world-alcanza-los-2 (accessed March 23, 2011).

International Monetary Fund. 2015. "Statement by the IMF on Greece." IMF Communication Department, June 30. http://www.imf.org/external/np/sec/pr/2015/pr15310.htm (accessed June 30, 2015).

———. 2012. "World Economic Outlook." April. http://www.imf.org/external/pubs/ft/weo/2012/01/pdf/text.pdf.

———. 2010. "IMF quotas." March 2010. http://www.imf.org/external/np/exr/facts/quotas.htm (accessed December 2, 2009).

———. 2009. "IMF Governors formally approve US$250 billion general SDR allocation." Press Release No. 09/283, August 13, 2009. http://www.imf.org/external/np/sec/pr/2009/pr09283.htm (accessed December 29, 2009).

———. n. d. "What is the IMF?" http://www.imf.org/external/pubs/ft/exrp/what.htm#member (accessed March 18, 2010).

Kirisci, Kemal. 2013. "Don't forget free trade with Turkey." *The National Interest*, April 15. http://nationalinterest.org/commentary/dont-forget-free-trade-turkey-8345.

Kitsantonis, Nikki, and Jim Yardley. 2015. "Alexis Tsipras, Greek Prime Minister, calls for new elections." *New York Times*, August 20. http://www.nytimes.com/2015/08/21/world/europe/greek-prime-minister-alexis-tsipras-to-call-new-elections-minister-says.html (accessed August 20, 2015).

La Vanguardia. 2015. "El Parlamento griego aprueba la convocatoria de referéndum sobre el rescate." June 28. http://www.lavanguardia.com/economia/20150628/54433074415/parlamento-griego-aprueba-referendum.html (accessed June 28, 2015).

La Voz de Galicia. 2013. "Merkel sugiere desbloquear el acceso de Turquía a la UE." February 13. http://www.lavozdegalicia.es/noticia/internacional/2013/02/24/merkel-sugiere-desbloquear-acceso-turquia-ue/0003_201302G24P29991.htm (accessed July 2, 2014).

Lorca-Susino, Maria. 2008. "The US dollar and the Euro: deus ex machina." *European Union Miami Analysis* (EUMA), Vol. 5, No. 9, April 2008, accessed at: http://www6.miami.edu/eucenter/LorcaFX-MP%20Theory%20Edi.pdf.

Mahony, Honor. 2015. "German MPs vote on Greece amid misgivings." *EUobserver*, July 17. https://euobserver.com/news/129680 (accessed July 17, 2015).

Maltezou, Renee, and Lefteris Papadimas. 2015. "Greek PM says time for action from lenders, IMF payment scrapes by." *Reuters*, May 12. http://www.reuters.com/article/2015/05/12/us-eurozone-greece-idUSKBN0NW10I20150512 (accessed May 12, 2015).

Martínez de Rituerto, Ricardo. 2012. "Turquía congela relaciones con la UE al asumir Chipre la presidencia." *El País*, July 2. http://internacional.elpais.com/internacional/2012/07/02/actualidad/1341248042_219571.html (accessed May 27, 2014).

Maurice, Eric. 2015. "UK to block Greece short-term funding solution." *EUobserver*, July 14. https://euobserver.com/economic/129637 (accessed July 14, 2015).

Monnet, Jean. 1943. "Algiers Memorandum." In *Building European Union*, ed. Trevor Salmon and William Nicoll, 20–21. Manchester, UK: Manchester University Press.

Morelli, Vincent. 2010. "European Union enlargement: a status report on Turkey's accession negotiations." Congressional Research Service. November 2. http://fpc.state.gov/documents/organization/152041.pdf (accessed March 29, 2016).

Munchau, Wolfgang. 2007. "Sarkozy jeopardizes the future of the Eurozone." *Financial Times*, July 2.

Mundell, Robert A. 2003. "The international monetary system and the case for a world currency." Distinguished Lectures Series n. 12. Paper presented at the Leon Komiński Academy of Entrepreneurship and Management (WSPiZ) and TIGER, Warsaw, Poland, October 23. http://www.wspiz.edu.pl/gfx/kozminski/files/badania_naukowe/distinguished_lectures/mundell2.pdf (accessed April 23, 2008).

———. 2002a. "Monetary unions and the problem of sovereignty." Columbia University, Discussion Paper 0102-06:1-32. http://www.econ.columbia.edu/RePEc/pdf/DP0102-06.pdf (accessed March 25, 2008).

———. 2002b. "The significance of the euro in the international monetary system." Speech, Henry George Lecture series, Pace University, New York. February 26. http://www.robertmundell.net/Menu/Main.asp?Type=5&Cat=08&ThemeName=Euro (accessed March 24, 2008).

———. 1999. "The euro and the stability of the international monetary system." Paper presented at a conference sponsored jointly by the Luxembourg Institute for European

and International Studies and the Pierre Werner Foundation on "The euro as a stabilizer in the international economic system." Luxembourg-Ville, Grand Duchy of Luxembourg. December 3–4. http://www.robertmundell.net/pdf/The%20Euro%20 and%20the%20Stability%20of%20the%20International%20Monetary%20System.pdf (accessed September 22, 2008).
——. 1998a. "What the euro means for the dollar and the international monetary system." *Atlantic Economic Journal*, 26, 3: 227–237. http://www.springerlink.com/ content/6715561141781038/ (accessed August 6, 2008).
——. 1998b. "The impact of the euro on the international monetary system." *The International Spectator*, XXXIII, 2 (April–June): 1–18. http://www.ciaonet.org/olj/iai/ iai_aprjun98.html (accessed July 28, 2008).
——. 1998c. "The case for the euro—I and II." *The Wall Street Journal*, March 24 and 25.
——. 1991. "Monetary policies for the new Europe." *Rivista di Politica Economica*, 21, 5: 71–88.
——. 1973a. "A plan for a European currency." In *The economics of common currencies*, ed. H. Johnson and Alexander Swoboda, 143–177. London, UK: George Allen & Unwin.
——. 1973b. "Uncommon arguments for common currencies". In *The economics of common currencies*, ed. H. Johnson and Alexander Swoboda, 114–132. London, UK: George Allen & Unwin.
——. 1961. "A theory of optimum currency areas." *American Economic Review*, 60, 4 (November): 657–658.
——. n. d. "World currency. The works of Robert Mundell." http://www.robertmundell. net/Menu/Main.asp?Type=5&Cat=09&ThemeName=World%20Currency (accessed December 28, 2009).
Nasseri, Ladene, and Mathew Brown. 2008. "Kuwait says oil over $100 is too high." *Bloomberg*, June 28, accessed at: http://www.bloomberg.com/apps/news?pid=2060108 7&sid=aJoz82F86Wis&refer=home.
National Bureau of Economic Research. 1991. "NBER Business Cycle Dating Committee determines that recession ended in March 1991." *NBER Business Cycle Dating Committee*. March. http://www.nber.org/March91.html (accessed September 14, 2009).
Nieminen, Ari. 2005. "Towards a European society? Integration and regulation of capitalism." Paper presented, with the permission of the faculty of Social Sciences of the University of Helsinki, for public discussion in the Auditorium of the Helsinki University Museum. March 19. http://ethesis.helsinki.fi/julkaisut/val/sosio/vk/nieminen/towardsa.pdf (accessed April, 23, 2008).
Nixon, Richard M. 1971. "Address to the Nation outlining a new economic policy: the challenges of peace." *The Nixon Library Foundation*, August 15. http://www. nixonlibraryfoundation.org/clientuploads/directory/archive/1971_pdf_files/ 1971_0264.pdf (accessed December 6, 2008).
Organization for Economic Co-operation and Development. 2011. *OECD Factbook 2011–2012*. December 7. http://www.oecd-ilibrary.org/economics/oecd-factbook-2011– 2012_factbook-2011-en (accessed December 2014).
Palop, Juan. 2012. "Merkel ratifica el pacto fiscal y subraya que sí habrá condiciones al rescate." *El Mundo*, June 30. http://www.elmundo.es/elmundo/2012/06/30/economia/ 1341025520.html (accessed June 30, 2012).
Peel, Quentin. 2010. "IMF likely to take lead if loans sought." *Financial Times*, March 29. http://www.ft.com/cms/s/0/f1f41fb6-3a87-11df-b6d5-00144feabdc0,dwp_uuid= 2b8f1fea-e570-11de-81b4-00144feab49a.html (accessed March 31, 2010).

Bibliography

Peel, Quentin, Ben Hall, and Tony Barber. 2010. "Merkel warns of hurdles in EMF plan." *Financial Times*, March 8. http://www.ft.com/cms/s/0/6fdeed16-2ad9-11df-886b-00144feabdc0.html (accessed March 8, 2010).

Poch, Rafael. 2013. "Merkel suaviza los impulsos antieuropeístas de Cameron." *La Vanguardia*, January 29. http://www.lavanguardia.com/internacional/20130129/54363211574/merkel-suaviza-los-impulsos-antieuropeistas-de-cameron.html (accessed March 21, 2013).

Ramírez, Luís. 2008. "La entrada de España en el euro infló la burbuja y disparó el precio de los pisos un 177%." *Libertad Digital*, October 14, 2008. http://www.libertaddigital.com/economia/la-entrada-de-espana-en-el-euro-inflo-la-burbuja-y-disparo-el-precio-de-los-pisos-un-177-1276340854/ (accessed September 13, 2009).

Randow, Jana, and Francine Lacqua. 2010. "Germany's Bruederle rules out bailout for Greece." Bloomberg. January 30. http://www.bloomberg.com/apps/news?pid=newsarchive&sid=aGSXppR4jJGk (accessed October 29, 2013).

Referendum "'NO' campaign." http://oxi2015.gr/ (accessed June August 2, 2015).

Reinhart, Carmen, and Kenneth Rogoff. 2010. "Why we should expect low growth amid debt." *Financial Times*, January 27. http://www.ft.com/cms/s/0/f4630910-0b7a-11df-8232-00144feabdc0.html (accessed January 28, 2010).

Reuters. 2015. "TEXT-Greece's request for a 3-year loan facility to the ESM." July 8. http://www.cnbc.com/2015/07/08/reuters-america-text-greeces-request-for-a-3-year-loan-facility-to-the-esm.html (accessed July 8, 2015).

Robins-Early, Nick. 2015. "Greece fails to meet IMF debt deadline." *The World Post*, October 15. http://www.huffingtonpost.com/2015/06/30/greece-imf-debt_n_7658084.html (accessed October 15, 2015).

RTVE. 2012. "El Parlamento alemán ratifica el pacto fiscal europeo y el fondo de rescate permanente europeo." July 29. http://www.rtve.es/noticias/20120629/parlamento-aleman-ratifica-pacto-fiscal-europeo-fondo-rescate-permanente-europeo/540788.shtml (accessed May 2, 2013).

———. 2011. "Entra en vigor el pacto fiscal europeo que lleva la austeridad al corazón de la UE." December 31. http://www.rtve.es/noticias/20121231/entra-vigor-pacto-fiscal-europeo-lleva-austeridad-corazon/591486.shtml (accessed December 3, 2013).

Schuman, Robert. 1950. "The Schuman declaration." In *Pioneers of European integration and peace, 1945–1963: a brief history with documents*, ed. Sherrill Brown Wells, 98–100. Boston: Bedford/St. Martin's.

Smith, Helena. 2009. "Financial markets tumble after Fitch downgrades Greece's credit rating." *The Guardian*, December 8.

Soriano, D. 2012. "El aumento de empleados públicos triplica al del sector privado." *Libertad Digital*, February 18. http://www.libertaddigital.com/economia/los-empleados-publicos-crecen-tres-veces-mas-que-los-del-sector-privado-1276405388/ (accessed May 2, 2013).

Steinhauser, Gabriel, and Tom Fairless. 2015. "Greece requests three-year bailout in first step toward meeting creditors' demand." *The Wall Street Journal*, July 8. Tejo, M. 2011. "España ya alberga a más funcionarios que comerciantes y hosteleros." *Expansión*, June 2.

Torrero Mañas, Antonio. 2008. "La crisis de la economía española." *Universidad de Alcalá, Instituto Universitario de Análisis Económico y Social*. Documento de Trabajo 09/2008. http://www.iaes.es/publicaciones/DT_09_08_esp.pdf (accessed on September 8, 2009).

Traynor, Ian. 2015. "Greece secures eurozone bailout extension for four months." *The Guardian*, March 2. http://www.theguardian.com/business/2015/feb/24/greece-secures-eurozone-bailout-extension-for-four-months (accessed March 2, 2015).

TRT. 2013. "Bağiş, sobre la presidencia de turno de Irlanda en la UE." January 1. http://www.trtspanish.com/trtworld/es/newsDetail.aspx?HaberKodu=5c1465dc-fe9c-46ec-a076-945550f87e2a (accessed March 2, 2014).
Vega, Jose. 2011. "España registra ya más emigrantes que inmigrantes a causa de la crisis." *Cinco Días*, July 1.
Vidal-Folch, X., and V. Carvajal. 1995. La peseta se devalúa un 7% para seguir en el SME. *El País*., March 6. http://www.elpais.com/articulo/economia/UNION_EUROPEA/ESPANA/UNION_EUROPEA/PORTUGAL/ESPANA/UNION_EUROPEA/UNION_ECONOMICA_Y_MONETARIA_/UEM/peseta/devalua/seguir/SME/elpepieco/19950306elpepieco_9/Tes/ (accessed September 2, 2009).
Viñas, Juan. 2011a. "Claves para entender la 'regla de oro' de la UE." *Cinco Días*, December 14. http://www.cincodias.com/articulo/economia/claves-entender-regla-oro-ue/20111214cdscdieco_3/ (accessed May 5, 2015).
———. 2011b. "La OCDE prevé tasas de paro altas en España hasta 2026." *Cinco Días*, May 26. http://www.cincodias.com/articulo/economia/ocde-preve-tasas-paro-altas-espana-2026/20110526cdscdieco_8/ (accessed May 24, 2014).
Walker, Andrew. 2011. "What is a Tobin tax?" *BBC News*, November 2. http://www.bbc.com/news/business-15555812 (accessed June 20, 2014).
Watt, Nicholas. 2011. "'Tobin tax' would hit City of London with missile, says John Major." *The Guardian*, November 18. http://www.guardian.co.uk/business/2011/nov/18/tobin-tax-city-london-john-major (accessed November 18, 2011).
Wunsch, Conny. 2005. "Labour market policy in Germany: institutions, instruments and reforms since unification." Universität Sankt Gallen, Volkswirtschaftliche Abteilung. Discussion paper, 2005-06. Sankt Gallen. http://www.iab.de/389/section.aspx/Publikation/k050426f32 (accessed May 2, 2015).
Zhou, Moming. 2014. "Crude extends fourth weekly decline amid supply glut." *Bloomberg*, December 22, 2014. http://www.bloomberg.com/news/articles/2014-12-22/crude-extends-fourth-weekly-decline-amid-global-supply-glut (accessed April 25, 2015).
Zschiesche Sánchez, Juan. 2003. "Reunificación Alemana: Aproximación a las consecuencias económicas y sociales para los Länder orientales." Universidad Complutense de Madrid, Papeles del Este, N. 5. http://biblioteca.ucm.es/cee/papeles/05/05.pdf (accessed April 3, 2014).

Index

acquis communautaire 111–13
Adjustment Program 35–8, 98, 105, 107
agenda 2010 xiii, 73–4, 76–7
Ankara Protocol 114

bailout 100, 105, 147, 154
bail-out rule 31, 99, 100
Barcelona Process 120
brain drain 78, 86, 91, 93
Brent 55–7, 63–5
Bretton Woods 13, 25, 75, 80, 148
Bundesbank xiii, 71, 74, 75
business cycle 25, 43, 50, 54, 64, 82–6, 156

capacity index 60
common currency xiii, 3, 4, 7, 9, 13–19, 24, 46, 74–5, 108–9
competitive devaluation 74–6, 80–1, 83, 85, 93, 138
crude oil 50, 54–7, 59, 60, 62, 64–5
currency snake 76, 82
Custom Union 116
Cyprus 4, 9, 12, 32, 37–8, 46, 111, 114–15, 121, 140

debt ceiling 42, 43
Delors Report 16
democratic déficit 5, 33, 137, 139
Dublic Regulation 125

Economic Adjustment Program 35–8, 98, 105, 107
Economic and Monetary Union xiv, 4, 7, 15–16, 19, 21, 26, 30, 33, 71, 108, 148–50
economic crisis 3, 19, 20, 26, 27, 29, 30, 32–4, 36, 38–40, 42, 44–6, 48, 52, 54, 59, 60, 62, 64, 74, 79, 81, 89, 93, 96, 108–9, 120, 131, 139, 140, 145
economic deficit 139
Economic Depression 13, 82
Estonia 4, 9, 12, 37, 46–9, 127
Eurobarometer 11, 12, 20–5, 139, 146, 149, 150
European Financial Stabilization Mechanism 32, 34–8, 104–5
European Agenda 111, 119, 124–6, 132–3
European Central Bank xiii, 15–17, 26, 34, 44, 74, 85, 89, 95, 97, 103, 150
European Constitution 4
European Financial Stability Facility xi, 35–8, 98, 107
European Identity 5, 114, 137–9,
European Monetary System 15, 76, 82
European Parliament xiii, 5, 18, 32, 97, 117, 140–3, 146, 148, 150
European social model 110
Eurosclerosis 25, 149
Euroskeptic 17, 18–9, 25, 29, 108–10
Exchange Rate Mechanism 76, 82

financial aid 32–7, 44, 46, 48, 80–1, 100, 116, 140
fiscal adjustment 43, 45, 46, 48, 110
fiscal austerity 39–41, 43, 45, 47, 49
fiscal pact 42, 110
fiscal policy 17, 42

Germany xiii, xiv, 4, 5, 8, 9, 12, 17–18, 26, 31–2, 35, 37, 42, 69, 70–8, 85, 91, 97, 99, 100, 119–21, 126, 138, 144, 154–5
Gold Standard 13, 25
Greece xii, xiv, 3, 4, 12, 17, 19, 26, 29–32, 34–40, 43, 45–48, 69, 71, 74, 76,

95–107, 119–20, 122, 124–7, 130–2, 140, 147–8, 151–2, 154
Greek Loan Facility 35, 38, 98, 106–7

Hartz Reform xiii, 73
hyperinflation xiii, 70

integration 3, 5–9, 12, 14–16, 18, 19, 21, 25, 70, 79, 108–9, 112, 120, 123, 128, 131–2, 138–9, 149, 151, 153, 154
international currency 17
International Monetary Fund 34, 38, 41–2, 44, 80, 97, 102–4, 140, 148–9, 151
Ireland xii, 3–5, 12, 26, 31–2, 35–8, 40, 43–5, 48, 69, 98, 108, 114, 120–1, 125, 140, 148
irrevocable fixing 33, 100

Laffer Curve 41
Light Crude 53, 55
Lisbon Treaty 5, 7, 8, 12, 15, 31, 38, 100, 107, 109, 140
London Ultimatum xiii, 70

Maastricht Criteria 82, 95
Maastricht Treaty 8, 12, 16, 17, 46, 99, 111, 128
Memorandum of Understanding 36, 98, 107
migration 9, 15, 73, 78, 87, 89, 91, 93, 119–34
Misery Index 86–91
monetary integration 19, 149
monetary policy xiv, 14, 16, 17, 29, 38, 71, 74, 80, 85, 113

optimum currency areas 14, 153

Portugal xii, 3, 4, 12, 26, 31–2, 35–8, 40, 43, 44–5, 69, 81, 98, 120–1, 127, 140, 147, 155
Progress Report 113, 150

referendum 5, 21, 103–4, 107, 109, 121, 128–9, 152, 154
Reform Treaty 4–6

refugee crisis 120, 124, 126–7, 129–31, 133
regional integration 3, 7, 8
reparation payments 70

Schengen Agreement 119–22, 127–8
Single European Act 8, 119–22
Social Charter 82, 109, 111
Spain xii, 3, 4, 12, 17–18, 26, 31–2, 35, 37–8, 40, 42, 45, 46, 69, 76–94, 98, 120–1, 138, 140, 148
Stability and Growth Pact xiii, xiv, 16, 25, 30–2, 40, 45, 71, 85, 95, 99, 109
stimulus package 38, 46, 151
Structural and Cohesion Funds 81
Switzerland 121, 126, 128–9
Syriza 101–6, 148

Tobin tax 109–10, 155
Transatlantic Trade and Investment Partnership 50, 59, 65
Treaty of Rome 12, 121
Treaty of the European Union xiii, 12
Troika 34, 44, 48, 103, 148
Turkey 59, 108–9, 111–18, 126–7, 129–34, 152
Turkish Stream 129

U.S. dollar 6, 10, 19, 54, 60, 62–4, 75, 80–3, 94
United Kingdom 62, 89, 108–11, 113, 115, 117, 120–1, 125, 128
United States xi, xii, xiv, 3, 5, 11, 14, 19, 21, 26, 38–40, 43, 50, 52, 55, 59–60, 62, 64, 91, 97, 116–17, 132, 138

Versailles Peace Treaty 70

welfare state 137, 143–5
West Texas Intermediate 55, 57, 64
Western Balkan Action Plan 126
World War xiii, 11, 13, 18, 40, 44, 50, 70, 73, 76, 78, 110–11, 115, 117, 127, 131–2, 137, 144–5

Taylor & Francis eBooks

Helping you to choose the right eBooks for your Library

Add Routledge titles to your library's digital collection today. Taylor and Francis ebooks contains over 50,000 titles in the Humanities, Social Sciences, Behavioural Sciences, Built Environment and Law.

Choose from a range of subject packages or create your own!

Benefits for you
- Free MARC records
- COUNTER-compliant usage statistics
- Flexible purchase and pricing options
- All titles DRM-free.

Benefits for your user
- Off-site, anytime access via Athens or referring URL
- Print or copy pages or chapters
- Full content search
- Bookmark, highlight and annotate text
- Access to thousands of pages of quality research at the click of a button.

REQUEST YOUR FREE INSTITUTIONAL TRIAL TODAY

Free Trials Available
We offer free trials to qualifying academic, corporate and government customers.

eCollections – Choose from over 30 subject eCollections, including:

Archaeology	Language Learning
Architecture	Law
Asian Studies	Literature
Business & Management	Media & Communication
Classical Studies	Middle East Studies
Construction	Music
Creative & Media Arts	Philosophy
Criminology & Criminal Justice	Planning
Economics	Politics
Education	Psychology & Mental Health
Energy	Religion
Engineering	Security
English Language & Linguistics	Social Work
Environment & Sustainability	Sociology
Geography	Sport
Health Studies	Theatre & Performance
History	Tourism, Hospitality & Events

For more information, pricing enquiries or to order a free trial, please contact your local sales team:
www.tandfebooks.com/page/sales

 **Routledge** Taylor & Francis Group | The home of Routledge books

www.tandfebooks.com